WORLD EDUCATION —
Revolutionary Concept

WORLD EDUCATION—
Revolutionary Concept

by

MORRIS R. MITCHELL

Library of Congress Catalog Card Number: 67-19755

Copyright © 1967 by Morris R. Mitchell

Published by Pageant Press, Inc.
101 Fifth Avenue, New York, N. Y. 10003
Manufactured in the United States of America

Pageant Press, Inc.   New York

Library of Congress Catalog Card Number: 67-19753

Copyright © 1967 by Morris R. Mitchell

All Rights Reserved
First Edition
Published by Pageant Press, Inc.
101 Fifth Avenue, New York, N. Y. 10003
Manufactured in the United States of America

Dedicated in Sorrow

to all who are hungry, all who are in prison, all
who are sick, all who are despised because of
race or beliefs, all who are poor, all who suffer
from the mass-murder we call war

and in Joy

to the world of peace and plenty that waits on
a new view of the role of education in the affairs
of the family of

Man

WORLD EDUCATION —

Revolutionary Concept

CONTENTS

CONTENTS

PREFACE

I am joyfully a member of the Religious Society of Friends and direct the Friends World Institute. If the Friends World Institute is the first college-level school to get underway that deserves the title of World Education, that is no accident. Held together by no creed, no doctrine, this always tiny band has practiced for 300 years the belief that there is that of divinity in every human, whatever the race, creed, color, nation, sex, or age. They have so cherished that belief that they have stood against capital punishment, against slavery, for equal rights for men and women, for prison reform, for humane care of the mentally ill, for feeding the hungry, for binding the wounds of victims of war on both sides, and against all war.

Worship with Friends usually consists of corporate search for truth without reliance on an authority figure. Meetings for business are a religious experience: the meeting of problems with such love, concern, for one another that no "minute" of decision is recorded if there is a vocal minority of even one in opposition. The wisdom of this practice lies in the fact that it keeps the minds and hearts of the majority open for further light. This is the democratic process raised to the ultimate degree. It is a slow way but the safest way.

Friends World Institute attempts to operate on Quaker practice, but this is not meant to be a Quaker book. Friends have no monopoly on human yearning for a peaceful and interesting world. There are a thousand or more efforts to build units of this new dimension of schooling—World Education.

This volume is written out of a sense of urgency that, in this hour of terrifying human disunity, the concept and purpose of World Education be known and made effective. It must attract students, teachers, administrators, interpreters, and donors. It demands the creation of an atmosphere of imagination, sympathy, and devotion.

This volume should at once be rewritten, so rapid are changes. World Education approaches the stage of worldwide movement. There is need of a clearing house for communication between all the varied efforts. Besides, this book has been written in such moments as could be snatched from the effort of helping to bring into being such a school.

Honor must be paid to Dr. George Nicklin, who initiated Friends World Institute and patiently and wisely coaxed it into being, also to each member of the Committee, now succeeded by the trustees, who met monthly for six years in long, tiring meetings, leaving at 12:00, 1:00, 2:00 A.M. to drive home. The doubters among them served a needed function. Those who gave deeply, became discouraged, and fell out were essential to their hour. Those who have given generously—12,000 in all— have supplied indispensable support, especially Mr. and Mrs. Henry Ittleson, who gave the Harrow Hill estate, and Mrs. Gerald Livingston, who largely gave the 90 acre Gerald M. Livingston campus on Lloyd Harbor. Finally, let us remember the several thousand members of the New York Yearly Meeting of the Religious Society of Friends who have shared in this concern and deliberately given their moral backing.

For their generous and able help in the preparation of

this little volume, I personally want to thank: Judy Ingersoll, Keith Helmuth, John Allerdice, Ruth Mary Hill, Collin Gonze, my wife Barbara, my daughter Nancy, and Amy Roosevelt. Amy kindly revised the entire manuscript. Without the devoted work of Ruth Dennis, the manuscript would never have reached the printer.

Harrow Hill
East Norwich, New York

CHAPTER I

World Education, Revolutionary Concept

A nebula of revolutionary social concepts is gathering
force, and only total war can stop their inexorable unfolding. For they are generated out of the "basic march-
ing orders of the universe," the basic processes of existence. They originate in the genes and chromosomes of
man's social being and development. Wanted, unwanted,
encouraged, opposed, ignored, they gather momentum
out of the womb of destiny.

Of recent emergence, and naturally so, they are the social aspects of puberty of the human race, and as un-
willed as physical puberty. They are predictable, like future stages of scientific progress, and are of the same
evolutionary matrix.

One of these, a creature of the past half century, is
world government. Many will put shoulders against the
wheels of time, but the most they can do is retard. Henry
Cabot Lodges are mired under. It is predictable that all
local government will be subordinated to world government. It is only a matter of time before world government will rest over the voice of all nations, including
China, and of all people in those nations.

Another is *racial equality*. Perhaps there will be more
Hitlers and Barnetts and Klansmen. But recognition of the
potential universal dignity of mankind is inevitable. The
growth toward *universal suffrage* has been a drama of
protagonists and antagonists, but the right to a voice in

government has been extended in this country regardless of sex, color, or property. The contests of the Martin Luther Kings versus the George Wallaces have been the superficial, local aspects of a universal upsurgence.

Another emerging concept is *social planning*. Hated in America when it burst into view in the Soviet Union in 1927, in the flicker of time since, it has become an accepted instrument of social growth, at every level from hamlet to the United Nations.

Still maligned by selfish interests, *regional development*, since its inception in the Tennesee Valley Authority Act of May, 1933, has spread almost unbelievably to areas of all political aspects, thus proving its potential universality. Clearly, it is only time before every major drainage area in the world will be under centralized, purposeful, deliberate development.

Consumer Cooperatives emerged as a workable concept in Rochdale, England, in 1844. The eight Rochdale Principles of consumer cooperation form the most ideal basis for both production and distribution that the mind of man has invented. Slowly, and so quietly as to be scarcely noticed as a movement, consumer cooperatives now enroll in the International Cooperative Alliance 131 million dues paying members. And cooperatives operate in the East, the West, and in the uncommitted countries, proving their universality.

Socialism, in a half century, has spread more rapidly and more dynamically than has any other concept in man's history. Czar Nicholas tried to kill it in its infancy with a stick. With all his power of state police, he and his forces were ground under the wheels of emerging forces. Then nations combined to aid the White Russians, and we sent millions of rifles, but to no avail. Stupidly,

15

we still rely on military might to contain a concept, as though with bases around the world even our billions could control the thinking of half the world, when Czar Nicholas could not control a handful of revolutionaries. Cuba! Korea! China! Vietnam! We must find a new adjustment between individuals and society so that, with our new-found means of production, we can abolish want and gain optimum freedom for all. This adjustment may comprise a fluid, shifting interrelationship of free enterprise, socialism, and consumer cooperatives, after the Scandinavian pattern.

The concept of *intentional community* is coming of age. The awareness of the rights and dignity and responsibilities of the local community will come forward, much more quickly than did these values for the individual. The earlier sporadic instances of utopian communities foreran the *kibutzim,* the *ejidos,* the thousands of intentional community developments in India alone, and elsewhere. Community will come of age.

World education is another of these emerging concepts.[1] Quite spontaneously, individuals and groups are responding to enlarged cosmological and anthropological per-

1. *The Idea of a World University* by Michael Zweig, edited by Harold Taylor, carries the same title as an article by Taylor in the *Saturday Review* for November 14, 1964. That article is included in the present volume and describes a program directed by Harold Taylor for the Committee on a Friends College in the spring of 1963. Zweig and Taylor have done the cause of World Education a profound service by this broad and scholarly treatment of the emergence of the World University concept. This volume treats the need for a world university, the developed alternatives to a world university, the history of the idea, proposals to international bodies, and some projects and experiments. The appendix includes an enlightening exposition of existing international institutions which approximate, or might become, world universities. Published by Southern Illinois University Press, Carbondale and Edwardsville, Illinois, 1967 and by Feffer and Simons, Inc., London and Amsterdam, 1967.

spectives, and are advancing plans for world schools, world colleges, world universities. So clear is this emergence, that there is friendly rivalry as to which group can first get underway with a creative, workable, universally applicable plan. But the concept has been conceived, and is an embryonic stage within a process as irreversible as pregnancy.

There are other universally applicable and acceptable concepts such as the *Scientific Method, Industrialization* and its late stages, *Automation,* and *Cybernetics.* They are all potentially interrelated, capable of augmenting one another.

If one of these emerging concepts is more basic and important than the others, it could be this one of world education. For through education that has made of itself a reverent search for universal truth appropriate to our age, mankind could creatively join with such impulses as these which shape destiny and hasten the progress that has been so needlessly tortuous.

Then, with love, we could begin to mend the scars man has inflicted on Mother Earth, abandon war, advance knowledge, abolish poverty, provide for the sick, lengthen life, and prepare for the creative enjoyment of leisure. This is the direction of the emerging concept, the revolutionary concept of World Education.

World Education must find a new focus for these critical times, a focus which will integrate certain historical values we cherish with new theories of reality and knowledge.

More specifically, World Education must bring into a single focus two great currents of human understanding: that ancient one which interprets reality by sense perception, and the new, sometimes contradictory, interpretation of reality as revealed by scientific investigation.

If we tolerate the compartmentalization of the traditional and the new understanding of reality, science will remain amoral, its destructive potentialities a threat, and religion and education will continue to be ineffective.[2] In our search for truth relevant to our times, we can, and doubtless will, continue to use traditional value words, but every word must assume revised meannig.

For example, among Christians the "divinity of Christ," at first threatened by the growth of objective understanding, loses its uniqueness and its superstitious qualities and becomes in a superlative degree that gift for sympathetic love with which every human is endowed.

Again, to listen for the "voice of God" is to open one's being, heart, and mind in earnest, "reverent" search for the meaning of the unfolding of the powers of truth. And a localized, personalized God becomes those all-pervasive forces and motives that govern every electron of every galaxy.

And what vistas are open as we glimpse the newer meanings of divinity as World Education finally views all as one family?

How can we relate our traditional notion of a static past and anticipated future with the relativist scientific awareness that the past in actuality does not exist, no longer exists, and that the future does not exist, not yet, and that that which we sense as the present is an infinitely

2. See film, *Power Among Men*, distributed by the United Nations. Thorold Dickenson and J. C. Sheers in collaboration with Alexander Hammond, G. L. Polidaro, V. R. Sarma for the film service of the U.N. Office of Public Information. Italy sequence, 1946, produced by Julian Bryan and directed by Victor Vicas; commentary spoken by Lawrence Hawey; music composed and conducted by Virgil Thomson and played by members of the New York Philharmonic.

18

thin sliver of "time," like a moving point, a point by definition having neither length, breadth, nor thickness? "Ye have no time but this present time, therefore prize your time for your soul's sake," said George Fox in 1682.

That is the central challenge. With our new understandings and the powers of science to create and destroy, can we modernize our ancient preconceptions based on faulty sense perception? Can we embrace, before we destroy ourselves, the actuality of an existence of such incredible complexity and magnificence as to make childish the myths of our bibles and our tribal histories? Can we still nurture the impulses of respect, sympathy, and love, that were inherent binding forces in tribal structure and yet deliberately outgrow the counterbalancing hostilities toward other tribes? Can we accept the reality that we are all of one family and all interdependent as, at once microscopic and macroscopic, we cling perilously to our incredibly complex globe?

Specifically, we must accept into our affection all those we now regard as enemies, those we may now fight, those we may now fear, those against whom we arm at such cost, with such danger, such folly. We must realize that, tragically, we have been confusing cause and effect. We have made men our enemy, when our real enemy was enmity. We have fought through fear when fear was our foe. We have reacted to individual and group responses to poverty, hunger, and degradation by fighting those made desperate, thus further victimizing the victims. This process rages this hour in a war of an uncertain state of enlargement.

World Education must replace this inverted perspective with an objective one built on the knowledge that all men share the same basic needs—sufficient nourishment,

19

adequate clothing, suitable shelter and privacy, sexual expression and physical health, economic security, mutual devotion, recognition and appreciation, recreation, education, the experiences of growth, the sense of sharing, the sense of purpose, and optimum freedom; and moreover, that we all subordinate these values according to the circumstances: all hungry men are alike in subordinating freedom, if necessary, to the demands of hunger. So we must learn that the only moral equivalent of war is the war on the causes of war.

Tribal attitudes must be replaced by a sense of the inescapability of world community before prevailing hostilities loosen powers that will ten-fold overkill us all, so that we can, together, as one human family, realize exquisite excitement, the sheer music of spinning daily the rounds of our globe in our galaxy, midst other galaxies flung through space.

We must accept a revolutionary change of attitude toward the nature and function of the educational process. For in content, too, we must outgrow the now universal, provincial pattern which employs education as a tool to transmit tribal beliefs, tribal attitudes, tribal structures, tribal skills, tribal habits, and tribal knowledge. Education must undertake a loftier purpose, an aim of new qualities, new dimensions. It must become for now a tool of human survival, and that assured, must assume as its ultimate goal individual and social growth, based on reverence for life, as an end in itself. Then education on a world scale will be the social counterpart of the creative forces that shape our destinies. Then we shall have achieved Plato's dictum that education is "process not product." Indeed, man may find such education the means of so identifying with the progressive evolution of his environment as to share, through his inherent creative ability, in the primal processes of change.

Education , in an almost new sense, must bring us into greater identity with the complex, systematic beauty of the universe, our world, ourselves. Then we shall know how unthinkably wrong war is. And we shall have the basis for proceeding to build an environment, physical and social, which will create through these infinite natural resources conditions for still finer beings to produce still finer beings.

With new found ecological and anthropological perspective, man—creature of environment that he is—may approach the longed-for freedom of will by deliberately changing his environment in order to direct universal human betterment. This would call for the discovery, for each time period, of universally applicable concepts by which a creative cycle might come to replace the past, downward spiral of destructive exploitation leading to further destruction. Already there are inklings of this prospect.

Let us call this new form World Education and seek to describe it. The task is made easier by the emergence over the world of a surprising number of proposals. There are believed to be a thousand or more of these plans, some started, some brewing, a few dating back to the turn of the century. Most have been put forward in the last twenty years, particularly the last ten years. Many are broadened college courses, student-exchange programs, teacher-exchange programs, travel study, junior-year-abroad programs. Some result from individual concern; others have come from various types of organizations. Some presume one large central institution; some are schools afloat. Many are fairly traditional in educational approach; several involve radical changes.

In examing proposals for polycultural education, Oliver J. Caldwell said:

"Education as we know it is tribal in character, dedicated to extolling and maintaining the differences between tribes rather than emphasizing the universality of man. When the earth seemed to be the center of the universe, when people lived in semi-isolated groups on a huge unexplored planet, tribal education was inevitable and necessary because it defended and augmented the strength of the tribe. Furthermore, it preserved and extended the only knowledge available. But now man no longer lives in tribes. Whether he likes it or not, man cannot isolate himself from his fellows. It is the earth which has become small, and man has gained a new perspective of himself and his universe. Effective education should reflect these changes. But the necessary changes in education lag far behind the changes in the body of knowledge, in man's environment, and in man's relations with his fellows."[3]

How quickly can we come to see prejudices of all sorts —racial, provincial, religious—as the partialities they are? Can we enjoy our innate sense of human sympathy without the rasping realities of escapable poverty and sickness and the bestiality of battle? Can we exercise our sense of beauty in the new-found abundance of freedom from grinding toil? Can we enter into a millennium where love and justice and respect find their optimum fulfillment?

3. Oliver J. Caldwell, "Polycultural Education," presented to the 19th Annual National Conference on Higher Education, April, 1964.

CHAPTER II

The Process of World Education

A profound change is needed in education the world over. The traditional "subject matter" basis of education is gradually being reappraised in favor of some degree of integrated problem solving. It is recognized that the simple storing up and recalling of facts can be done better in our era by machines. In our generation, it must be the prime function of education to teach men and women to think, constantly to re-examine the "facts," and to aspire to wisdom in the proper mastery of the machines.

Resistance to change in educational processes is so widespread, that one needs to remember some of the underlying reasons for it. Man has a built-in eagerness to make sure that the techniques of civilization are passed on from generation to generation. Unfortunately, a host of undesirable pieces of "knowledge" are also transmitted —different errors in different regions. Thus the most ancient superstitions are continually being reborn in modern shapes. As an example, one might recall and compare the teaching of the cut and dried "facts" of genetics in 1925 in Tennessee, in 1938 in Germany, and in 1945 in the Soviet Union.

The eagrness to teach, to perpetuate the legends, to indoctrinate according to the will of the passing generation has a counterpart in the child's eagerness to learn. Curiosity is a natural hunger, like the hunger for food. Teachers often impair the student's curiosity, because they accompany their eagerness to teach with authority instead of permitting that curiosity to lead the student to true learning.

Universal problem solving allows for the development of thought and curiosity, re-examination of facts, wisdom in the proper mastery of machines, and a release from tradition and authority so that the individual can realize his own potential. Students must be free to discover the truth and to recognize the folklore, whether they are in Moscow, Mississippi, or Munich. Therefore, World Education must be based on the process of universal problem solving.

Before considering recommendations for a philosophy of World Education, let us look at prevailing patterns. Theodore Brameld[1] finds four chief systems of thought governing education, i.e., Perennialism, Essentialism, Progressivism, and Reconstructionism. He makes no attempt to present the four as mutually exclusive nor even as points in a continuum. Instead, he suggests that they are overlapping systems of discourse, of points of view, with none completely or exclusively held to by any author or school of thought.

The most reactionary is Perennialism. Its central aim is the search for eternal truth, truth, without change, that defies time and space. This description might fit no one school exactly, but there are educators who embrace and defend this view. They are apt to stress the "great books," the great thinkers of the past.

The conservative schools are Essentialist, because they

---

1. Brameld, Theodore. *Patterns of Educational Philosophy,* World Book Co., 1950, later published with revisions in two volumes: *Philosophies of Education in Cultural Perspective* and *Toward a Reconstructed Philosophy of Education* by Henry Holt and Company, Inc., New York, 1955.

seek to conserve the "essential" knowledge of our accumulated culture by reducing it to textbooks and textbook teaching. This group comprises the great majority of schools, public and private. There is much subject matter emphasis in Perennialist schools, but Essentialist schools are hide-bound in subject matter, with administrative supervision, testing, grading, and promotions on the basis of factual knowledge. The process begins with the first grade and reaches beyond college and graduate school into economic life. A good report is a good meal ticket.

Progressivism seeks to stimulate and release an individual's natural power. Like processes of growth, *it involves continuing change and improvement through experimentation. Through self-directed activities appropriate to the individual's level of growth,* rather than through the external compulsions of authority, it seeks *to develop the whole person.* Advocates believe education at any age should be a natural growth involving physical, mental, moral, social, and spiritual experiences adapted to the age, health, interests, and abilities of each pupil. Progressive Education, then, in John Dewey's meaning, comprises the continual reconstruction of experience. Experience embraces thinking and doing. Dewey's analysis of the thinking process is central to Progressive Education.

Building on Progressivism, Brameld goes beyond to describe what he calls *Reconstructionism,* a philosophy differing from Progressivism in that it is geared to our crisis culture. *Reconstructionism would make of education an instrument for confronting and directing revolutionary change.* By wedding knowledge to basic values for choosing between the critical alternatives of our time, it would help students to become agents of constructive social change. The subject matter learned would be that needed

25

for the purposes at hand. Thoroughness of such learning is assumed, but knowledge is regarded as a means to important ends, not an end in itself. If Perennialism is timeless but oriented to the past, if Essentialism conserves the past and Progressivism deals with today, Reconstructionism is future-oriented.

Brameld promoted and made specific the discovery that there are emerging in our cultural crisis creative impulses, far less obvious than their destructive counterparts, but which have the magic quality of being universal in appeal. This universality makes them, if understood, natural bridges of reconciliation between conflicting ideologies in our chaotic world.

What do these four views of education hold for the emerging concept of World Education?

Perennialism stresses the search for basic truth. World Education will borrow this devotion to the search for truth, but within a relativist, not absolutist, framework. Every year, one might almost say every day, research scientists and mathematicians add to our equipment for understanding, both the microcosm and the macrocosm. No longer can education content itself with an acceptance of the world of our sense perceptions and the whole body of related superstition-ridden concepts of theology, religion, and moral conduct. It is time now, if time there is, to make a renewed search into the meaning of being and the place and the role of man in it.

The emergency related to our capacity for self-destruction can only move in the direction of increased knowledge of new methods and more dangerous devices of annihilation. Search for the socially constructive counterparts is imperative. Collective study will be part of the search, but much of it must be done individually, each for himself. Each man is a creature of the central creative power and process, and each is thus rightfully heir to his own creative capacities. Among these are curiosity, imagination, analysis, synthesis, critical reflection, and such emotional endowments as give worth to such wonderings: sympathy, affection, and reverence. The respectful search for the essential meaning of being and for the emerging truths of our times must take on renewed dignity as pursued with all the tools we have at hand. This, without its authoritarian overtones and absolutism, we borrow from Perennialism.

Essentialism stresses the importance of knowledge translated into textbooks as subject matter. It is obvious that knowledge is the very essence of education, provided the word "knowledge" is interpreted broadly enough. Knowledge is more than facts. Learning involves changes in the whole being: habits, feelings, attitudes, ideas, information, and ways of behaving alone and in relation to others.

The knowledge explosion has led to a crisis in education as in all phases of social being. Programs based on subject matter served well through the more static centuries. Only a century ago a scholar could master most available subjects. Today, the expansion of knowledge is so great that there is no longer a core of information—such as English, Latin, Greek, and mathematics—that can mark a man as educated. This same expansion makes a man feel like an impostor if he seeks to be broadly educated and walls him off from others if he specializes.

More and more facts have been added to the textbooks, and the fields of specialization are becoming so subdivided that the curriculum is fragmented. This condition has led to the elective system under which the student

27

selects certain categories of knowledge that preoccupy him, to the neglect of an enormous array of subjects not elected. Even in the courses chosen, the student gains an encyclopedic knowldege unrelated to a search for a value system. In social studies, the arts, and humanities, he is likely to presume an outmoded theory of being and nature of reality. His course is a status quo affair, not only with reference to the field of knowledge, but to the socio-economic realities of the life he is to lead. He prepares for a job that soon may not exist; and if it does, it is too often a job that he selects because it will pay well, rather than because it will satisfy personal or social needs.

The consequence is uncritical drifting into quite dangerous situations. Individuals find themselves trapped, unorganized, and voiceless against the institutions' mass media. National policy is little more than a moment of forces of closely related business, military, and political institutions. Just when governments, through a soundly educated people, could eliminate nearly all of man's oldest enemies, they are so armed and so hostile that the people might be better without national governments.

At all educational levels, no one really knows how to outgrow the subject matter approach. The pattern fits neatly into our passion for standardization. It is measurable, as only quantitative matters are. Education, however, should be chiefly qualitative. The products of true education should be as unique in their differences as the products of our assembly lines are alike.

Let's examine the students' race to cram their heads with facts. Intuitively we know this is wrong. The mind is a remarkable repository indeed for storing and recalling facts, but an electronic computer is many times more efficient.

28

Unlike the electronic computer, man has a built-in value system. His values operate deliberately to select facts that have meaning in advancing purpose. Learning in man should be relative to interest and the state of readiness to advance his purpose, hopefully in terms of values. Vigorous living sends the center of purposeful attention magnetically scouring over the universe of one's knowledge, revitalizing by repetition of awareness that which is useful, slowly cleansing the mind of the superfluous and useless. The mind perceives the relevance of knowledge as though by centripetal force or magnetic attraction, throwing in facts and digesting them in a residuum of experience, "the apperceptive mass." By opposite selective action, it throws off unrelated data as though by centrifugal force or negative magnetic influence. Even the subconscious mind sifts the fleeting bits of information, attracting the related, rejecting the irrelevant. So the poet or the scientist, any creative thinker, "broods and mulls" over his area of concern. When a new meaningful relationship appears, usually in a relaxed mood of contemplation, the conscious mind glows with interest, even excitement. This has been the manner in which all great minds have worked and all great discoveries achieved.

Required courses of study are a violence to the mind's natural selective purpose as well as to nature's method of growth. They teach facts, but there are apt to be concomitant learnings in attitude, such as docility and complacency, rather than vigor of curiosity. Crammed facts, learned for such extraneous rewards as grades and degrees, are worse than useless except to that breed of "quiz-kids" that our schools are grinding out. Facts so taught clutter the mind. They displace more meaningful personal goals by making their mastery an artificial, imposed purpose.

To assign "lessons" to a class, sometimes to classes of hundreds, is to assume that all minds are to be programmed alike with reference to an identical mass of knowledge. Much common knowledge will result from purposeful education, but it will come from self-directed inquiry. Compulsory assignments infringe on the free spirit of the learner and are emotionally crippling. Actually, with such rapid social change and the explosive enlargement of knowledge, no two people should share the same required inventory of knowledge. The beauty and wonder of the individual should be in the richness of what he has chosen from the storehouse of knowledge through the selective processes of his own concerns.

Nature's way of learning, not facts alone, but complex matters of habit and attitude, is awe-inspiring. It involves the whole person in relation to his physical and social environment. We shall have fewer persons with emotional blocks, fewer emotionally sick or institutionalized, when education becomes an extension of the natural growth process. Man's unique creative gifts can meet this challenge.

Due time for reverent meditation, individual and group, is essential for continual reorientation, reassessment of objectives, the nourishing of determination to seek and follow the light of conscience. Meditation serves an integrative purpose as well. This puts it on a level of importance with study, discussion, travel, play, and work. Specifically, educators are aware that, in the rapid expansion of knowledge, specialization has led to the increasing inability of scholars in different fields to communicate with one another. Each tends to become encapsulated in his increasingly restricted area. Scores of attempts have been made to "cross-fertilize" knowledge by various schemes of during the latter years of the depression). Generally, the problems which were pursued were those that arose naturally, even accidentally, for spontaneity was a part of the cult, and suggestions from the teacher were taboo. Therefore, they were immediate and local, unless the teacher saw his role as putting the problem in its larger context.

A bicycle rider was struck as he pedaled to school. Was the problem to repair the damages or investigate the reasons? In one such case, investigation led to a study of the traffic ordinances, even those about the use of bikes being too legalistically worded for the youngsters. That led to their proposing to their city council a reformulation of their own which was adopted.

A child was one hour late because of a change of time. The problem could have been considered simply one of proper disciplinary handling. The teacher, in this case, raised the many questions involved in chronology, such as relativity and means of measuring time. The children made sun dials, water, weight, wax candle, and spring-driven clocks. Art work centered about the concept of time.

The absence of a child with typhoid fever in Collings' "An Experiment with the Project Curriculum" led to health studies of the situation. Remedial measures were taken that set the pattern for the curriculum. Through such approaches to many problems, the community advanced measurably in a number of respects.

In Winnetka, the project method was employed in meeting such needs as the purchase of school supplies, re-

integration. Many of these have involved team teaching; many have pursued courses of "general education." Interdisciplinary programs have become a part of the jargon of the day. These have generally proved disappointing and sometimes have seemed to lead to "cross-sterilization" instead.

One of the most basic, vigorous, and long-sustained of these efforts has been that of the Foundation for Integrative Education,[2] of which Fritz L. Kunz is the leading figure. The assumption of this group of eminent scholars is sound: all knowledge is a proliferation from a dynamic core of central and related truths. These student-scholars have sought the common, basic, conceptual elements in their various disciplines. Their search has been illuminating not only in the areas of ontology, axiology, and epistemology separately, but, even more profoundly, in the nature of the underlying unity of these three.

Should such a search finally succeed, it will chart the pattern of truth but will not specify a manner of learning. It will, however, emphasize the soundness of deep respect for the related purposes and personality of the learner and of group purposes and community character in group study.

For the moment, let us compare the positive quality of learning with the negative quality of forgetting. From a teacher's carefully prepared lesson plans flow ten thousand facts. Most are forgotten, relearned, and eventually hazily retained. Some stealthily slip away. In Florida, the Seminole Indians, never conquered, still recognize their tribal laws as higher than our state and federal laws. Regularly they have entered their children in school for

2. Foundation for Integrative Education, 777 U.N. Plaza, New York, New York.

the first time when ten or eleven years of age. What must one think of the importance of all the careful lesson plans of the teachers those first few years, when experience shows that these children, who often come with no English, are soon abreast of the other pupils?

A factor that encourages an exaggerated appreciation of formal learning is that knowledge which is taught readily lends itself to objective tests. By such testing, one can measure not only the success of the student but also of the teacher. Unfortunately, these are tests of "progress" but not of direction. Therefore, it happens that the most literate nations of the earth have produced not only the greatest abundance of socially useful goods but also the greatest flow of destructive goods.

We plead then for a broad interpretation of learning. Every part of every day is a part of the process. Even learning the judicious amount of sleep is part of the learning process.

Change to the problem solving approach will be difficult, certainly most difficult in the areas where academic habits of curriculum, testing, and point credits are most firmly congealed. The process can succeed only if viewed as a whole and understood in detail.

To aid in the search for truth and the broader interpretation of knowledge, *World Education borrows from Progressivism its problem solving approach.*

John Dewey himself did not know how his theories should be applied. He taught about a theory which was inconsistent with the method he was using. He hardly made a gesture toward problem solving as he lectured.

The chief interpreter of Dewey was William Heard Kilpatrick. Kilpatrick held hundreds spellbound, aroused interest, and excited enthusiasm with gifts that often

proved misleading. He oversimplified. Kilpatrick skillfully divided Dewey's educational philosophy into componen[t] aspects and approached these through ordered questions For each question he provided appropriate references He divided his large classes into groups of ten for discus sion. Then he assembled these smaller groups and raise[d] the questions they had considered. In this manner, he ha[d] direct or indirect discussion with a class of two hundred Finally, he would summarize each question and each topi[c] with such succinctness that everyone felt he had brilliantl[y] voiced a consensus. His students went out, captivated b[y] a philosophy that had come too easily, to practice th[e] "project method," to follow the student's "interest," an[d] to initiate an "activity program."

Some who believed in Dewey's philosophy were wor[ked] derfully successful, e.g., Ellsworth Collings in *An Exper[i]ment with the Project Curriculum*,[3] and the thirty bett[er] Progressive schools which were carefully paired and com pared with an equal number of traditional controls in th[e] *Eight-Year Study*.[4] The findings of the latter study we[re] deeply significant. Not only did the students in the Pr[o]gressive schools make greater progress in character d[e]velopment, they did at least equally well in the maste[ry] of subject-matter; and students in those schools whic[h] departed furthest from tradition did best.

Even in its heyday, Progressive Education was confine[d] to elementary and secondary schools (except for Comm[u]nity Education courses in some teachers' colleges a[nd] some programs called Functional Education that flare[d]

3. *An Experiment with the Project Curriculum*, Macmillan, New Yo[rk], March, 1923.

4. Aiken, Wilfred. *The Story of the Eight-Year Study with Reco[m]mendations and Conclusions*, Harper and Bros., New York, 1942.

pair of bicycles, sale of pets, and insurance of dishes to set up four kinds of business enterprise: competitive, monopolistic, cooperative, and socialistic. In this way, the children had some experience in connection with their classroom study.

There were enough successful examples of such kinds to fill volumes.

Through a problem approach based on existing purposes, each learner amasses his unique treasure of knowledge. Although most of it is common to others, it is garnered in the course of processes both self-disciplined and free.

Dewey's *Democracy and Education*[5] was written before World War I, and reflects a relatively static culture. There is greater alertness now to the critical problems of our day, such as civil strife, shameful poverty, cost of arms, and threat of the escalation of war. The problems of mankind, which elude assigned learning in compulsory schools, may indeed have no ultimate answers. Nevertheless, if World Education aids in producing enough seekers, we can yet escape the dangerous frustrations of our crisis culture.

In World Education one learns more, quantitatively and thoroughly, because the learning is acquired through the motivation of purposes beyond the learning itself. In Essentialism the acquisition of knowledge is the aim, the end, of schooling. In World Education, knowledge is a valued by-product of a purposeful process which is the meaning of Plato's "Education is process, not product," and Arnold's "Education is a growing and a becoming, not a getting and a having and a holding."

---

5. Dewey, John. *Democracy and Education*. Macmillan, New York, 1916.

We now arrive at a central question: In the problem approach of World Education, will scholarship result? For now, let us put aside the stereotype of academic scholarship and analyze the learning process to which Plato referred. Here we relate Essentialism and Progressivism.

Knowledge is, in part, attention become memory. Such learning is rather well understood. It is an exercise between the ears, though affected by the entire body and by the environment. It follows certain rules, called "the laws of learning": as "learning is in direct relation to the number of attentive repetitions." There are rules indicating the plateaus of learning and even rules to avoid forgetting what has been learned.

In the broader sense, however, knowledge is viewed as a consequence of experience. Experience is seen as encompassing a range of reactions along a continuum; intellectual abstraction is at one end and feeling at the other. Thought can never escape the bounds of that continuum. The further we approach the extreme of abstraction, the less is feeling involved, hence the less the involvement of the whole body, the less motivation to action, and the more elusive the content. Without an element of feeling, thought would attain a pure absolute and vanish into nothingness, the only absolute. On the other hand, the further we approach the extreme of feeling, the less is the element of rationalization, the more the involvement of the entire self, the stronger the motivation to action, and the more retentive the impulse. There must be some element of idealization or else the victim of extreme emotion loses all awareness (including self-awareness) and is "mad," hence incapable of learning. These two basic factors are equally imperative to all experience and learning.

The Roles of Feeling and
Perceiving in the Thinking Process

Let us say that a man is crossing a street. While attending to such matters as direction, unevennesses of the road, the persons in sight, the stores around, the signal lights, the hazards of traffic, and while maintaining largely by habit his balance and forward motion, in addition to all these, he slowly becomes aware of a feeling. The feeling actually was so buried in the subconscious (latent but inactive on the continuum we call thought) that he was halfway across the street before the awareness arose to consciousness. Then, by imperceptible degrees of gradation, that awareness takes hold as a sensation, at first only a vague, uneasiness, the opposite feeling from that of well-being he had enjoyed in the pleasure of motion in sunlight and comfortable temperature. But involuntarily the sensation of anxiety gradually increases, and by the time he has reached the sidewalk, the discomfort has become so pronounced that it over-shadows all other concerns, and, temporarily setting aside his former purposes, he gives attention to this pervasive feeling.

"What troubles me?" he asks himself. Under question, under attentive inquiry, the feeling begins little by little to seem less vague, less permeating, until, with a mild, mild sense of relief, it localizes in the area between the right arm and the right side. On further attention, this localized feeling takes on a new qualitative aspect, a qualitative aspect which, like the original feeling of uneasiness, arose out of the subconscious. At first both faint and vague, then stronger and clearer until he can vocalize it, "There seems to be some improper emptiness here between side and arm." He moves the arm a little outward. Then follows, again gradually (though the whole episode lasts only a minute), a more definite sensation, though a negative one only at this point, of absence of a wanted pressure against the two parts of the body involved. "What is missing here?" he asks himself.

Then, finding no clue immediately, he begins the more rational step of deliberately seeking an explanation. "What had happened that underlay this discomfort? Well, where had he been?" He had crossed the street. That seemed, felt, unrelated. He had just been in the barber shop. Still no inkling of cause. Where before the barber shop? The shoe store.[6] Then quickly now, he knows. He has left the box of old shoes at the barber's. And so his direction is reversed. He retrieves the package. He has completed an act of thought in which feeling and thinking have each performed its characteristic function. The one has retained a purposeful impulse to action, the other has provided definition of direction. This dualism illustrates one aspect of the theory of reality suggested in the first chapter.

Feeling is the generating element of thought; perception is the directional factor. Both must be present in every act of thought. From the standpoint of time, either may procede the other in importance of function. One's random speculations may lead suddenly to the perception of a hitherto unrecognized relationship between two facts or ideas, giving each a new significance, and strong emotions may result from this new meaningful insight. Likewise, feeling may precede perception.

The scientific method, critical reflection, and speculation are similarly parts of a continuum in the process of

6. In this case, the shoe store was what John Dewey would have called the "key datum."

38

thought. Science is only a tool to understanding, not understanding itself. It has no value system, no morality. It is equally subservient to the purposes of war and peace, poverty and prosperity. The scientific method of thought stands at the opposite end of a continuum from speculation with its freedom of imagination in the dimensions of range and depth. Pure speculation is unreliable, only suggestion. There are, in each of these extreme forms of thought, some elements of the other. The scientist must postulate his thesis, and the imaginative thinker must test his speculations, if they are to have the slightest profundity.

Between these two methods of thought is the great middle ground of critical reflection, which is the method of everyday life and the most appropriate for general problem solving. The extremes of thoughtful experience, imaginative speculation, and scientific testing can be united in critical reflection.

Let World Education accord due emphasis to every aspect of the whole range of the thinking process. Although science is now so much in ascendancy, so highly regarded in the popular mind, we must not be misled into overestimating its bounds of usefulness. Germany was the mecca of science. What Germany needed in the twenties was an army of Martin Luther Kings. It should be a purpose of World Education to produce such men suitably equipped to function in all the different areas of human tension: racial, political, economic, and psychological.

Thinking, then, can be viewed as the purposeful definition of feeling. This definition is very different from the basis presumed in Essentialist education. The thinking process, as defined by Dewey in *How We Think*,[7] is the new

7. Dewey, John. *How We Think*. Heath, Chicago, 1933.

39

logic, and is as basic to a philosophy of World Education as Aristotle's logic has been and is to the subject matter approach of Essentialism. One needs only remind oneself of the syllogistic approach of Aristotle in which the regular form of logical reasoning or argument consists of three propositions, the first two called the "premises," and the third the "conclusion." Aristotle's was logical logic; Dewey's, psychological logic.

Since we are proposing reliance on pragmatism, let us review Dewey's foremost contribution in his analysis of a typical act of thought. Let us scrutinize its stages for the kinds of learning that are corollary. These are crucial in answering critics who fear that the problem approach will not lead to "scholarship." Actually, the problem-solving approach has engendered most of the creative scholarship of the past, now mummified in textbooks.

Typically, according to Dewey, there are several stages (not always in this order nor always complete in number):

1. There is an ongoing activity directed toward a purpose. The freer the growth, the more the learner feels this purpose to be his own. Assigned lessons originate with the teacher or the text and are part of the basic assumption that teachers know better than students what students should want to know and in what order they should want to learn it. Growth in the use of freedom is one consequence of self-motivated learning, of pragmatic scholarship.

2. In the pursuit of this purpose an obstacle is encountered. Otherwise, there is routine or habitual response, not the adjustment that involves thought. The habit of adjustability is a natural by-product of purposeful education and therefore, in Dewey's meaning, a part of learning, of the new scholarship.

40

3. The learner reacts to this encounter in one of two basic and opposite manners. Either he accepts the challenge to his pursuit of purpose, or he reacts negatively with irritation or anger, discouragement, hopelessness, or perhaps violence. This positive-negative "choice" is a learned or conditioned response. Already acquired attributes of attitude such as health, self-confidence, and emotional self-discipline enter into the response. A response is an aspect of learning because it is a further factor of conditioning. The habit of emotional control whenever one encounters an obstacle is learned. A long, long sequence of encounters shapes character in these vital regards. Consequently, they are essential to moral learning, which is essential to valid scholarship.

In Essentialist schools, students are motivated by authority for extraneous rewards such as grades leading to a report, graduation, a job, financial security, and perhaps wealth—all extraneous to the assignment. Under these circumstances, acceptance of a hard assignment and application to master it lead at best toward docility, at worst toward discouragement, resentment, rebellion, and withdrawal from school. Indeed, it is not far-fetched to argue that nations made up of the products of Essentialist teaching may be counted on to acquiesce in national policies that become involved in brutal war, because obstacles to national purposes were not recognized in time as occasions for reflective consideration.

4. Presuming a positive emotional reaction in meeting the obstacle, the learner next defines the problem. For example, a student bends closer and closer to his book in the late afternoon as the room grows slowly darker. This discomfort may continue for some time and gradually increase before he recognizes the problem and flashes on

41

the light. Or a white man becomes embroiled with a Negro by sitting at dusk on the Negro's small child who was lying on the dark-colored seat of a coach. All the emotions involved in present racial attitudes tended to obscure the recognition, the analysis, the definition of the unintended error. Such definition of hindrance can become a learned habit and, of course, should. Such learning is part of the moral aspect of education, and an illustration of how education and religion must become, and be recognized as, parts of one another. The habit of carefully defining the problem is an aspect of functional scholarship.

5. Imagination is brought into play in search of ways to circumvent the obstacle. Imagination rests both on a native quality of the mind, employing the intricacies of classification of experience, memory, and selective recall, and on the accumulation of related experience, hence related learning. We cannot imagine apart from a basis in experience. Even within the realm of experience, we are far less inventive than we are prone to think. Space craft are indeed ingenious inventions, but they are little more than the culmination of a sequence of thousands of minor steps, some of which, such as the wheel, eluded mankind for thousands of years. Similarly, bottles were known and also wire. It was recognized that electric current would make a wire glow and that oxygen was needed for burning a wire. Yet it took Edison's brilliant, inventive mind to place a wire in a bottle from which air had been excluded and turn a switch.

Obviously, when the student in fulfillment of his purpose approaches an obstacle with hope and self-confidence, even courage, he stands a far better chance of solving his problem and thereby strengthening these constructive attributes. For the hopeless one this encounter is a further discouragement. Imagination is an elusive power, a precious product of purpose and emotional health that does not flourish on destructive emotions: anger, hopelessness, helplessness, rejection, docility, insecurity, disappointment, or fear. Education must prepare the seed-bed for creative imagination, an aspect of true scholarship.

Dewey spoke of three qualities of imagination that now come into play: range, readiness, and profundity. It would seem that the operation of the first two must precede in time the exercise of the third. The native gift of temperament as well as experience enter into the outcome; so does environmental conditioning. One cannot assign exercise of imagination; imagination is the magic servant of purpose. It usually operates best in times of relaxation or quiet contemplation, when the subconscious mind, at work on a problem, brings into meaningful relation factors not before connected. Schools are too hurried with their cramming of facts to provide time or place for contemplation. Besides, Essentialist education rarely calls for the exercise of imagination, as both problem and answer are provided to be "learned." This process puts the cart before the horse, while problem-solving puts problem and answer in the natural order.

The student, pursuing a purpose and encountering an obstacle which he has recognized and accepted, now imagines one, or a series of, possible solutions. A bright animal, say a dog, faced with a problem also "thinks," in that he tries one plan after another until he succeeds, if he succeeds. But if he weighs possible plans at all, the process is quick and shallow, for he seems guided by one impulse to action after another.

6. In selecting between the imagined solutions, the student exercises another quality of genuine scholarship,

43

judgment, which is rooted in a value system. He judges with care because of involvement in the consequences. If his purpose is a world of peace and plenty, the obstacles are as real as life itself, and the stakes are the highest.

7. Having selected one course from several, the learner now goes into action with his purpose in mind as the goal and the reward. In education through extraneous rewards, application at this point in the learning process, if there is a counterpart, calls for the exercise of what is called "will power." I suppose that "will power" in this sense is the power to make oneself do what one knows one ought to do in order to avoid worse alternatives or to gain a good grade. This is basically a slavish affair in which teachers have been well termed "masters" (who serve under headmasters"). Those students who are not so impelled are sometimes called "lazy." This word should not exist, for no one is really lazy. "Laziness" is an indiscriminate epithet for one who is perhaps sick, tired, hungry, or discouraged by feelings of insecurity, rejection, inadequacy, loneliness, or the like. Too often the "stupid" child is the victim of unstimulating, unwholesome conditioning. "I.Q.s" camouflage causes.

At this stage in Dewey's thinking process, the learner is not forced but is drawn by the prospect of achieving his purpose. He makes himself do what he recognizes as necessary. The process may be "hard" in the sense of being prolonged and difficult, but it has no tinge of coercion. It is free. It is this kind of free, disciplined man that the world needs, this kind of scholar.

The goal is attained, or, if not, a second alternative is tried. At the moment of success, there is a sensation of fulfillment, of completion. If the way has been hard and long, there may even be something of that ecstasy of the consciousness of growth. Thus, the earned sense of well-being and increased self-confidence rightly have moral overtones because the problem was met creatively, not evaded, not attacked with irritation, anger, or violence.

8. Finally, the learner, having completed a typical act of thought, reviews his course, evaluates it, and fixes at least the crucial factor of choice in memory. This step Dewey calls "the reconstruction of experience." That which was sought with reference to one goal has become acquired knowledge ready for use in the pursuit of some new objective. The achievement of one purpose becomes a steppingstone to future purpose. If the thinking process was a joint one, the art of constructive cooperation was learned in addition.

In listing possible new goals and selecting one, the student exercises continuing value judgment. It is by the wise exercise of value judgments that he threads his way toward his own life's objectives, and he becomes increasingly differentiated from others through the fruition of that uniqueness that is the potential endowment of every individual. Learning, in the Dewey sense, is far broader, richer, more dynamic than in the Essentialist sense.

To the often raised question, then, will problem-solving education produce scholars, one must ask the questioner whether he refers to Aristotelian or Dewey scholarship, formal or pragmatic, old or new, relatively static or dynamic.

Illustration of the Thinking Process

A student who was looking for an opportunity to make a laboratory exercise of the thinking process was advised to watch for a situation of irritation or anger and see if he could substitute resolution of conflict through the Dewey analysis of a typical act of thought.

On a farm in Georgia, the student chanced to see a farmer leading a mule from the barnyard out to work. A few yards outside the gate, the mule balked. The farmer encouraged the mule to go but she refused. He scolded, he cursed. He strapped the mule with the lines and then began kicking the mule. As the student approached, there was the same angry expression on the faces of the man and the mule.

Student: "I've been looking for an opportunity to apply the typical stages in Dewey's analysis of the thinking process, and I wonder if you will let me help."
Farmer: "What the hell do you know about a mule?"
Student: "I know little about mules, but you know a lot about them. And I want to understand the thinking process and try it out experimentally."
Farmer: "I don't half understand what you are talking about, but I was getting nowhere. Go ahead."
Student: "What are the types of causes that could make a mule balk?"
Farmer: "She's stubborn."
Student: "What makes her stubborn?"
Farmer: "She's mad."
Student: "What sorts of things can make a mule mad?"
Farmer: "Well, she could have a rock caught in her hoof."

Then the farmer showed the student how to run his hand down the mule's leg and lift one foot at a time. This was accomplished but no stone was found.

Student: "I wouldn't need to know much about a mule

46

to know that she needs to eat and might be angry if she weren't fed."

Farmer: "Now, I fed her myself."

Student: "What about water?"

Farmer: "She's had water. I told Henry to water Maude."

Student: "Dewey said to verify one's data. Henry, did you water Maude?"

Henry: "Naw, doggone it, I forgot to."

This remark produced in the student what some psychologists call the "Aha reaction."

Student: "Let's see if Maude will go back to the watering trough."

And sure enough, as though Maude had been listening to every word, she went willingly back, drank her fill, shook her head patiently, turned, and went willingly to work.

Through a long series of such experiences, that student, who drew the accompanying cartoon, made great progress in gaining habitual self-control.

In his later teaching, problem-solving was central. If a boy raised his hand to ask to be excused,

Teacher: "Why do you ask me if you may be excused. Only you know if you need to. This way you make an authority figure of me and place yourself in a position of willing submission to such authority. Why not go when you need to?"

Student: "But suppose my parents phoned and wanted me. The principal wouldn't be happy if he found you didn't know where I was."

How Do You Solve a Problem?

Thinking this problem through, the class arrived at a workable plan of having a board with hooks individually labeled. There were six hooks marked, Toilet, Library, Gymnasium, Principal's Office, Playground, Infirmary. On leaving the room, students indicated their whereabouts by putting their paddles on the correct hook.

Beginning with such immediate problems, the program gradually moved outward to the problems of the community and the world.

Our proposals for World Education, it should be clear now, are both eclectic and elastic. But, as yet, we have made no mention of our borrowings from what Theodore Brameld calls Reconstructionism. Brameld differs from the classical Progressivists in his feeling that they did not sufficiently appreciate the impact of social forces on individuals. He emphasizes the significance of group conflict and allegiances as well as group "conditioners." In this same spirit, we propose to focus World Education on a number of determining societal factors which might well form our "core curriculum."

First, man can learn to plan with foresight so as to direct his destiny. He can decide between the paradoxical alternatives of human suicide and the achievement of such a plateau of existence as would make clear that the ancient dreams of an uneventful Eden and a bodyless heaven were childish fictions.

The objective of Reconstructionism is an ever-planning society, not a planned world community. Even the most enlightened contemporary planning can be disastrous when it is imposed by a small group of planners.

For example, in the Anti-poverty Program, we attack the symptoms, never questioning the causes. We siphon off from excessive profits just enough to make tolerable the poverty that results from that excess, and measure the urgency of avoiding such eruptions of violence (Exp. Watts) as can kill thirty-four people and wantonly destroy fifty-million dollars worth of property. This material destruction is repaired by further funds from the top.

Through planned cooperation the world over, this planet could be air-conditioned, moderating the extremes of the poles and the tropics by speeded up, channeled air currents, accelerated and redirected ocean currents, innumerable vast air storage chambers to be alternately filled under pressure and released to forestall the violence of storms. Swamps could be drained, deserts irrigated, and population stabilized. Agricultural and industrial production could become so automated that the need of manual labor would fade in significance. The present violently conflicting policies of ownership and distribution would give way to a computerized method of registering production needs and distribution quotas to eliminate poverty and release time and energy for beautifying our earth and our lives on it.

Second, man must realize that all men are alike in their basic wants, and that the absence of the means to attain them results in desperate devices which cause some wants to be sacrificed for others. To illustrate, hungry men will forego freedom to attain food; but when basic, essential needs are met, effective demand for freedom follows. If Americans understood this fact of life, an alternative would present itself in Vietnam, for instance, that otherwise would never even come to mind. Instead of sowing dragon teeth, we would join with Communists and all others in building dams, generating power, establishing industries, improving canals and other transportation systems, attending to health needs, and rebuilding homes. In

50

a land of plenty, freedom blooms as naturally as a cared-for garden. No people want totalitarianism except as a temporary expedient. Therefore, we should be working with the Peoples' Republic of China, through their government, like it or not; and, in the same manner, with every government.

Third, in accepting the problem-solving approach, we must do so with the ultimate purpose of discovering solutions that will work universally. We are today in a period of metamorphosis when old institutions are degenerating, and we feel ourselves in that moribund state of the pupa. We need to reflect on the meaning of metamorphosis to realize the real significance of the day's crises. Analogies, admittedly, can be fallacious; they can also be illuminating.

Consider the nature of the changes in the caterpillar and the process of metamorphosis. After a life of crawling and feeding on leaves, quite automatic changes lead to the operation of glands that secrete a silken filament. Instinctively, the caterpillar begins to twist and turn to the end of encasing itself in a cocoon thus made.

Within that protective case, the caterpillar undergoes changes that resemble death. The moist, green skin becomes hard and brown. The organs within lose identity and appear as a gelatinous mass. Clearly, it can never again exist as the creature it was.

Within this seemingly moribund protoplasm there is the germinal promise of a new form, microscopic in dimensions. Slowly the old substance reforms into the new design. In due time, there emerges not the belly-crawling worm but a creature of flight on iridescent wings.

The tortuous progress of man, for hundreds of millennia earth-bound and slow as the creeping of the caterpillar, can now give way not only to physical flight in space but flight in imagination into a realm of being more interesting and exciting than man's childhood visions of heaven.

The pupal stage is the last before the ultimate development. The potential society of tomorrow is foreshadowed in emerging concepts, emerging truths, that are aspects of our cultural unfolding as a tiny segment of the ever-changing, unfolding universe.

In this context, we might well look to some of the concrete challenges to which all persons must be prepared to respond. We might call these the Triple Revolution[8] plus one: the cybernetic, nuclear, and human rights revolutions, and the question of population growth. The effects of all four are already changing our style of life and our expectations. Our responses are, for the most part, *ad hoc*, fragmented, hysterical. World Education must help provide the tools to integrate solutions. It is the cultivation of these potentialities that dwarfs the provincialism of present educational stereotypes, and, if humanity is to survive, reveals the true dimension, the vision, the challenge, and the necessity of World Education.

If World Education can promote free search the world over, then man will arrive.

World Education's Need for an Accrediting Agency

At present, there is no suitable accrediting body for World Education schools at the college or university

---

8. The term Triple Revolution originated in a document demanding "a fundamental re-examination of existing values and institutions" in the areas of cybernetics, weaponry, and human rights prepared by an Ad Hoc Committee of American scientists, educators, social leaders, and critics. Printed in *Liberation*, April, 1964.

level. Especially is this true for such schools as plan centers in various parts of the world. Local, regional, and even national accrediting associations are naturally reluctant to give recognition to schools that extend beyond their boundaries. They even hesitate to approve the local unit of a World College, on the ground that they have no such authority and, besides, would need to inspect regularly at the school's expense each such distant unit.

For reasons given elsewhere in this volume, the U.N. and Unesco have been unwilling to set up such an agency. And their reluctance is understandable in terms of expense, the complexities involved, and even more in terms of the risks of appearing arbitrary, unsympathetic, or unfair in establishing standards.

So these new ventures find themselves caught between the impropriety and unwillingness of local accrediting bodies to pass judgment and the absence of a world agency of competence, authority, and willingness.

The best hope seems to lie in seeking local approval, state and regional, for each local unit, while working toward the formation of a world-wide accrediting association.

The former tends to be further complicated if the program is based on universal human problems rather than on subjects. And many World Education ventures tend to follow Dewey in this respect rather than Aristotle. The tendency even in accredited schools is toward seminars, tutorials, replacing textbooks with reference materials, studying problems, abolishing grades. However, the faculty are measured by the conventional subject matter standards of scholarship. And so, accrediting officials count degrees. And faculty degrees are on a rising market, are costly.

But the doctorate is no evidence that the holder has well integrated knowledge, a wise, balanced outlook, or has had life experience with any of the momentous concepts that hold such promise for the future. The probability is the reverse. So the emerging World College must play two games at once: satisfy conventional requirements —faculty-wise, financially, in terms of plant and library— while pioneering into a realm that redefines the terms, gives them new meaning, and establishes new criteria.

While playing this dual role at the local and regional levels, World Education must work toward a new world accrediting association. All colleges and universities are moving in the international direction, and they have their International Association of Universities with headquarters at 8, Rue Franklin, Paris 16. But this is purely an association of already accredited institutions.

There is a way out, a simple way, proved historically and thoroughly acceptable to Unesco. And that is to have several World Colleges (there are no real world universities now except in name) meet and form an association for purposes of mutual assistance but, specifically, to establish criteria of their own, with appropriate stages from perhaps mere registration through correspondence and candidacy to full accreditation. Then this association, we have been amply assured, would be welcomed into membership in Unesco as a non-governmental organization.

This is the historic pattern by which all accrediting associations have come into being. And the weight of authority would rest, as it should, on the quality of standards and their appropriateness to the purposes of this emerging form, World Education.

An example of this procedure is already afforded in the International Schools Association with headquarters at the

International School, 62, Route de Chêne, Geneva. This Association has membership in Unesco, and, through generous foundation grants, International Schools Examination Syndicate has been formed to bypass the present need in International Schools to also prepare different students for the exacting requirements of the several regional associations involved in the students' choices of college.

Progress has been made in developing syllabi and examinations, especially in the social studies field, that are already widely accepted. And the program is being extended to other areas of study.

The next step at the college level is to call preliminary meetings of interested World Colleges. It has been suggested that one such meeting be on the West Coast, one on the East Coast, and one in Geneva. Such meetings, hopefully, would be followed by a world meeting at a time and place determined by a committee appointed at the earlier meetings.

Until a clearinghouse emerges for World Education, those interested in such meetings are invited to contact to Friends World Institute, East Norwich, New York 11732, Phone 516-MA 6-1310.

CHAPTER III

World Education, An Example
Friends World Institute

Growing out of six years of planning by the Committee on a Friends World College, and after an experimental project in the summer of 1963 directed by Harold Taylor,[1] Friends World Institute[2] opened in September, 1965. Thirteen buildings, formerly part of the Mitchel Air Base, were rented from Nassau County. Forty students[3] and ten faculty members assembled to begin a bold enterprise, perhaps the world's first truly world undergraduate program.

---

1. This program was described by Harold Taylor in "The Idea of a World College," *Saturday Review*, November 14, 1964.

2. In New York State, "college" and "university" are protected words and cannot be applied to a school without the consent of the State Department of Education. The requirements are, properly, high. The school must have a minimum of $500,000 in assets; $3,000,000 are recommended. In these days of giants, starting a college requires much more than purpose and ideas; accreditation becomes increasingly essential. There are steps provided in attaining accredited status; but they are high steps for infant legs. Only bold students, if they have the choice, will attend a school that cannot call itself a college, cannot grant a degree, does not have available loans from most lending agencies (as the United States Student Loan Fund, a federally-sponsored agency). Such beginning schools seek status as *Candidates for Accreditation* from the Middle States Association of Colleges and Secondary Schools. But the requirements are high, even regarding administrative qualification. And if the goals of the school are unconventional, the process of evaluation is, naturally, made harder. Then, if the methods of the school are also experimental, the obstacles mount. One would think that in this day of so much dissatisfaction with colleges as they are, so much alienation among the students, experimentation would be encouraged, even as-

Students participating in the pilot project of the Committee on a Friend's World College, Summer 1963

Students and faculty had worked for three weeks put-

---

sisted, by the associations of accredited schools. But this is not so. Fortunately, the way for advancement opens a crack if three or more accredited colleges are willing to give credit for well-done work of students who might transfer. In the case of Friends World Institute, Goddard College, Antioch College, Pacific Oaks College, and Western College for Women have kindly given such assistance.

(Just at press time, net assets stand at $1,000,000 and application for a college charter is being made to the Regents of New York State.)

3. Entrance requirements are largely reversed. The student chooses the school, more than the school the student. There is little need of tests of intelligence, for no dullard comprehends the significance of such a program; little need of test of academic aptitude, for granted intelligence, such a program brings into play latent abilities in the past too seldom challenged.

The tuition per year in dollar equivalency is, except for personal extras, $2,625, including food, lodging, tuition, use of books, intra-regional and inter-regional travel. In regions where such charge would be prohibitive, special plans are being studied, such as the use of counterpart funds to cover the expenses of all seven regional groups while in India, in return for the expenses of Indian students around the world. Grants are hoped for.

ting into usable condition the buildings that had not been used for several years. The opening exercises were held out of doors, with Committee members, faculty, students and friends numbering about 200. There was in the bright, crisp air a sense of pioneering and a suspicion that this occasion might prove historic in the annals of education. There was the unspoken question, "May this prove to be the first in a revoluntionary turn from provincialism to humanism?"

Dr. George Nicklin[4] spoke as follows:

> Freud said there are three imperfect professions. These include: Psychoanalysis, Politics, and Parenthood. To this should be added Education.
>
> We should be prepared for a natural anxiety over our imperfections in these areas. The practice of Education today involves politics, parenthood, and psychoanalysis. A good education is a therapeutic environment, or it can be anti-therapeutic.
>
> The Friends' (Quaker) concept of education involves belief of "that of God in every man." This sets up a self-fulfilling prophesy which encourages the best of people.

---

4. George Nicklin, M.D., had long been Chairman of the Committee on a Friends World College and had been the strongest and most persistent promoter of the purpose. His motivation came largely from a high school course on the Cause of War, his undergraduate years at Haverford, an A.F.S.C. work camp experience in Mexico, and participation in World War II, in which he was seriously wounded. Having become a Friend, he introduced the idea of a Friends World College at Westbury, L.I., Meeting. New York Yearly Meeting of the Religious Society of Friends was asked to appoint a committee to investigate the propriety of establishing a Friends College in the New York State area. The resulting Committee worked long and hard, often meeting well beyond midnight, then adjourning to widely scattered homes. At first the thought had been to have a Quaker college north of Philadelphia and east of Ohio. But nearness to the United Nations and world developments, such as the launching of satellites, early expanded the proposal to embrace the world.

58

nor on the premise of the importance of great patience. We do persist, and with compassion, eventually overcome. We are participants in the greatest discovery since the Wheel; i.e., the concept of education, the discovery that data sticks to the bits of protoplasm we call People and in so doing catalyzes the creative process, which is revolutionary. Indeed, this revolution probably preceded the wheel. We are here to further that revolution, to enable it to spread Man's understanding and compassion for himself and his fellow man.

The road into the future is paved with our heartbeats, which generate our ideas. Our heartbeats are limited, but our ideas are unlimited. It is important to use both wisely. The phenomena of Society, such as cities, churches, universities, colleges, nations, and this Institute, represent collections of heartbeats and ideas. It is apparent in the way in which these appear in Society, that a master plan with some flexibility is built into our biological structure.

You, and we but especially you, the students—are the Future. We intend you to help catalyze the world of the Future into peace as we follow Life's Destiny of a unified mankind.

Norman Kuebler, one of the students, made these remarks:

To be a part of this searching education has left me for the moment numb-full of excitement and eagerness to learn, yet hesitant in my plunge into knowledge, looking for a handle to grasp.

The college is new. The word *new* has in the American vocabulary an almost isolated meaning that is separated from the rest of the language. Women in stores go al-

59

most stark raving mad over seeing brightly colored boxes and gaily decorated pink and gold cans with that word *new* sprawled across the label. Certain people come close to the point of ridiculous insanity when new cars, new televisions, or whatever the gadget is comes out for the first time. However, even with my obviously slanted remarks about the word, it does create a sensation of stirring people and getting attention. I as a student feel this and feel fortunate to be *new*—something I have not been for nineteen years.

We are students from extremely varied backgrounds. We naturally and rightfully wish to be separate individuals. I hope for myself and for my fellow students, however, that we do not become so individualized that we forget that concept of "oneness" that I believe I came here to find and that I hope others did also. Oh, it's nice to dream of living a life isolated somewhere, to think with God. But we are a world community—a community that during the next four years we hope to come to know better and to be a greater part of.

I warn myself not to be overly pessimistic and discouraged with what I see now and will see later. As we look around Mitchel Gardens there are houses falling apart, lighting fixtures hanging from the ceilings, faulty plumbing, and so on. But as we look outside of those barbed wire fences that the Air Force has left us to keep out the Indians and buffaloes that exist on Long Island, we find a world of governments that are falling apart, missiles and bombers hanging from the sky, and faulty uses of natural God-given resources. In that short, short period since the Friends World Institute was graciously given the old homes of Air Force personnel to lease, much hard work has gone into making the homes livable.

I like to think that this same type of physical and

mental work can be applicable to that world outside the barbed wire fence. The result may not be immediately as apparent as it has been here, but it can and must be done to make the world livable. I am not quite sure whether or not it is the spark of "newness" that has spurred people on to renovate Mitchel Gardens. If it is, we must light the fire to create another spark of newness to renovate many of those old and outdated methods being used in today's world community. With all of this I am happy. I am happy to live and to exist. I am happy that I am not alone in my search. I have long known that I have had the guiding hand of God with me, and I now know that in all of you there is the God within to help me also.

Three Revolutionary Concepts

1. This was clearly to be the first college-level institution to employ the world, literally, as its campus. It embraced the concept of several Centers of World Community, each bearing its local designation. For there is no natural cultural center on the face of our sphere. Community must grow as from the joints of a web, tying by its filaments all mankind into a sense of oneness. The plan for a world campus would be to send students systematically around the earth with six-month stops at each of the seven centers and to engage in thousands of miles of studytravel in each of seven regions.

2. The program of study breaks with the traditional subdivision of curriculum into subject areas; seeks the basic unity of all knowledge in common truth; seeks knowledge not as an end in itself but as a means to human goals; and is based on direct and vicarious experience in recognizing, defining, and solving major problems

in our crisis culture. The curriculum evolves and grows out of the continual reconstruction of experience.[5]

3. Teaching yields its honored role to the humble one of seeking; the Quaker subordination of the preacher to the inner authority of conscience in each worshipper's quest for truth correspondingly makes of faculty and students a fraternity of junior and senior scholars; the object of the quest is those universally applicable concepts which are emerging today as the counterpart of the destructive forces which threaten human survival.

The World As Campus

The accompanying diagram shows the plan by which the world is being made the campus. Seven loosely defined regions are, largely for convenience sake, the subdivisions: Africa, South Asia, East Asia, North America, Latin America, West Europe, and East Europe.

The plan is to admit students, ultimately 100 every six months, at the Study Center within each of the seven regions. Each student attends first the Center of the region of his origin. Then by plane he moves to the next Center to the East for the next six months. The direction

---

5. The program comprises the wise use of the entire day. There is variety in each day and from day to day, so that vacations away from school are almost unnecessary.

All share in caring for the property, preparing meals, and other duties. There is no other help. There is good equipment so as to minimize routine work and duties are rotated. There are staff members to help those who are unfamiliar with such matters. (At the beginning of the summer program 1963, some of the students were so unfamiliar with dishwashing that two dozen quart bottles of detergent were used the first week. Suds billowed shoulder-high while the washer poured in more.)

Work is important to maturing, if only through understanding the millenia of human experience in making and doing through periods of inescapable scarcity.

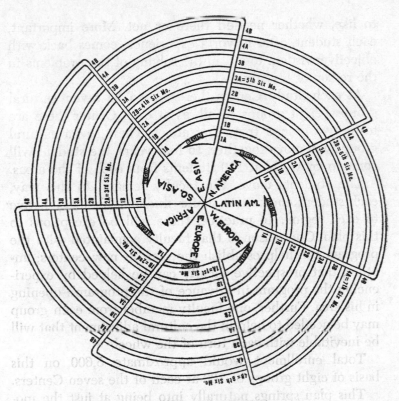

World Education Symbol

is arbitrary. By seven such stages, the student encompasses the globe. Observe that in this plan a new group of 100 is to enter every six months at each Center; and at each Center, one group is to be graduated every six months.

Since there are eight six-month periods in the four year program, but only seven Study Centers, each student automatically returns to his own area for his last study period. This fact obviates the tendency of some, in other plans, to remain in whatever area they visit and happen to like, whether needed there or not. More important, each student, after a world experience, comes back with objective wisdom to aid in the solving of the problems in the region of his origin.

At each Study Center there are to be seven cultural groups (eight groups in all, as at each Center there are to be two groups from that area). These seven cultural groups will move together. In four years, the student will come to know about 100 students from each of the areas.

The students move, the faculty remain. In this way, each student encounters senior students (faculty) native to each region. In practice, there will be exceptions to this plan. One reason is that faculty acquainted with the program can help establish the plan in new centers; another, that prospective faculty can be helped by experiencing the program in advance of the program's opening in his area. Further, one faculty member from each group may be needed to help in the cultural adjustment that will be inevitable with each turn of the wheel.

Total enrollment would approximate 5,600 on this basis of eight groups of 100 at each of the seven Centers.

This plan springs naturally into being at just the moment in civilization when man's mastery of the arts of communication and transportation enable him to relate instantly to the antipodes. The plan, logistically, is timely.

The physical set up at each Center will differ. But the plan as it is developing in three Study Centers will be described.

North American Center

A campus of 93 acres for the North American Center of Friends World Institute was made possible by the gen-

erosity of Mrs. Gerald M. Livingston in memory of her late husband, for whom the Center will be named. This plot faces on Lloyd Harbor, with more than 1,000 feet of waterfront. The 30 acres near water height may be used by all groups for tennis, riding, volley ball. It is hoped to have a small fleet of sailboats. To the south of this area, the land rises rather sharply by 120 feet. On the 60 acre plateau above, 400[6] students are to live and study.

The present plan involves four stages, the first of which will be completed in time for the fall term of 1967. This involves making ready the existing buildings and installing equipment and the library. Then, in succeeding stages, eight villages will be developed around a central core comprising a Meeting, a main library, eating facilities, science hall, arts and crafts building, and administration quarters.

It is planned that each village will accommodate 50 students and ten faculty members. It will consist of a number of simple cottages with apartments for three or four students, each apartment with two bedrooms, living room, kitchenette, and bath. These cottages will surround a Meeting large enough to accommodate 60 or so, kitchen and dining room for that village, and a small working library of perhaps 5,000 volumes, the books most used in the program.

The following outline sketch of the projected library system of Friends World Institute was proposed by Charles Vertanes, Library Consultant. His paper is in-

---

6. Four hundred students for the reason that half of each group spends half the time in field study. The logistics for moving so many students in seven areas will call for a special office, possibly a computer. It's like the truck driver who kept beating on the side of his huge van because the axles would hold only half the weight of the load of canaries, so he had to keep half of them flying.

cluded as an illustration of how the simple, basic idea of the world-as-campus unfolds in hundreds, thousands of consistent, but, from the beginning, scarcely envisioned, ways. So with the curriculum, so with admissions, administration. The financial projection from the one million dollar mark in assets achieved in 1967 is to reach nearly five million by 1972. If the plan of having eight hundred students at each of seven Centers is fulfilled, the tuition, including scholarships, will amount to $14,700,000 annually.

Proposed Library System for Friends World Institute

The library system of Friends World Institute is projected as consisting of the coordinated acquisition and centralized processing of the library and audio-visual resources of all the centers and divisions of the Institute, and the independent administration of these resources at each of the centers and divisions. The system will embrace the resources as well as the facilities and services of the world-wide-centers of the Institute's current program, of the resident four-year college that is now being considered, and the Conflict Resolution Study and Research Center that will be established either at Harrow Hill or at the Livingston campus.

It is anticipated that within the next three or four years, when the form and functions of the various centers and divisions of the Institute will be fairly well-defined, a plan will be developed and the means will be sought to automate fully the library system of the Institute along the lines of the ESEA Title III Operational Grant project, SLAP, designed by the author of this paper, for the implementation of which about $400,000.00 has been allocated by the U.S. Office of Education. By that time, the art of library automation will have been so far advanced, and the Library of Congress itself will be so far ahead in its plans to offer standardized services in this new area of library technology, that the automation of the Institute's library system will be greatly facilitated. It is with this objective in mind that the plans for the organization of the system are now being made, and procedures established that will readily lend themselves to mechanization and automation. It may be worthy of note that the Austrian Center of the Institute already has access to a computer in Vienna through a console located on the campus.

Because of the world-wide distribution of the Institute's centers, the Universal Decimal Classification system is being adopted as the basis for the organization of the library and audio-visual resources. The schedules for the social sciences and the humanities of the UDC will be expanded to meet the curricular and research needs of the Institute, and its faceted, analytical classification devices will be exploited fully to give ready and many-sided access to information resources. Full advantage is also being taken of the structural and functional flexibility of the UDC—features which neither the Dewey Decimal Classification nor the Library of Congress Classification system possess to any significant extent—to meet the bibliographical and information needs of the Institute.

In this scheme, for one thing, it will be possible to catalog the holdings of the Institute—no matter where acquired and whatever the language of the text—from one processing center or in any given locality, and have the results equally usable anywhere, without the necessity of revision or adaptation for use in any other location. It will also be possible to use the basic bibliographical information on the L. C. catalog cards, and perhaps even make some use of the suggested classification and the subject headings on these cards, if such a procedure may promise to be more economical and/or more efficient than otherwise for the FWI-UDC cataloging scheme.

The geographical codes provided in the UDC system will make it possible to identify an item's regional location immediately. They will also make it possible to reassemble items on shelves primarily on a regional basis, when this becomes necessary, and at the same time to maintain the hierarchical subject arrangement within each region or country or other geographical division. When the need is no longer there, or if the maintenance of the new arrangement is no longer desired, the items on the shelves can once more be rearranged in the original order, giving priority to the main subject code. And this can be done, back and forth, as often as desired, without adding or deleting a single numeral or letter from the classification number used as the call number of the items.

The Livingston campus, or any other location that may become the overall administrative center of FWI, will also be the administrative and technical processing center of all the library and audio-visual centers of the Institute. The basic cataloguing of locally acquired materials in given instances, such as in languages not within the competence of the central library agency to handle, will be done locally, but in accordance with procedures established by the central agency of the library system. UDC lends itself to a good deal more uniformity in this type of decentralized cataloguing than either the DC or LC classification system. A copy of such locally catalogued information will be sent to the technical processing center, where it will be checked, edited, and the result printed on cards

In multiple numbers and the appropriate number of copies distributed to the respective libraries of the Institute.

It must be stressed that while a great many acquisitions in each region will be made locally, a good deal of the basic cataloguing and organization of the materials will be done at the administrative headquarters of FWI, at least in the early years of the development of the Institute. Any other course would be too costly and impractical.

The centralized processing center at the administrative headquarters will provide fully-printed-ready-to-be-filed catalog cards for all the library A-V centers of FWI, so that in each center there will be a complete catalog of all the holdings of all the centers and divisions of the Institute; except, of course, materials that are ephemeral in character and of strictly local interest. For the sake of uniformity, all material will be catalogued in transliteration in Latin characters, with translations of the titles and annotations and the abstracts in English. In each region where necessary or desirable, local and regional materials may also appear in the catalog in the character of the languages that do not normally employ Latin characters; and translations in any one or more of these languages of the titles and other data on cards may be added.

The FWI library system will also provide depth access to selected items that contain important, significant, and unique materials. Where necessary, such material in any one center may be made directly accessible to any other or all centers by means of microfilm or microfiche copies. Microfilm and microfiche readers will be amply provided in all centers, and most periodicals and all rare materials of relevance will thus be made accessible to students and faculty.

Federal funds are presently being sought under Title II of the Higher-Education Act of 1967 for the purchase of a 3M microfilm reader-printer, three 3M microfilm readers, microfilm storage cabinets, the *New York Times Index* for the years 1913 to 1967, and microfilm files of scattered groups of years from 1913 to date of the *New York Times, Nation, New Republic, Literary Digest, Business Week, Newsweek,* and the *Saturday Review.* The request includes also a grant for the purchase of a basic collection of reference works and reference tools for the weeding and cataloging of the more than 20,000 titles now at Harrow Hill. The *New York Times Index* for the years 1914 to 1966 is also important as a means to gain access to the extensive Broadman Collection.

Work is currently going on for the conversion of the first floor of the main building on the Livingston campus to house the bulk of the collection now at Harrow Hill, with work rooms set aside for the acquisition and cataloging of materials. The main reading room of the Library will be placed in what used to be the music building of the Livingston estate. The shelving in the two buildings is scheduled to be ready for use sometime in July.

At present, Friends World Institute possesses library resources and is planning library facilities for its programs as follows:

1. The collection of over 20,000 titles at Harrow Hill, already referred to, has much of it fully relevant for the undergraduate program of the Institute. The collection is still growing through gifts from friends. Part of it is divided into major subject areas on shelves at their present location. It has been subjected to a cursory weeding process. More thorough work needs to be done in this respect on a systematic basis, and what is retained needs to be fully catalogued.

2. The cursory weeding referred to has yielded a "Quakeriana" collection of about a thousand volumes, now housed separately at Harrow Hill. This may very well be combined with the extensive Quaker archive of manuscripts and other rare materials of the New York Yearly Meeting housed in the vaults of the Fifteenth Street Meeting in New York City and incorporated in the projected library system of the Institute, probably in conjunction with the Conflict-Resolution Study and Research Center contemplated for the Institute.

3. A small library at the temporary Mitchel Gardens campus, organized functionally for use by the present student body.

4. A library of about 10,000 volumes, most of them in English, mainly in the field of the social sciences, at the Institute's Austrian Center, owned by the director of the Center.

5. A modest collection at the Institute's Center in Mexico City, in time to be enlarged into a library.

6. The vast Broadman Collection of newspapers, periodicals, pamphlets, mounted cartoons, and other materials covering the period from 1914-1966, assembled systematically and with diligence from various parts of the world, and devoted to the subject of war and peace. The collection is now in storage in a large two-story garage building in Scranton, Pa. This collection may well serve as the nucleus of the library of the Conflict-Resolution Study and Research Center.

7. A beginning may be said to have been made in this connection with 26 cases of documents the Institute has recently acquired from Germany.

8. The Institute has also arranged for the use by its students and faculty of the library facilities of Bangalore

University, Bangalore, India, and of the American University in Cairo, Egypt, both within the Institute's designated Asian and African centers.

9. Similar arrangements will probably precede the establishment of the Institute's own library facilities in Kenya, Japan, and the Soviet Union, where regional centers and programs are being contemplated.

10. If the four-year resident college program in the Institute's plans is established elsewhere than on the Livingston campus, that too will require separate library facilities.

11. It is possible that through negotiation with the American Friends Service Committee its vast body of organizational papers of great historical and social value may also be organized by and within the FWI library system and designated portions of it made accessible to the world of scholarship. Such program could well be carried on in conjunction with the Conflict-Resolution Study and Research Center.

12. At present, a study is being made of the foreign area programs and library resources in the United States, with a view to discovering where and how relations may be established with them by the Institute that may enrich the information resources accessible to both.

The Problem Approach in a Crisis Culture

Personal problems and world problems are interbound. The widespread alienation is certainly partly a reflection of a deeply divided, fearful, and hostile world. More and more, police try in vain to stem rising violence at home, while ghastly violence is part of our national policy and is escalating abroad. We live in a war economy, and, sub-

72

consciously, minds reflect the destructive emotions that so largely direct us.

The students today want to bring their personal problems into the open; they must seek their own identity; must resolve tensions about sex, alcohol, marijuana, LSD, obscenity, tobacco. Many communicate their rebellion in obvious ways. We try to treat these manifestations as symptoms only and attempt to get at basic causes.

Some of these problems are dealt with in programed meetings, with suggested readings in advance and resource persons as leaders of discussion. The discussions sometimes continue day and night, making heavy competition for the broader social problems.

The great problems that divide mankind and so impede progress are rather obvious and easily listed: danger of thermonuclear war, cost of armaments to the world, poverty in the midst of affluence, urban sprawl, race prejudice, population explosion, disintegration of family life, waste of natural resources, improper use of mass media, individual and social suicide, denial of civil liberties, illiteracy, physical-emotional-mental disease, and crime. Such problems comprise the heart of the study program, coupled with learning from the contacts and experiences of each day. At present, we spend the first two and one-half months on these problems and the search for related, universal concepts which, if applied in unison, could resolve the major problems.

Different Centers utilize different approaches to the program of study. At the North American Center,[7] the

7. For the various Centers, there are Directors of Development: Ruth Mary Hill, North America; Robert Duckles, Latin America; Adolph G. Anderson, West Europe; Samuel Corson, East Europe; Ernst Winter, Acting Director East-West European Center; Mary-Cushing Niles, India; Barbara Mitchell, Director of Studytravel.

73

procedure is as follows. Each morning after breakfast and time for cleaning up, all gather in the Meeting. There is a half-hour of meditation, which some use in the exercise of openness to the leading of truth; some to more self-directed contemplation of the topic for the day. The Meeting is informal but reverent, arranged generally in a circle. All are invited to renew their purposes in being at the school, to put aside trivia, and settle down to the business at hand, search.

Since seeking is the purpose of the school, meditation is as important a part in the learning process as reading or discussion or recreation or travel or work. Meditation has a special function in relating knowledge to feeling, making of learning an experience that alters attitudes, and strengthens character. Too often "scholars" are wise only in the thoroughness of the rationalizations of attitudes unconsciously learned even at the mother's knee. For example, three "scholars" testifying at a Senate Committee hearing on American attitudes toward the People's Republic of China gave well-informed reasons why we should extend communications and trade, while three other "scholars" in succeeding sessions advised exactly the opposite.

As Richard Bowman has written, "My first requirement would be that principal, faculty, and students think out individually and discuss together the kind of future world they want to work for. We should be able to know where we agree and where we differ in the vision that inspires us."[8]

Following the Meeting, study guides are given out which announce the resource leader, frame the question

8. Richard S. Bowman, *International*, publication of the International Peoples College All Students Union, Nos. two and three, 1963, p. 3.

or problem, and present an annotated bibliography. In the center of the Meeting room is a table for this material; those who will, display books and pamphlets they recommend and discuss them briefly. The walls of the Meeting room are lined with shelves for those books most pertinent to the problems and concepts that comprise the curriculum. These number only a few thousand, and the checking-out system is informal. Journals and papers are also available in the Meeting room. Since we often work close to the growing edge of society, we watch some developments so new that not even pamphlets are available, only letters or mimeographed materials or word of the innovator himself. The larger collection of books is available as needed. After Meeting, the group breaks for study. In the evening, it is usual to have a documentary film on the topic under consideration. Use may be made of records, tapes, posters, or plays arranged by the group.

Usually the following day, after meditation, the resource person engages the entire group in discussion. He tries to encompass the scope of the problem and indicate its relation to the other major problems.

Dewey said, "A philosophy consistently applied reveals itself in every detail." Group arrangement and group process are not to be minimized. Class seating in rows with the teacher in front is autocratic, even military, in arrangement. The center of attention is the teacher. Students look at him or at one another's neck. "Lecturing," it has been said, "is talking in other people's sleep." If we abandon the dominant role of the teacher, then student inexperience with processes of democratic self-discipline results in substitute domination by some of the students and continued passivity by others.

Elements of democratic discussion must replace the

order of the lecture room. One of the techniques of group dynamics is to have an appointed "observer" who reports from time to time or when asked to do so by any member of the group. He may report the number of times, without names, that the members have spoken, from say none to 241. Hearing such a report, the most talkative, suddenly self-aware, speaks again: "Ain't science wonderful." The good discussion leader usually raises a very few provocative questions at the beginning of the period, tries to hold discussion to this field of discourse, encourages the reticent to share, and discourages the overly talkative by indicating another, as "let's give Herb a chance to get into this." The leader may serve for a day or longer, but the responsibility is shared. He is assisted by a "chairman" who gets the meeting organized, makes (and invites) announcements, and gets any business details out of the way. The discussion leader may also be assisted by an "orienter" who carries a special responsibility to remind the group when it has left the agreed-on track or is otherwise wasting time.

Surely one of the best ways of presenting a problem for discussion is by the use of the Socratic method. The questioner must have thought through, if not to the answer itself, at least to the nature of the problem. Then the questions should be so ordered that those questioned discover at least as much as the leader knows.

Dr. William Heard Kilpatrick was a master of the Socratic method as illustrated by this instance. Asked by an honorary fraternity to speak under their auspices at a college of 3,500 students, he wished to make clear that while he would do so, he regarded even honorary fraternities as undemocratic. The questions saved him the embarrassment of expressing his opinions by leading the committee that waited on him into self-discovery. He asked these questions:

Kilpatrick:	"Do you have social fraternities here?"
Committee:	"Oh, no."
K:	"And why not?"
C:	"They are undemocratic."
K:	"And what harm do they do?"
C:	"They make all excluded feel rejected, unhappy."
K:	"Well, what about those who are elected; is there any harm done them?"
C:	"Yes, they gain a false sense of superiority. Such fraternities are undemocratic and we do not have them."
K:	"Now tell me, please, how your honorary fraternity differs."
C:	"Ah, it is open to all."
K:	"To all? Are there no restrictions?"
C:	"No, no restrictions. Any who do well enough in their grades."
K:	"Is there a limit to the number admitted?"
C:	"Yes, the 40 highest."
K:	"Do you mean that if all 3,500 students tried hard enough they could squeeze within the limit of 40?"
C:	"No, I guess not."
K:	"Tell me how do those feel who try but don't make it?"
C:	"Oh, badly."
K:	"Finally, (You don't have to answer this question), What harm might inclusion do to those who do make it?"
C:	"We hadn't thought of it in that light."

77

Kilpatrick's ten questions were ordered and inescapable. But often the questioner does not himself see so clearly the conclusion. Then teacher and student seek together, and Dewey has said that "learning often takes place best when student and teacher learn together."

After a pause for snacks, it is usual to break into smaller groups of five or ten for discussion till lunch. Afternoons are for study and recreation. The present evening schedule for the North American Center is as follows:

Monday: Workshops in fine arts: Music, Sculpture, Ceramics, Creative Writing, Drama, and Dance.

Tuesday: Documentary films of high quality, usually related to the area of study currently involved.

Wednesday: Meeting for Worship (unstructured).

Thrusday: Meeting for Business. The Meetings for business which open with a period of meditation are conducted after the manner of Friends. A Friend presides, because of his familiarity with the method of resolving group problems and arranging affairs. This method is regarded by some as the foremost contribution of Quakers. The Clerk presides, and a secretary reads the Minutes. After consideration of each item on the agenda, a "Minute" is proposed. Members of the group who assent, so indicate by a nod or "I approve." Opportunity is given for objection. Such objection, if any, leads to further consideration until the Clerk is able to state as "the sense of the Meeting" a Minute to which none expresses opposition. This the secretary records and reads the "Minute" to the group.

There is no rule by majority, no votes or counting of those "for" or "against." Actually, "the sense of the Meeting" that notes the conclusion of discussion is quantitative as well as qualitative. For degrees of "concern" enter into the conclusion. The deeper involvement of some, or their deeper experience or wisdom, is weighed against the more casual interests of others. The purpose is to come to a conclusion that expresses the optimum of interpersonal respect and affection.

When a majority overrides a minority in the Democratic process, bitterness is often the result, while in the Friends way, one member can postpone action for further discussion. In this postponement, he bears a responsibility that prompts him to examine his objectives.

Norman Whitney tells the story of a Meeting at which one of the prominent members, an influential Friend, felt differently from most about the subject under discussion. During a long discussion the Friend voiced his feelings. The Meeting as a whole agreed upon a procedure of action contrary to the Friend's opinion. The Clerk of the Meeting read the minute embodying the "sense of the Meeting" as he understood it. The minute was approved. The differing Friend had not objected. Following the Meeting, this Friend went up to the Clerk and said, "I think this is the wrong decision, but if we are going to go forward in this effort it will be at some cost and I want to help." The Friend handed the Clerk a check of considerable amount.

Any problems of conduct come before the Meeting for Business. Ideally, each group should meet first informally and agree on its own guidelines. But because social expectations differ with each culture, it seems best to have a basic set of continuing (but modifiable) guides. These are guides only, however, and there is latitude for individual and group discretion. Only deviations that seem to hurt the purposes of the program or threaten the welfare of the individual or the reputation and viability of the school are considered at Meeting.

Guidelines for the North American Center may serve as illustrations.

For the North American Center

SOME STANDARDS FOR GUIDANCE

"Law can provide a path, but conscience is the only vehicle that can follow it." Spencer Grin, at Friends World Institute, January, 1966.

1. Unless prior arrangements have been made, all members of the community are

expected to be present at all scheduled
meetings and meals.

2. It is requested that all persons refrain
from smoking in the Meeting Room and
in the Dining Room. Fire Marshal's regu-
lations prohibit smoking in the student
apartments.

3. The use of illegal drugs and intoxicants
cannot be condoned in a community like
ours without involving others in involun-
tary risks and affecting the unity of the
whole.

4. It is expected that men and women will
respect the privacy of each other's apartments, and that there will not be inter-
visitations after 11 p.m. All apartments
will observe quiet hours after this time.

5. Arrangements for rooms and meals for
guests on campus must be made in advance. Rooms: $1.00; Meals: Breakfast,
$.40; Lunch, $.60; Dinner, $1.00.

6. Out of consideration for others with
whom one lives, attention should be given
to personal cleanliness and tidiness.
Among other things, this would relate,
specifically, to the orderly care of rooms
and neatness in dress and appearance in
the Dining Hall, particularly at dinner.

7. As a matter of both convenience and
courtesy, students leaving campus for

81

	over-night or longer should register their addresses.
Friday:	Art activities. There is an "Activities building" largely for the Arts, and specialists[9] come to help with Sculpture, Ceramics, Drama, Music, Painting. These groups occasionally give concerts, plays, and exhibitions.
Saturday:	Saturday morning is for Journals. These are the records kept by the students of their growth, gained through study, reading, conversation, contemplation, work, recreation, travel, et cetera. Ideally, these Journals should be kept because of promptings akin to those of the early Quakers who recorded in their Journals their spiritual adventures and encounters with obstacles. In different terms, spiritual needs are as great today. Years of assigned learning have left too few with the will for self-directed intellectual-emotional venturing. Left without prompting or requirement, we find some do superlatively; a greater proportion make sporadic efforts; some do little. Any requirement deadens the spirited, and the laggards lapse into obedient lethargy which defeats the basic purpose. We do not know how long it would take for most over-directed students to find self-motivation. Some have done so in two, three or four months. Some have not in six. One student, anxious because he was

9. Herbert Arnold, Arlene Diamond, Jane Meyer, Janet Olstein, Beth Strode, Lorraine Pekula.

82

not responding to the challenge, went of his own accord to a psychiatrist. He became convinced that he had made of the Journal a symbol of "growing up." His early life had been so unhappy that he had developed a subconscious block against becoming like the adults he knew. Only children were admirable. And so the day came when, surrounded by the affection of adults and near adults, he gladly took his pen in hand and wrote well and with ease.

Journals are more than a reminder of growth, an outlet for the expression of thoughts and feelings, a means of communication, an exercise in writing. They are the chief basis for evaluating the student's success in terms of conventional standards. And so, at the end of each six months, the student meets with his faculty advisor, and they translate the growth that has taken place through this integrated process into conventional terms. Guidelines for this translation are distributed in mimeographed form and are elaborated in discussion. Entries are then made on a transcript form to be consolated at the conclusion of the student's course. The following suggestions for preparing transcripts were formulated by Dr. Anthony Pearce of the faculty.

The basic principle we follow is that each student knows best what he or she has accomplished. So the first step is for each of you to prepare a careful summary of your varied learning experience in the last months. The second step is consultation with your

83

advisor, who will work with you on checking the transcript and assigning an appropriate number of semester hours of credit. (No grades will be assigned for any work.) Checking the tentative transcript will involve two main questions: first, is the transcript complete, or has the student overlooked any specific learning which should be recorded?; second, is the record of learning expressed in language intelligible to conventional colleges and prospective employers? While our methods may be unique, our subject matter often overlaps the subjects of conventional college courses. Wherever possible, we should attempt to describe the general structure of our learning in communicable terms.

Student and advisor will work together on allocating appropriate semester hours of credit. As a general guide, we might recall that one semester hour of credit certifies that during one semester (fifteen to sixteen weeks) a student spent one hour a week in a classroom and about two hours outside the classroom fulfilling class responsibilities. (What does this actually mean in learning? God *may* know!) So if you have spent the equivalent of a week (forty to fifty working hours) on any program of learning, you can note down the equivalent of one semester hour of credit.

This may result in a very varied and complex list of subjects which would be unwieldy—for example, you may list 1½ hours on music, ¼ on sculpture, and ⅛ credit hour on painting or ceramics. We suggest you consolidate such related courses as: 2 semester hours of fine arts (music, sculpture, painting).

Almost half of our program has been based on two general programs of learning: the consideration of world problems in the first six weeks and the Southern Studytrip. We suggest that all of us could consider these learning experiences as more than the equivalent of two conventional courses: the first six weeks could be called "The Sociology of Community Development: study and field experience." Each six-week period could be considered the equivalent of at least three semester hours of credit.

May we finally remind you that your Journal is intended as the permanent and visible record of your learning. When assembling appropriate credit hours, how far does your Journal help you and your advisor assess your achievements? The vital record of your learning is in the re-structuring of your thought, your judgment, and your feelings. The Journal only helps us to know some parts of your experience in objective and schematic form, but it would serve as assistance of great value.

As a check on this informal approach to learning, the students know that at the end of their fourth year they will take the Princeton Graduate Record Examination. It is hoped they will not study with these examinations in mind, beyond questioning from time to time as to whether they are learning both broadly and deeply.

This is not a new procedure, but was first used 30 years ago by New College of Columbia University and for the past 15 years by the Putney Graduate School of Teacher Education. Colleges have accepted these transcripts. Several colleges have stated that they will accept Friends World Institute students by transfer on this system.

Sunday: Sundays are given to collecting one's thoughts and weaving new learnings into old. Meeting for worship after the manner of Friends is the spiritual center of the program. All students, faculty, and staff are encouraged to attend the school's own Meeting or other nearby Meetings or churches of their own choice. Obviously, one cannot require worship, but the unstructured Meeting for Worship can be one of the most important parts of the year. At these meetings, it is hoped attenders will enter with no intention to speak, no intention not to speak, but with an open seeking attitude and a readiness to share if moved to do so.

The Following Schedule for the Fall Term, 1967, Illustrates the Structure for Seminars:

WED., SEPT. 28
1:00-6:00 Students arrive. Tea in Dining Room
6:00 Dinner
8:00 Meeting in Library—Welcome—Folk Singing

THURS., SEPT. 29
7:30 Breakfast

86

8:30	Meeting in Library—Introductions
10:15	Coffee
10:45	Continue Introductions
12:30	Lunch
2:00	Meeting in Library—Handbook and Details of Community Life
3:00	Field trip to Hempstead Harbor—Look at Incinerator, Discuss the Pros and Cons of Putting it in, Economically and Ecologically—Richard Proskauer
8:00	Meeting for Worship—Library
8:30	Films in Dining Room

FRI., SEPT. 30

7:30	Breakfast
8:30	Study Groups—Personal Conduct and Community Goals at F.W.I.
10:15	Coffee
10:45	Seminar—Library—Discussion of Study Croup Reports Continue Introduction to Life at Mitchel Gardens and Expectations
12:30	Lunch
2:00-5:00	Afternoon for Work (Painting, Fixing up rooms, etc.)
6:00	Dinner
8:00	Meeting for Worship—Library
8:30	Dancing—Folk and Other—Dining room—Refreshments

SAT., OCT. 1

7:30	Breakfast
8:30	Seminar—Philosophy of F.W.I. and World Education — Morris Mitchell (See study guide for this)
10:15	Coffee

87

| 10:45 | Continue Seminar |
| 12:30 | Lunch |

SUN., OCT. 2
8:30	Breakfast
10:30	Visits to Local Friends Meetings
1:00	Dinner
2:30	Beach Party
7:00	Supper
8:00	Films—Dining Room

MON., OCT. 3
7:30	Breakfast
8:30	Seminar—Man and Nature—Richard Proskauer
10:15	Coffee
10:45	Continue Seminar
12:30	Lunch
2:00	Seminar—New England Study Trip Plans —Arthur Meyer
6:00	Dinner
8:00	Meeting for Worship

TUES., OCT. 4
| 7:30 | Breakfast |
| 9:00 | Leave for New Hampshire |

WED., OCT. 5
TO
MON., OCT. 10   New England Study Trip

All friends of Friends World Institute are welcome at all meetings without charge. Meetings run from 8:30 a.m.-12:00 a.m.

Tues., Oct. 11 *Survey of Problems and Concepts on the Individual Level*

| | 8.30—study groups |
| | 10:45—seminar |

Wed., Oct. 12	*The Individual and the Family*
	8:30—study groups
	10:45—seminar—Mr. Irwin Lesser

| Thurs., Oct. 13 | Morning and afternoon: Advisement, reading, journals |
| | 8:30 p.m.—conversation: "My Life as a Work of Art," Newton Garver |

Fri., Oct. 14	*The Individual and the School*
	8:30—study groups
	10:45—seminar—Morris Mitchell

| Sat., Oct. 15 | *The Individual and Problems of Communication* |
| | 8:30—seminar—Newton Garver |

| Mon., Oct. 17 | *Community Meeting*—Problems and concerns facing our own community |

| Tues., Oct. 18 | *The Individual: Physical and Spiritual Health* |
| | 8:30—study groups |

Wed., Oct. 19	*Love and Sexuality*
	8:30—seminar—Dr. George Nicklin
	9:30—study groups
	11:00—seminar

| Thurs., Oct. 20 | Morning and Afternoon: Advisement, reading, journals |
| | 8:30 p.m.—Conversation—"Gandhi"—Labhu Vyas |

89

Fri., Oct. 21	*Survey of Problems and Concepts at the Neighborhood, Municipality, Regional and Global Levels* 8:30—study groups 11:00—reports and planning
Sat., Oct. 22	*The Individual and the Concepts of Labor and Work* 8:30—study groups
Mon., Oct. 24	*Automation and the Cybercultural Revolution* 8:30—seminar—Alice Mary Hilton
Tues., Oct. 25	*The Concepts of Labor, Work, and Alienation from the Marxist Viewpoint* 8:30—seminar—Allen Krebs
Wed., Oct. 26	Arbitration, Conciliation, Mediation 8:30—seminar—James Hill
Thurs., Oct. 27	Morning and Afternoon: Advisement, reading, journals 8:30 p.m.—conversation—"Black and White Thinking"—Bob Duckles, Chuck Fager
Fri., Oct. 28	*Automation in Production and Service Industries* 8:30—seminar—Hildreth Strode 10:00-5:30—field trips to several automated industries in the New York area
Sat., Oct. 29	*Summary: The Individual and Goals in Life* 8:30—seminar—Newton Garver 10:45—study groups

Mon., Oct. 31	*The Origins of the City* 8:30—seminar—Tony Pearce
Tues., Nov. 1	*Suburbs and Integrated Housing* 8:30—study groups 10:30—seminar—Morris Milgram
Wed., Nov. 2	*Intentional Communities* 8:30—study groups 10:30—seminar—Winifred Rawlins
Thurs., Nov. 3	Morning and Afternoon Advisement, reading, journals 8:00 p.m.—conversation—Bradford Lyttle
Fri., Nov. 4	*The Use of Computers in Decision-Making* 8:30—study groups 10:00—seminar—Kenneth Knowlton
Sat., Nov. 5	*Changing Public Opinion—Approaches to Social Change in the City* 8:30—Introduction—Chuck Fager 9:30—Film "The Language of Faces" 10:30—study groups
Mon., Nov. 7	*Action Research in the Study of the City* 8:30—Seminar—Steven Yale—Urban Agent of Metropolitan Associates of Philadelphia
Tues., Nov. 8	*Violence and Conflict in the City* 8:30 — seminar — Ross Flanagan — Director Quaker Action Project on Community Conflict 8:00 p.m.—Films—"Men of Rochdale"; "Barpali Project"—Orissa, India

91

Wed., Nov. 9	*Cooperatives*
	8:30—seminar—Morris Mitchell
	8:00 p.m.—Films—"The City" parts III and IV

| Thurs., Nov. 10 | Morning and Afternoon Advisement, reading, journals |
| | 8:00 p.m.—Conversation "The Influence of Yiddish Drama on the American Theater" —Dr. David Lifson, Professor Monmonth College |

| Fri., Nov. 11 | 8:30—Leave on study trip to Rochdale Village for seminar on this cooperative apartment complex |
| | 2:00 p.m.—Community Meeting |

| Sat., Nov. 12 | *Youth in the Ghetto* |
| | 8:30—seminar—Barrington Dunbar, mobilization for Youth, N.Y.C. |

| Mon., Nov. 14 | *Preparation for Mexican Semester* |
| | 8:30—seminar—Robert Duckles, Director. Latin American Center |

| Tues., Nov. 15 | *Highlander Research and Education Center* |
| | 8:30—seminar—Conrad Browne, Dir. Highlander Center |

| Wed., Nov. 16 | Advisement and Journals |

| Thurs., Nov. 17 | Study Trip to N.Y.C. to Study Urban Problems |

| Fri., Nov. 18 | Study Trip to N.Y.C. to Study Urban Problems |

| Sat., Nov. 19 | *Destructive Pressures of Modern Society* |
| | 10:00 — Workshop — Westbury Meeting House. Newton Garver—Opening Speaker |

| Mon., Nov. 21 | *Port of New York Authority* |
| | Barry Conforte—Director Public Relations, Port of N.Y. Authority |

| Tues., Nov. 22 | *The Uses of Silence* |
| | Labhu Vyas, Winifred Rawlins, Brian Wenk |

| Wed., Nov. 23 | Advisement and Journals |

| Thurs., Nov. 24 through Sun., Nov. 27 | Thanksgiving Recess and time for continuation of individual study of "The City" |

SCHEDULE OF SEMINARS ON PROBLEMS AT THE GLOBAL LEVEL

First Week

Monday, November 28:

A general meeting of responses to the question: "At this time, how am I planning to help create peace throughout the world?"

Tuesday, November 29:

8:30-10:30 "What are the principal organized approaches to the creation of world peace?"—Tony Pearce.

11:00-12:00 Meeting of development groups; planning visits to resources in New York.

Wednesday, November 30:
8:30 "How can we begin to understand hostility and war between nations?—Students are asked to read aloud brief passages from philosophers, historians, novelists, and poets which speak to this question.

Thursday, December 1:
Advisement, journals, reading.

Friday, December 2:
8:30 "How can we begin to understand the problems of developing the human and material resources of the poverty-stricken majority of mankind?"—Titus Podea, economic consultant.

Saturday, December 3:
8:30 "How far has India been able to develop her human and material resources?"—Labhu Vyas.

Second Week

Monday, December 5:
"What are the prospects for arms control and disarmament?"—Newton Garver.

Tuesday, December 6:
"What are the major trends in nuclear deterence and in 'conventional' warfare?"—Col. Stewart, N.Y.U., Air Force R.O.T.C.

Wednesday, December 7:
Development groups visiting resource persons and libraries in New York City.

Thursday, December 8:
Further visiting of resource persons and libraries. 8:00

p.m. Attend SANE rally, Madison Square Garden—I. F. Stone, Erich Fromm, Gunnar Myrdal, Floyd McKissick, Norman Thomas.

Friday, December 9:
8:00 p.m.   Conversation—Albert Bigelow
Advisement and journals

Saturday, December 10:
8:30-12:00 Preliminary drafting of written reports in development groups.

Third Week

Monday, December 12:
Tuesday, December 13:
Final drafts of written reports in development groups. (To serve each and all of us, the world problems planning group requests each of the development groups to prepare written reports setting out the main points of its special approach. Such reports will be mimeographed and distributed widely, so they should be kept fairly brief— say 1,500 to 2,000 words. Each group is encouraged to exercise its initiative and imagination to the utmost within the general theme of different approaches to the development of India.)

Please plan to begin cutting stencils of these reports on the afternoon of Tuesday, December 13, and to finish all stencils by the following afternoon. Reports will be mimeographed at Harrow Hill and distributed on Thursday and Friday. (Kindly plan to read these reports over the weekend.)

Wednesday, December 14:
8:30 "World Government and World Law"—Richard Hudson, Editor, *War Peace Report.*

Thursday, December 15:
    Advisement (3:00-5:00 p.m.: Rehearsal for offering on December 20).

Friday, December 16:
    Visit to the United Nations.

Saturday, December 17:
    Unscheduled day, left free primarily for final rehearsals for the Drama Workshop offering to be presented at Harrow Hill this evening at 8:00 p.m.

Fourth Week

Sunday, December 18:
    8:00 p.m. Myra Roper, Australian educator and lecturer —"China, the Surprising Country" and film taken by her on four trips to China.

Monday, December 19:
    Final rehearsals in development groups for our International Dialogue.
    7:30 p.m. Norman Thomas—Dialogue on "Today."

Tuesday, December 20:
    Friends World Institute presents: *AN INTERNATIONAL DIALOGUE ON THE DEVELOPMENT OF INDIA.*

    We will imagine that a distinguished group of Indian citizens, deeply concerned over the slow development of India's human and material resources, have invited to one conference groups of advisors on development from: the United Nations, the United States of America, the Union of Socialist Soviet Republics, and the Peoples'

Republic of China. The Indian group presents its proposed solutions to the India problems of development, and, in turn, the other delegations present their proposed solutions. An exchange of views follows.

"I do not want my house to be walled on all sides and my windows to be stuffed. I want the cultures of all lands to be blown about my house as freely as possible. But I refuse to be blown off my feet by any."
—Mohandas K. Gandhi

Wednesday, December 21:
Advisement and Journals
Cleaning apartments for the next group of students.

Thursday, December 22:
Homegoing for Christmas and the New Year.

FRIENDS WORLD INSTITUTE

presents

An International Dialogue on the
Human and Material Development of India

The schedule of the dialogue
 8:30 - 9:00 a.m. Period of silence
 9:00 - 9:40 a.m. Reports by representatives of India
 9:40 - 10:00 a.m. Questions on the Indian report
10:00 - 10:40 a.m. Reports by representatives of the United Nations
10:40 - 11:00 a.m. Questions on the U.N. report

(Noon: Lunch will be served to all the delegates, by courtesy of Friends World College, Indian Center.)

1:30 - 2:00 p.m.	Reports by representatives of the U.S.
2:00 - 2:15 p.m.	Questions on the U.S. report
2:15 - 2:45 p.m.	Reports by representatives of the Soviet Union
2:45 - 3:00 p.m.	Questions on the Soviet report
3:00 - 3:30 p.m.	Recess
3:30 - 4:00 p.m.	Reports by representatives of the Peoples' Republic of China
4:00 - 4:15 p.m.	Questions on the Chinese report
4:15 - 5:30 p.m.	Free debate between different delegations
6:30 p.m.	Dinner for all delegations and guests
7:30 - 9:00 p.m.	Summaries by delegations—limited to fifteen minutes for each national delegation and twenty minutes for the UN and Indian delegations and proceeding in the following order: China, Soviet Union, U.S.A., UN, and India.

Art Program for first semester of 1966

October 13 Evening seminar for explanation of art program, introduction of art faculty, and sign-up for different activities.

List of possible activities are:

Sculpture .... Herb Arnold
Ceramics .... Janet Olstein
Music .... Arline Diamond
Modern Dance .... Loraine Pekula
Drama .... Beth Strode
Play Readings .... Newton Garver
Poetry .... Wini Rawlins
Photography .... John Phillips
    Robert Duckles

98

Programs which have been set up on a regular weekly basis are: sculpture, ceramics, music, modern dance, and drama. These activities meet once a week for 2-4 hour sessions.

Music ....1-3 Tuesday
Sculpture ....1-6 Tuesday
Ceramics ....2-4 Monday
Modern Dance ....1:30-3 Tuesday
Drama ....1-4 Monday and Wednesday

Groups meeting once a week will have met 10 times during the semester. Drama will have met 15 or 20 times counting rehearsals and workshop performance December 17.

Play readings meet about 4 times for 1 or 2 hours each time. Photography is completely individual, and there is no way of judging the amount of time put in by various students. Poetry is also done on an individual basis. Students take their poetry to Wini, and they sit down and discuss it for the afternoon or evening.

In addition, several evening programs have been planned:

Portrait Demonstration at Herb Arnold's
Piano Concert given by Arline Diamond
Poetry Reading given by Wini Rawlins
Minority Drama lecture by David Lifson

Film Schedule; Fall, 1966

September 29, 1966
The Living Stone—The Eskimo's approach to carving is closely bound up with his belief that a spirit exists in all things, and these spirits of nature can be influenced by releasing the image the artist sees imprisoned in stone and

99

other objects. The film is in the form of an old hunter of Baffin Island recounting a legend to children.

Life in the Woodlot—Long shots and closeups of animals and plants in a woodlot on a farm in the eastern Atlantic woodlands show the seasons of the year, man's use of the woods in spring and fall, and the balance of nature when uninterrupted by man.

The Red Balloon—A fantasy about a little boy who makes friends with a balloon.

October 16, 1966
The Plow That Broke the Plains—A moving film about the dust bowl and the government's agricultural wartime policy.

October 18, 1966
Day After Day—Imaginative photography, skillful editing, and an unusual sound track combine to reveal impressionistically the stultifying effects of the routine existence on a worker in a Canadian paper mill.

Children Adrift—A poignant and beautifully-photographed, poetic film of children living in a refugee community near Paris.

Willie Catches On—The story of one boy growing up, and of how the seeds of prejudice are indirectly sown by adults through their unconscious attitudes toward other groups.

October 23, 1966
Children Without—A moving and sensitive film study of the double role of schools in regard to children from families

100

of low socio economic levels—not only to teach but also to counteract destructive influences at home and in the neighborhood through using new methods of dealing with children and of parent education.

Glass—The art of hand-blown glass is dynamically contrasted with the mechanical production of glass in this unusual musical and visual fantasy.

October 25, 1966
A Drop of Water—A Mexican public health film showing the minute organisms in water, the diseases they cause, and the processes used to purify water used for drinking.

Protoplasm—A scientific film studying life through various forms of protoplasm and experimenting with it in different ways.

A Fresh Start—About the Job Corps in New Bedford, Mass. It goes through the many months of training and adjustment of a boy from the slums of New York.

October 30, 1966
No Hiding Place—A CBS-TV award-winning film from the East Side-West Side series concerning integrated communities and the problem of real estate block-busting practices. Arguments for and against integrated communities are realistically, if emotionally, expounded by members of a typical suburban community.

November 1, 1966
The City—Part I—Heaven and Hell—Outlines the opposing forces inherent in the city—creative and destructive. It shows the elements which helped create the first cities about five thousand years ago, and the forces which now threaten to destroy it.

101

The City—Part II—Cars or People?—The problem of people versus cars is studied, as well as the ability to plan our cities to allow for free flow of traffic.

November 6, 1966
Superfluous People—The camera records the faces and words of New York City's "superfluous" people—the unwanted babies, the aged, the derelict, the drop out, the victim of urban renewal—and asks the question why any affluent society should contain so many "superfluous" people. Prominent social workers, psychiatrists, and clergymen assess the sense of dignity necessary to every person regardless of his circumstances and point out that everyone has a responsibility towards those less fortunate.

November 8, 1966
The City—Part III—The City and its Region—Shows how the migration from the city to the countryside is creating "suburban cities" and destroying much of the "country's" natural beauty. Ways of solving this problem are also studied.

The City—Part IV—The Heart of the City—Surveyed is the "modern" city—congested, architecturally sterile, and lacking in social vitality. Possible solutions to this problem are discussed.

November 13, 1966
Albert Schweitzer

November 15, 1966
The City—Part V—The City as Man's Home—Discusses the problems of slum clearance versus urban renewal. The sterility of modern housing complexes as compared to the social warmth of old "neighborhoods" is studied and possible solutions given.

The City—Part VI—The City and the Future—Examines the effect of low-grade urban sprawl on the city's function as center of business and art. Alternatives to this type of development are examined.

November 17, 1966
   On the Bowery

November 20, 1966
   Nanook of the North
   The Annanacks

November 22, 1966
   Lines
   Very Nice, Very Nice
   Mekong River Development

November 27, 1966
   Minister of Hate
   H-Bomb Over the U.S.
   A Short Vision
   The Magician

November 29, 1966
   The Hole
   Night and Fog
   Trial at Nuremberg

December 4, 1966
   Food or Famine
   Overture
   The Population Explosion (N.V.)

December 6, 1966
   Unseen Enemies
   The Rival World

December 11, 1966
 Latin America—2 parts
 The Rising Tide

The Following Illustrates the Kind of Study-guide Provided for Each Seminar:

October 3

All friends of Friends World Institute are welcome to all meetings without charge.

Topic: Man and Nature

Resource People: Dick Proskauer and, for New England Studytrip, Dick Brett and Silas Weeks.

Schedule: Seminar (Dick Proskauer) on Monday, October 3: Studytrip to Vermont and New Hampshire from October 4- October 10.

BIBLIOGRAPHY:

I. Long Island:

Directory of Commerce and Industry
Long Island Assn., 320 Old Country Road., Garden City, N.Y.

Your Nassau County
Office of the County Executive, Mineola, N.Y.

II. Man and Nature:

Royal Bank of Canada—Monthly Letter—Vol. 41, No. 4, 1960

Joseph Wood Krutch—*The Great Chain of Life*

Karl Von Fritche—*Man and the Living World*

William Vogt—*Road to Survival*

Ellsworth Huntington—*Human Habitat*

Louis and Margery Milue—*The Balance of Nature*

Rachel Carson—*Silent Spring*

Yearbook of the U.S. Dept. of Agriculture—*A Place to Live*

Julian Huxley—*Essays of a Humanist*

Marston Bates—*The Forest and the Sea*

Frontiers of Modern Biology

E. John Russell—*World of the Soil*

III. Vermont and New Hampshire:

Elspeth Huxley—*A New Earth*

Historic Tours of New Hampshire

Dorothy Canfield Fisher—*Vermont Tradition*

Ralph Borsodi—*Education and Living*

Vermont—WPA Western American Guide Series

A New England Reader

The Great Outdoors

Beyond the Cabin Door

Birth of a Forest

Rachel Carson—*The Sea Around Us*

The Following Illustrates the Itineraries Provided for Each Studytrip

New England Studytrip
Tues., Oct. 4-Mon., Oct. 11, 1966

Tues., Oct. 4	9:00 a.m. Leave Mitchel Gardens 4:30 Arrive Pawtuckaway State Park, Raymond, N.H., set up camp.
Wed., Oct. 5	9:00 a.m. Talk with Silas Weeks, Extension Economist, on the Rural Area Development Program of N.H. and on the Agricultural Extension Service. 12:00 Lunch in cafeteria—University of N.H. 2:00 p.m. Talk with George Frick of the College of Agriculture on the use of linear programing in Farm Management Decisions. 4:00 p.m. Visit the farm of Charles Burwell and talk with him on the subject of Farm Management and Planning.
Thurs., Oct. 6	10:00 a.m. Talk with Dr. Nelson LeRay,

Sociologist, on Human Problems in Community Development.

12:00 Lunch in cafeteria—University of N.H. Afternoon is free for small group visits to areas and activities under direction of Silas Weeks.

On Wed. and Thurs evenings we will have the opportunity to take part in the activities and the program of the University of N.H. We will also plan to meet with any of the County Rural Area Development Committees which may be meeting in nearby counties on these evenings.

Fri., Oct. 7   9:00 a.m. Leave for East Barnard, Vermont. Each car will travel independently, visiting areas of interest in small groups. Some of the possibilities are: Daniel Laufman and Subsistance Living Group in Canterbury, N.H.; State Planning Board, Concord, N.H.; Dartmouth College Public Affairs Institute and possible talk with Dr. Francis Smallwood on Community Development and Planning from the point of view of the professional planner.

4:00 p.m. Arrive Hawk's Hill—Set up camp.

8:00 p.m. Talk with Burt Croft on Woodlot Management and an introduction to Hawk's Hill.

Sat., Oct. 8   Small group work projects in tree stand improvement, pruning, cleaning, etc. Instruc-

107

tion in the use of Sandvik, chainsaw, and axes, etc. Visit two examples of poor wood-lot management in the area.

Sun., Oct. 9   9:00 a.m. Meeting for Worship.

10:00 a.m. Talk with Richard Brett on the background and philosophy of the Hawk's Hill property and tour of the property with him. The remainder of the day will be free for continued work in the woodlot or visits to points of interest.

Mon., Oct. 10   9:00 a.m. Leave for Mitchel Gardens. Possibility of a picnic lunch at Powell House and a talk wth Francis Hall.

5:00 p.m. Arrive at Mitchel Gardens.

Truths for a Crisis Culture: A Search

UNESCO would be the single most fitting agency to promote, institutionally, world education. For now, UNESCO believes it should not. How the movement would surge forward if that body (especially after the admission of China) were to establish a world university system, creating an administration, building units where needed, and providing standards for accepting into membership qualifying units of whatever origin!

But even then, there would be need of independent efforts to broaden the base of experimentation. The need is great, at the world level, for curriculum and method based on the universal objective of a world of peace and plenty. Billions are poured annually into industrial and scientific experiments; so little goes into social experiments.

Friends World Institute, then, is one deliberate experiment, responsive to the antinomy of our time.

One might question the propriety of any religious sect presuming to organize such an all-inclusive enterprise, especially such a small sect—indeed one of the smallest, with only about 250,000 members who are widely scattered and bound together by no hierarchy, indeed, by no creed. The truth is, the Religious Society of Friends is just what the name indicates. The members are religious in the sense of having a reverent attitude towards life and an awareness of the potential beauty and divinity of all persons. They are religious in being devoted to a search, individual and collective, for those central, emerging truths that for now are the spirit of creation, a creation which did not finally create but which is forever creating. It is a society, not a church (though some groups do use churches instead of "Meetings"). Members believe in friendship as a way of life and for 300 years[10] have witnessed, with admirable devotion, opposition to all oppression, notably: slavery, abuse of prisoners, maltreatment of the mentally ill, capital punishment, and war. They have stood for the equality of rights of all persons regardless of race, creed, color, or sex. There has been a universality to the concern of the Friends that surely qualifies them as one group worthy of this great undertaking. Their impartial and vigorous programs, scattered over the world, are indicative of the courage of this small band to act on policies arrived at, not by voting, but by the still more democratic process described above.

10. Howard Brinton, *Friends for 300 Years*. New York: Harper and Brothers, 1952.

For now, Friends World Institute seeks to integrate, at the undergraduate level, a world view of education and the Friends' loving view of life, which by definition and practice has been world embracing. Since thinking involves the whole being, education should be concerned with the health, the vigor, of the whole self, mind and body, perceiving and feeling. Related action is the fulfillment of thought, its essential consummation, which is why right education should involve interrelated doing and thinking. Learning generally takes place in a social context. Accordingly, wholesome group living is essential to optimum learning.

Efforts at such integration must be experimental. Thus the first group at Friends World Institute followed only two guidelines of conduct: 1. conscience in individual matters; 2. consensus in group matters. The consequence was that some, unaccustomed to such absence of an authority figure, at first took advantage of the freedom, with too little regard for responsibility. Some said they had been rebellious but felt a little lost in a situation where there was no one against whom to rebel. But the irresponsible exercise of freedom naturally led to problems. These were aired with sometimes astonishing openness. Actually, much time was taken up with discussions in which the group tended to scatter along a continuum. There were a few who wanted conventionality, wanted to get down to work on the program of study as planned in advance, thought "rules" were a necessity, were rigid in posture as a cover for inward insecurity. There were a few, conversely, who tended toward anarchism and hedonism, were highly experimental, and felt that the discussion of the problems within the group should for the time being constitute the core of the program (as it largely did). A book could be written on those six months, and many records are available. But none will know with certainty for years, if ever, whether this policy of loving trust afforded optimum growth. For though an environment of loving trust involves risks, requires almost unbearable patience, and exposes the whole venture to being misunderstood, I rather think the end results will appear worth the price. And if any confuse un-Quakerly conduct of a few with tenacious holding to Quakerly process, let it be recorded that in six months there was not, during long, long hours of meeting, at least, an incident of anger. And there was abundant evidence of profound affection in the group. That affection bound like a centripetal force, ever bringing back into the fold tangential thrusts.

With the second group, seven guidelines were prepared in advance and presented to the group. Outwardly, the program ran more smoothly. Some said the guidelines were reasonable, but they felt they should have been arrived at by the whole group, faculty and students. They were advised of the cost, with the first group, of not having such guides. But one wonders whether students are in bed earlier or only less open about it. Journals are handed in more regularly, but these seem less spontaneous. Rebellion is less than on most campuses, but one feels it is there, latent.

Central emphasis in the program is on the definition of man's major problems. Individual problems are scheduled as well as social. Effort is made to see all these problems in interrelationship, personal and social and the social with one another, as poverty with population increase, poverty with diet and health, with ignorance, with violence. And effort is made to make clear that these same problems will be met and studied for the four years around the world.

111

SILENT VIGIL. Three students at the Friends World Institute who went on a fast Sunday night protesting war in general and the war in Vietnam specifically without troubling to publicize their action sit in the institute's library yesterday. They are, from left, Jane Echenhofer, 18, Jim Eisenberg, 19; and Robin Keeler, 19.

Peace Goes With Quiet In Student Fast on Viet

Mitchel Field—A rabbit scampered across the headlight beams as the car moved slowly down a dark, private road, past decaying military barracks, and rolled to a stop near three dim silhouettes.

"Can you tell us where the anti-war vigil is?" the driver asked. There was a silence, then a slightly embarrassed reply. "I guess this is it," said one of the silhouettes.

Quietly the figures moved into one of the former barracks, which is now a library weighty with political tomes. Under the dull electric lights, the silhouettes were revealed as three open-faced college students. Together they make up one of the nation's gentler demonstrations against the war in Vietnam.

The three youngsters—two boys and a girl—are students at the Friends World Institute, a Quaker-sponsored college that is being housed temporarily at Mitchel Field. Along with a fourth student, they began an anti-war fast Sunday night, and say they plan to eat nothing and drink nothing except water for a week. It is a protest like a thousand others that have been held across the country in recent months, with one major difference. This one was begun with no fanfare, no calls to the newspapers, no television interviews. Its initial purpose, the students said, is to affirm their convictions for themselves.

"It is an expression of personal commitment," said one of the fasters, Jane Echenhofer, 18, of Horsham, Pa. "A witness to your beliefs," said Robin Keeler, 19, of Los Angeles, "doesn't have to

be a public thing." Only the third youth expressed a slightly different viewpoint. Asked why they were not calling public attention to their fast, Jim Eisenberg, 19, of the Bronx, said apologetically, "We haven't really got organized yet."

The students said they are planning a public vigil at the end of the week, in conjunction with a nationwide series of anti-Vietnam war demonstrations scheduled for the weekend. "It may be outside a bank, or outside the Westbury Village Hall, if there is such a place," said Eisenberg. "We really don't know Long Island very well. We just got here three weeks ago." But first, they said, they want to fast for themselves.

The students were beardless, well-scrubbed, shy and a bit nervous. "I've never been interviewed by a reporter before," said Eisenberg. Their fast was discovered accidentally last night. They took the opportunity, when prodded, to express pacifist views. "You can't defend peace with arms," Miss Echenhofer said. All said they believed the U.S. should withdraw its troops from Vietnam. But when asked what message they had for the public, Eisenberg spread his palms far apart and said simply, "Just one big word: think."

The fourth fasting student, Peter Cass, 17, of Florida, was off campus last night, attending a concert. Several other students in the class of 17 were also off campus, eating pizza. "I hope they don't bring any back," Eisenberg said.

NEWSDAY, March 22, 1966—A NEWSDAY article reproduced and distributed by Committee on a Friends College, East Norwich, New York

But the third characteristic—after the world as a campus and the problem approach to learning—is the search for a unified perspective on man in our particular moment in cultural evolution. This is the most distinctly Quakerly aspect of the school.

The reverent search is for more than some ill-defined "truth." It is in part to deepen human affection, to attune one to the social and cosmic forces about, and to strengthen the resolution to live by convictions. Thus the students decide to take part in civil liberties campaigns, go on week-long fasts,[11] to aid a school need.

Moral education and practical education must be as interrelated in the search for truth as the warp and woof of fabric, and growth in the art of purpose is the essence of morality. Growth in choosing and applying means is the essence of the practical.

But the deeper substance of the search is for constructive concepts that are quietly emerging as the governing principles in the present unfolding of history. Destructive forces are obvious. Ours is a patient, disciplined search for emerging nebulae of truth which bear up under the all important criteria of universality of applicability, not only in theory but in political practicality.

And here we come to a special difficulty in carrying the argument further. For to name such concepts is to contradict the process of search and discovery. Further, to list such concepts is to open oneself to the charge of formulaism. Finally, such concepts depend for their evaluation on the background and experience of the individual, who may accept or reject in terms of emotional bias. So there is no set of concepts that are taught.

---

11. *Newsday* article on fasting, March, 1966.

Yet there are such emerging truths. They are present to be discerned and understood and implemented. They do stand the test of universality. And they are all clearly interrelated and mutually supportive.

But before making bold to suggest several of these emerging concepts, simply for illustrative purposes, a special problem that has arisen in the school program must be mentioned. The problem is:

If a student has been brought up in comfort (and nearly all of ours have, otherwise they could not afford the $2,625 annual tuition), then his interest is such a problem as the juxtaposition of poverty and affluence can only be academic. He reads Galbraith's *The Affluent Society* and Gunnar Myrdal's *Challenge to Affluence*. He is interested in and puzzled over the fact that we have 100,000 millionaires in this country, and sixty million who are poverty-ridden. He watches with sympathetic interest films on migratory workers, on the plight of most of the American Indians, the mass of American Negroes, or impoverished slum dwellers who exist in areas spread like a cancerous growth in the sides, or sometimes the center, of every major American city. He reads, he sees, but he cannot be expected to feel deeply what he has experienced only vicariously. These depressions are quick in passing, and conversation soon becomes as intent about the dessert for dinner.

The crux of this special flaw in the problem approach is that a student cannot be expected to take a profound interest in the solution of a problem he has never felt deeply. His interest in the answer is of the same academic kind as his interest in the problem. (Of course, some are far more sensitive, more empathetic, than others, and most reformers have been of the Thomas Jefferson, privileged type, rather than the Benito Juarez type, that sprang out of dire poverty.)

So we now try to expose students through first hand experience to these problems. They go down to the Bowery with a few pennies in their pocket and attempt to stay even two or three days and nights. They may be reduced to pawning their watches. They smell the stench; I have watched one such student retch. They experience poverty, and, possibly, if they have been gently brought up and are intelligent, that experience will last for life.

But then the further problem lies in the fact that he doesn't begin to comprehend the reason why in this richest of countries such contrasts exist. He only knows now that they do. He is more ready to seek the solution. But he cannot do that until he has discovered the cause. It is hard for him to perceive the cause, because he has been brought up in America and has no contrasting experience.[12] Later he will go to several countries that have few resources, nearly none compared with ours, yet no slums, urban or rural, and practically no poverty (as Denmark,

---

12. "At one time in my career I ran educational study-trips for the Newark State Teachers College and found the individual backgrounds of the students made a great difference in their understanding of the social processes observed as well as sight observation that we interpreted in the light of their own experiences. As an example, I remember one trip through the slums of St. Louis where many lived in literally tin and paper shacks, toilets were coal shovels, cooking was done on an open fire, and water was drawn from one tap in a six or eight square block area. The understanding and appreciation of the problems involved, and the written observations of the students, were strictly related to their own past experiences. Some just saw the filth and squalor; others realized and wrote about the sociological problems that caused the slums and the reason why these people lived under these conditions. I remember another instance of first-hand observation where a woman who had taught school for a number of years stood on the levee at New Orleans and asked where she should look to see the levees I had described in lectures. When I told her she was standing on one, she expressed sur-

Sweden, Switzerland). He reads Hudson Strode's *Sweden, Model for a World*; he can stand an examination on it. But he won't really understand the functional causes until he has had a greater variety of experience.[12] Thus conceptual growth will be a continual process as the student proceeds around the world. For now, explanations of American poverty are academic, necessarily complex, and lacking in challenge to one for whom there has always been enough of everything.

Oversimplify the answer, blame it all on "economic imperialism," and the student turns to radical answers, especially if his personal life has had an overdose of hostility as against a parent or parents.

Conceptually, there is no one answer. But the student can be brought to study types of socio-economic means of production and distribution from capitalism (badly named because all systems, and equally, require capital) to Communism (both systems being fluid and hence defying exact definition).

For instance, it is likely that he has scarcely heard of consumer cooperatives.[13] Give him books on this subject,

---

prise and told me her mind-picture of a levee was two boards with dirt between them." Quoted from a letter by Arnold M. Hess, Board of Education, Newark, N.J., March 18, 1966.

13. American Cooperatives: (1) *Where They Came From, What They Are, Where They Are Going,* by Jerry Voorhis, Harper & Brothers, New York, 1961, $4.95; (2) *Studies in the Social Philosophy of Cooperation,* Paul Lambert reviews the ideas and practices of cooperatives since pre-Rochdale days and evaluates them vigorously. *Cooperative League,* Chicago, 1963, p. 000, $3.00. (3) Films: A. *As Consumers We're Owners.* Neighbors join as owners and customers of a supermarket. What it means, how they do it, what they achieve. Color. 13½ minutes. Cooperative League, 59 East Van Buren St., Chicago, Ill., 1958. $125 a print, $5.00 rental. B. *Men of Rochdale.* Twenty-eight weavers open their store in Rochdale, England, in 1844, struggle to make it succeed. B&W. 50 minutes. Cooperative Union of Great Britain, 1944, $100 a print, $4.50 rental.

and he may be surprised at the prophetic nature, the utterly democratic quality, and the potential universality of the eight Rochdale Principles, as established in England in 1844. He may be surprised and interested, too, to learn that since that date the paid membership in the International Cooperative Alliance numbers some 130 million. He lifts his eyebrows in academic surprise to hear that such a cooperative in Chicago operates the largest supermarket in that city, and that the cooperative at Greenbelt, Maryland, now does $32,800,000 worth of business annually.

But visit with him the Hyde Park Cooperative in Chicago or Greenbelt Consumer Services in Maryland. He is not apt to be moved. Not now, at least. He sees only the stores. They look so familiar. They are like the best of supermarkets, but no better. And as to the principles, they get lost somehow in the market baskets or at the checkout counter. Only momentarily did he feel the problem, so he seeks to avoid the whole business, seeks out some faults in administration, as for example, too few members attend the business meetings. He turns his back and says, "Let's go have some interviews with senators" or "There's a demonstration in Washington. Let's make some placards and march. Let's do something."

It's hard, especially when the students have lived mostly in school, from age 6 to 16. But open to him the meaning of capitalism, fascism, socialism, cooperatives, communism, and cybernetics, let him study these institutions in historic perspective, and he will perceive that, while the rights and responsibilities and the dignity of the individual must forever be defined and defended, in a technological age socialization as a concept is irresistably emerging.

All the creative concepts for which we seek, each relative, each fluid, each dynamic in potentialities, are obviously related. And most of them have crept quietly into being, born of human want of one kind or another, in rather recent times.

So world government sixty years ago was never discussed, was advocated by Hamilton Holt in the *Independent*, but by few others. Yet in half a century, it has sprung into being as an organization soon to embrace all mankind in membership and is destined, if we survive this lingering era of fanatical nationalism, to serve as a political vehicle for world government.

Regional development, thrust on this country only 34 years ago, has, by the might of its own inherent soundness, leaped oceans; and the Tennessee Valley Authority (T.V.A.) pattern has taken hold in all political areas of the world: in Russia, the Volga-Don complex; in China, the Yellow; in India, the Damodar; and many others. With such appeal to all political factions, the river valley authority as a concept for our time is demonstrating its constructive possibilities and its universality.

And so with the concept of social planning. Announced first in the U.S.S.R. as an active procedure so recently as 1927, rejected for decades in conservative countries, it is now an accepted instrument of social progress almost everywhere, even in Putney, Vermont.[14]

So with the intentional community development. Scattered Utopian ventures not so many years ago, now as

___

14. It has been said that Vermont is not a republic, nor a democracy, nor a theocracy, nor a state, but rather a state of mind, where a lot of lovable but stubborn people are strewn through a rugged terrain, where they wait all year for Town Meeting so they can gather to elect officers from whom they will take no orders and choose leaders they will refuse to follow. If social planning will work in Vermont, it will work anywhere.

ejidos in Mexico, *kibbutzim* in Israel, communes in the U.S.S.R. and China, and by the thousands in India, intentional community developments are responding at the local level to a universal human impulse to rise above accidental social sequence and establish, deliberately, a constructive cycle of progress.

Again, the concept of racial equality has in recent years come vigorously to world attention. Twenty years ago, Clarence and Florence Jordan and the Martin Englands were pioneering this simple concept of racial equality at Koinonia Farm, near Americus, Georgia. History will record the heroism of that small band standing against the bigotry of the Klan and the White Citizens Council. Burned out, bombed, shot at, turned out of the church in which both Clarence and Martin were ordained ministers, beaten, boycotted so completely they could not buy feed, seed, fertilizer, or gasoline, nor insure cars, trucks, nor houses, they pioneered the tidal waves on which more recent heroes still bravely ride, or die.

Even earlier, history will tell, Myles and Zilphia Horton made a frontal attack on this ancient, arch-foe of world embrace. It was Rosa Parks' dignified refusal to stand and give her place to a white man that touched off the Montgomery bus strike, the first major gain in the civil rights program. Let it be remembered that Rosa Parks had recently come from attending the Hortons' Highlander Folk School, where she had been accepted into such equal respect and fellowship that she found strength to refuse to give up her new-found dignity and the right to equality. And let it not be forgotten, that under minute pretext, the Courts of Tennessee closed Highlander and confiscated the property. Remorse, shame, will come, but will

119

never atone or repair the injury. One pauses to meditate reverently on the thousands, in a broader sense, the millions, of Negroes who have suffered every form of persecution and indignity, slavery, murder, lynching.

World education differs from earlier schools in that it would not leave to Jordans and Hortons and Kings and the like this challenge to human progress. In the old schools, "teachers" taught in segregated schools and took their checks monthly for personal security; never mentioned that their schools were segregated, but by their lives taught segregation. How tragic that some universities, denying the very meaning of their name, became the strongest bastions against this world concept of human equality and had to be forced by armed militia to open their doors.

In contrast, take the following episode.

We have traveled interracially through Tennessee, Mississippi, Alabama, Georgia, North Carolina, and now came to Virginia. Always we had asked if we could eat together, but now in the Old Dominion State presumed we could and simply entered an attractive restaurant near South Hill. Experience teaches that integrated groups should avoid trying restaurants with small windows and dark curtains as evidences of exclusiveness. But this one was made largely of plate glass and brightly lighted.

The manager called me and asked, "What is the race of those people?"

I: "I have known them only six months, and it never occurred to me to ask. Shall I call some of them so you can ask?"

He: "Oh, no, no. I can tell. That fellow is a Negro. And

you all can't eat here. If you did, most of these people would leave and many would never return."

I: "There must be a hundred persons here, and we don't want to hurt your business, but I wonder if you are right. My friend, do you believe in the freedom of speech?"

He: Yes, yes," relieved to get on a different subject.

I: "Then you can't object to my asking the customers?"

Then, taking advantage of his confusion, I addressed the patrons:

"Friends, I am traveling with students from China, India, Africa, Jamaica, Haiti, and the United States. The manager says we cannot eat here because you would be offended, and many of you would leave. If he is right about that, then we want to leave, because we don't want to hurt his business. So I'm going to ask any of you, when I give the signal, to raise your hand if you would rather we leave. But first I want to tell you that these are all my friends and good friends, and that John Noble, for instance, escaped from Southwest Africa by jumping off a running bus some miles before it reached the border, then made his way at night through lion-infested country in order to hitch-hike 12,000 miles to reach a land of freedom and democracy. Now any of you who would be unhappy in eating in the same room with this man, please raise your hand; don't creep it up, hold it high. And if there is one, we will leave and have sandwiches in the forest."

I waited a long time, a little fearfully, but a long time. Then, turning to the manager, asked, "May we be served?"

"Yes," he said, and we were. A white girl left her place to join us, as did a professor of education at Duke. I think even the room took on a hum of greater congeniality.

I am happy to report that on returning recently, a few years later, I found many Negroes eating in this restaurant. Route 185 by-passes this spot, and trade had declined. The manager said that one-third of his customers are now Negroes, that only one white had taken offense and left, and that I could see that one at the moment at an indicated table. The manager even went so far as to speak well of the deportment of the Negroes. "If anyone comes in wearing a hat, it is never a Negro." The manager said the one-third of his customers who are now Negroes are essential to his continuing in business.

I offer this small example as suggesting the fitting role of education in helping society discover the modern day necessity of interdependence. Particularly in race relations.

Finally, then, schools have been creatures of tradition, rather well-designed to conserve tradition,[15] teaching until recently languages, two millenia dead. The curriculum was a catch-all trap into which fell an amazing assortment of facts and myths, all of which became sanctified; a trap from which there was little exit. Those who taught had entered this trap at a tender age and, upon graduation, often afraid of life, had stayed on to keep the wheel in motion. Now it is clear that we must break with this intellectual in-breeding. Students by the tens of thousands are questioning the whole enterprise and are turning to existentialism, Zen Buddhism, to fill a value void: or, striking against this moral vacuum, are seeking ways to be different from their well-heeled elders, even if it means donning the disguise of a beatnik and rebelling

15. *The Sabre-toothed Curriculum*, J. Abner Peddiwell, McGraw-Hill, New York, 1939.

against training in cleanliness and refinement of speech.[16]

Fortunately, there are many students who make out through docile acceptance of the status quo, and, better, a few who find genuine outlet through civil liberties participation, Peace Corps, International Voluntary Services, VISTA, and the like. For such rewarding efforts, some choose to leave school. But schools need to change, so that students are not forced to make this choice between schooling and more vital, if less structured, education.

Schools must now become agents of wise social change through making students and faculty learner-seekers, as together they grope towards tomorrow's potential design. The outlines are emerging as a nebula of universally applicable, universally acceptable, concepts, all relative, all fluid, all dynamic, all spelling out, each in its own related way—world community.

Studytravel

In addition to about 35,000 miles in zigzagging around the world, largely by plane, students will travel about

16. "Why does Socrates appeal to contemporary students? They respond to his fearless assertion of his right to determine his own conduct despite powerful opposition from the majority of his fellow citizens. The conflict between individual freedom and socio-political authority which he dramatizes expresses their own central dilemma. These students have outgrown the discipline of parents. In college, various authorities—the college administration, campus mores, and student cliques—vie for their allegiance. They are also uneasily conscious of the different standards of the professional and business worlds they are about to enter. The sensitive student, confused by these uncertain values, is thrilled when Socrates, the original rebel who became the "father" of philosophy, tells his fellow Athenians that he loves and cherishes them, but chooses to obey only his own vision of the right and good. Socrates' example can still engender a revolutionary fervor in youthful hearts. It was hardly an accident that the campus rebellions at Berkeley, and earlier at the University of Colorado, were led by philosophy majors." J. Glenn Gray, *Harpers*, May, 1965.

5,000 miles in the area of each regional Center. Generally this will be by small buses. The first group traveled to Mexico in five VW micro-buses, equipped with a carefully selected assortment of books, a modern, light, easily erected tent, a cook stove, food, 30 lbs. of duffle per person and a sleeping bag, some typewriters, and, of course, cameras.

The present group on Long Island used similar equipment for their study of the South, and five busses are in use in Europe.

In essence, the purpose of the trip is to experience, at first hand, problem areas and solutions being attempted. Sharp distinction is made between mere do-good efforts that attack the symptoms of the problem, and those that, in terms of the conceptual guide-lines above mentioned, seek to get at causes, that seek to be curative, even preventative.

Before the Southern United States trip, the group will have had an intense urban experience, seeing the worst and the best of remedial efforts, coming away wondering whether all the efforts are not merely palliative: city planning, urban renewal, anti-poverty, head-start, anti-narcotic, drug addiction withdrawal, children's courts, boys' clubs, settlement houses.

Under sponsorship of the American Friends Service Committee, students will have experienced a well-planned weekend in a mental institution, including discussion with a psychiatrist, seeing a film, a briefing by the administration and director of recreation. They visit each ward and try to find ways to be helpful, with games, group singing, conversation, getting up a Saturday evening entertainment. At the end, an evaluation leaves the students with questions. Is this the way to deal with the emotion-

Pruning trees at Hawk's Hill

Richard Brett explaining the Hawk's Hill Project

ally ill? What is causing the increasing incidence of such illness? What kinds of communities produce the lowest per cent of such sickness? How does the experience relate to the madness on the world scene?

The group will study ecology through the Hawk's Hill project developed by Richard and Elizabeth Brett near East Barnard, Vermont. At this project they walk over the 70 acre demonstration of the interrelated and balanced phases of forest care, soil conservation, moisture conservation (including a series of beaver dams and aeriation dams), recreation, wildlife, and natural beauty. They work at a project carefully laid out in advance, thinning a half acre of forest and pruning as indicated, constructing an eighth-mile of road with an underdrain, or making markers to advise that this is an experimental area.

Let us look at the Southern U.S. trip in some detail, but realize that travel about each region will be unique. The Southern trip is designed to see one region whole, just as in four years the students are to see and feel the world whole. They view the study film *Face of the South*,[17] which shows the four distinct sub-regions of which the South is comprised: mountain, piedmont, plantation, and coastal plain. It outlines the history and the problems of each and suggests solutions to these problems. They set out to experience each of these subregions and a fifth region, not mentioned in the film, the region of the T.V.A. which brings into effective coordination the peoples of the mountain, the piedmont, and the plantation in a single integrated whole.

In passing, the group stops to see urban sprawl, un-

---

17. George Sinclair Mitchell, *Face of the South*, a 25 minute talk film on the South produced by the Presbyterian Church of the U.S.A.

planned rural slums, magnificent but labor exploiting truck farms, planned communities, as Greenbelt and Reston, consumer cooperatives. At Greenbelt, there is opportunity to study a well-organized consumer cooperative. The students question the citizens of Greenbelt, the officials of the town, and the employees, directors, and customers, all co-owners, of the Co-op. By contrasting this cooperative store with chainstore supermarkets certain aspects of the reading and discussion of their first six weeks comes into more vivid focus. Similarly, the Credit Union is studied and compared with small loan company practices. Visiting, then, producer cooperatives such as Southern States, the concept of a "cooperative society" emerges as a reality. The John Bellers tract of 1696[18] takes on serious significance. The Rochdale Principles of 1844 appear as possible guidelines.

What if most businesses were organized on principles of open membership (anyone being eligible regardless of race, creed, or nationality); democratic control (each member having one and only one vote); neutrality in all matters of religion and politics; operating on member-owned capital; selling at prevailing market prices; paying a low, fixed rate of interest; returning savings above costs and reserves to the customers in proportion to their trade; and expanding through constant education? By what magic, unless its appropriateness to man's universal needs, has this movement grown from 28 members in 1844 to 131 million members in the International Cooperative Alliance, with dues being paid on both sides of the Iron Curtain? Could it be that consumer cooperatives consti-

---

Note 18. *New View of Society*, John Bellers, 1696. This is a rare volume in the library of the Co-operative Union Ltd., Manchester, England.

tute one of the emerging universal concepts appropriate to our period of metamorphosis, and that, with many other universals, they could give new meaning and new design to tomorrow? What has been the role of cooperation in Denmark, Sweden, India, the Soviet Union, in Berkeley, California, in the Hyde Park Co-op, of Chicago, Illinois, in Maynard and Fitchburg, Massachusetts, as in Greenbelt, Maryland?

Twelve miles farther south the group stops for first hand observation of Congress at work; talks with Congressional leaders about issues of the day; appraises the grandeur of marble facades in classical style while serving functions never then dreamed of. The students attend museums; visit Arlington to wonder what came of the human sacrifices buried there, that might not better have come through conciliation; talk with representatives of different political parties, with leaders of would-be reform movements; observe problems incident to school and housing integration.

Then the Skyline Drive for geographic perspective, to overlook the Appalachian geosyncline, the Shenandoah; dip into one of its limestone caverns for geologic perspective, see stalactites and stalagmites millions of years in the making (and still being made) by the redeposition of particles of lime first formed there eons ago when that area was beneath the sea, hundreds of feet in depth of deposits of microscopic shell creatures. For World Education means, among other learnings, coming to have a reverence for the enormous span of time whose constant changes we inherit.

There is a visit to the Cherokee Reservation where the Superintendent gives a briefing, naturally with real effort to share the Indian point of view. But tell the story as one will, it is a sordid, sorry affair of arms and greed, hunting down and shooting many helpless people, most finally fleeing, some hiding out and holding on to where they are now. We observe the school (so like others); the handicrafts retrieved or invented; the dual system of government, federal and tribal; the tourist exploitation as "braves" in gaudy headgear and trappings for the occasion show children, for 25¢, how to shoot with a bow and arrow; and enough more to leave with questions as to whether the remaining culture of these people should be encouraged to remain as a social inheritance, or integrate their culture with ours for the benefit of each.

In the Appalachian Highland, the area of present widespread concern, poverty has always been characteristic. Only recently has America come to care. John C. Campbell in the early nineteen hundreds studied these quiet people. Men came down out of the mountains occasionally with horse or donkey, bringing skins or tanbark or liquor to sell, and bought gingham dresses and other needs for the family. Campbell wrote a book *Men of the Mountains* and advocated Scandinavian type folk schools as a partial remedy for the backwardness and the poverty. After his death, his widow studied folk schools in Denmark. And at Brasstown, North Carolina, in 1923, she established the John C. Campbell Folk School. In that immediate area, great changes resulted from improved agriculture, cooperatives, credit unions, handicrafts, drama, folk dancing, music. Here Jack Holt, when asked how he could find such wonderful horses in a block of wood, gave the famous answer, "I just whittle away what ain't horse."

Later more and more individuals and groups came to help solve the problems of Appalachia. Thomas Hughes had come in the eighteen hundreds to establish a utopian

131

community at Rugby, Tennessee, for the younger sons of landed gentry. The project was a failure, but some of the houses, the beautiful church, and the library are still to be seen. His financial loss was great, and there was little gain for the local region.

Mrs. Roosevelt took a special interest in Ravenscroft, Tennessee, an abandoned mining community. Heroic leadership was made available, but the futile effort to build on no firm economic foundation invites study.

We visit the efforts of as many more pioneers as time permits, for there are profound lessons to be learned at each: Big Lick, Tennessee, where Eugene Smathers tried to build a community about the church with better farming, a health center, a stone church built by the residents, a community wood processing plant, and modern charcoal kilns, only to have the community drawn off to various nearby centers of transportation and communication. Crossville, Tennessee's Cumberland Homestead, and Skyline, Alabama, where the Farm Security Administration poured several millions into these planned and hopeful communities with emphasis on such principles as balance of industry and agriculture. Many church groups have made community building efforts in these highlands: the Seventh Day Adventists in 13 centers (most notably the hospital and college at Madison, Tennessee), usually with low cost health provisions; the Quakers; the American Missionary Association where Pleasant Hill Academy was operated as an educational project in community building from 1884 until recently; the Brethren in various centers of Western Virginia; the Macedonia Cooperative Community, six miles north of Clarkesville, Georgia, which operated from 1935 to 1957 on the basis of twelve principles of community organization as derived by students at New College of Teachers College, Columbia University. This project of 1,000 acres followed the Rochdale principles of cooperation, practiced continual democratic planning, controlled the entire area as a unit, sought to balance industry and agriculture, sold refined products rather than the raw materials, was self-supporting but not self-sufficient. A good dairy, excellent forest, and a factory that turned out the well-known Community Playthings were some of the tangible results. The growth of those involved was even more impressive. After 22 years as a cooperative community, Macedonia became a Christian communal group by joining the Society of Brothers and moved to other centers.

These and many other projects preceded the present concern about poverty in Appalachia, and wisdom demands careful study of their successes and failures, lest hundreds of millions be wasted in repeating errors; more important, in the hope of great success.

In the mountains, the traveling students see typical areas of Appalachia, as at Alice Lloyd College at Pippa Passes, Kentucky, and the isolated cove community of Decoy. In Habersham County, Georgia, they experience a forested, mountain area at first hand. There they:

Visit the headquarters of the Chattahoochie National Forest of the State Forest Service and of the county agricultural agencies for briefings on their programs.

Learn to use a chain saw and a *sandvik* (Swedish for "bow saw"), both under expert instruction.

Learn from a local woodsman to swing an ax, cut a "unit" of pulpwood, and load it.

133

Visit the interrelated enterprises of a portable saw mill and a centralized saw mill whose by-product of shavings is litter for poultry houses producing 12 million broilers annually.

Visit the egg producing units turning out the 12 million biddies, and the processing plant where they are slaughtered and processed.

Visit the rural electric cooperative that serves four counties and helps make such enterprises possible.

See the pastures (recently forest) now bulldozed into rolling enclosures made green year round by seed choice and abundant use of chicken manure mechanically applied.

Observe a half million dollars worth of Aberdeen Angus cattle on a single poultry grower's land.

But they see, too, the plight of the ignorant and unemployed, visit one of their dynamited stills. One boy, by pushing buttons, is now producing 75,000 broilers each nine weeks. Automation has thrown thousands out of work who had raised broilers in a less automated way. These things the students see, and from them they learn much about this mountain area.

Clearly they learn:

1. These mountain people are basically as admirable and lovable as any they have known.
2. Under the same conditions, they themselves could have done no better.
3. Education is gradually relating itself to the problems of

134

the people (as at the North Georgia Trade School), but is still too remote.

4. Physical work is a hard way to make a living. (40 students together earned $16 in a day, their first and only day of cutting and loading pulpwood.)

5. All phases of economic life are related and tend to be interdependent.

6. Race prejudice can be overcome, manfully, by local citizens who declare they will observe the law, and that the group may eat where it will.

7. This is a region in rapid transition, so that the exciting talk given by Alice Mary Hilton on cybernation becomes a reality.

One of the more striking efforts was the Highlander Folk School begun by Myles Horton and Jim Dumbrowsky in 1932 at Monteagle, Tennessee. Myles Horton has carried on through the years, throwing courageous and skillful energy into problem area after problem area; now labor organization through a school for labor leadership, now handicrafts and folk music, now cooperatives, now race problems. It was at Highlander that the theme song of the Civil Rights Movement, "We Shall Overcome," originated. It was at Highlander that George Mitchell's talk on the *Face of the South* was first given, and the film of that talk was being shown when marshals entered to arrest the staff. The state then confiscated all the Highlander Folk School property, land, buildings, Horton's home, the library. This desperate and shameful act is a measure of the power of Highlander in sparking the Civil Rights Movement. Myles Horton directs, from the present Highlander Center, 1625 Riverside Drive, Knoxville, Tennessee, the students' study of the many-sided struggle for equality.

Most scholarship seems so sterile when compared with a thorough study of an area like Appalachia in which the purpose is to find workable remedies for the misery that has smouldered in cabins tucked away in cove after cove. Technically-trained men have come in increasing numbers to every county: experts in forest care, forest fire fighters with observation towers and fire fighting equipment, general agriculturists, home economists, doctors and public health specialists, conservationists, resource technicians, and better and better equipped teachers.

But these people have tended to be compartmentalized, and in consequence relatively ineffective. Let us take one example. The forest service has told farmers that they are cutting the forest too close, that it takes 25 or 30 years for a pine to grow 10 inches in diameter at breast height when, at $30 a thousand board feet, it is worth on the stump 60¢ but that if a man waits an equal period longer, the tree grows to be 20 inches in diameter at breast height and is worth on the stump $10.44. That is, the tree increases 17½ times as fast the second period as the first. This the farmer has heard and believed, but the forester has not told him how to eat during that second period of 25 to 30 years. So when the tree will buy three loaves of bread, it is sacrificed to necessity. And the forester is helpless to resolve the problem, because his knowledge is specialized to the point of being encapsulated. And so the vicious circle of poverty has continued: early cutting, continued poverty.

We need a new scholarship based, not on studying such subjects as forestry, but beginning with human problems and then reaching deeply, deeply into every phase of forest care, economics, tree growth, diseases, insects, balance of nature, wildlife, recreation, aesthetics. For then it becomes apparent, in the instance cited, that what is needed is cooperation between the forest service and some lending service such as the Federal Land Bank Association, so as to average out the income from a forest under optimum care and supervision. Such a plan would be much more than self-supporting, would multiply the income of the forest farmer many times above costs, and result in a magnificent stand of trees that is now neither beautiful nor productive.

Fortunately, we observe such overall concern in some of the newer developments as the Water Shed Projects and Rural Area Development groups under the supervision of the State Extension Service.

We also study and observe vast expenditures under the Appalachia Redevelopment Agency, with thousands of miles of highway being constructed, electricity brought into remote areas, industry being carried to the mountains, and other measures.

Watching all these efforts, from those of John C. Campbell to the present major plan, the students are watching for social processes, the facts without which plans are futile, and asking over and over, "What can we learn here that could be useful in resolving problems over the world? What universal concepts are to be found?"

Poverty experienced in Harlem and in remote coves of Appalachia will already have given more vivid meaning to the earlier study of poverty in the midst of affluence. But only by reading and seeing such studies as Erskine Caldwell and Margaret Bourke-White's *You Have Seen Their Faces*, seeing films such as Pare Lorentz's *The River* and Eli Kazan's *The Wild River* can students of this generation appreciate the transformation that has taken place in the drainage area of the Tennessee since 1933.

We must not study T.V.A. in an academic way, preparing to answer questions on the number of billions of KWH produced. We must catch something of the creative impulse that led Senator George Norris to plead with administration after administration for its enactment. George Norris was not taught regional development. He envisioned it as a concept, and its myriad aspects are the unfolding of corollaries he saw only in general:

1. the building of a dam at Paducah to impound one of the longest artificial reservoirs, 184 miles, to Pickwick Landing, where the ferry would be replaced by a roadway over a dam that would back water to the Wilson Dam, Wilson to Wheeler, Wheeler to Guntersville, and so on to Hales Bar, Watts Bar, Chicamauga, Ft. Loudon, and to all the catchment basins on the river's tributaries;

2. flood control, to lessen the flow of the Tennessee's 52 inches of rain a year into the Ohio when the floods of these two would, at terrible cost of life and property, be added to that of the Mississippi;

3. a nine foot (now 11 foot) channel for the use of barges on 660 miles of the river through a series of locks;

4. the harnessing of electric energy at each of the major dams;

5. the coming of industry to use much of the power including now steam generated power;

6. health measures such as the destruction of the anopheles mosquitoes that had long been so costly in sickness and death;

7. recreation to add a needed dimension to the lives of the valley's impoverished people and

8. conservation, without which the reservoirs would have silted to the brim.

Now those visions are fulfilled, and the original dream continues to expand. The shore lines now total more than 10,000 miles. Locks have had to be enlarged, and that at Wilson is now the largest in the world. More than 2,000 industries have found their way to the Tennessee Valley. Race relations have improved more rapidly than elsewhere. Unpainted mountain shacks have given way to comfortable homes. Concrete roads make the whole area available. Charges that there would be little demand for so much current have proved ridiculous by the ever-increasing number of generators that have been added with each additional dam and by the building of steam generating plants so large that one of these alone produces more power than all the hydro-electric plants combined. Nor could Norris have foreseen that in the comparable development of the Cumberland River, a 90,000 acre National Recreation area, the Land between the Lakes would come into being; nor the building of Oak Ridge, nor the carrying on of the T.V.A. concept to each tributary of the Tennessee in such developments as those on the Chestuee, the Beech, Bear Creek, Clinch-Powell, Upper Duck River, the Elk, Upper French Broad, Lower Hiwassee, Upper Hiawassee, the Sequatchie Valley, South West Virginia Area, Yellow Creek, Twin-State Development Association, Walker, Catoosa and Dade Development Associations, and the Emory River Development Association. In time, every tributary of the Tennessee will be a sub-regional development.

During the ten days given to the study of the T.V.A., the group begins with inspecting such tributary dams, including the highest one, Fontana, and Hiwassee, where in off-peak hours the generators are used as motors, and the turbines as pumps to pump the water back into the reservoir so that it will be available for use again in peak demand hours. They see how these dams may be drawn down 60 feet or so to make storage room available in seasons of heavy rains. In Knoxville, the group meets with officials who answer questions and make available movies on any aspect of the program. Demonstration farms are visited, factories, locks and mainstream dams, the Atomic Museum at Oak Ridge, the steam plant at Kingston. Here, freight cars are inverted by giant machines, the coal powdered and blown into the furnaces. Tributary area developments are visited and studied in all their aspects. Officials are willing to explain any aspect of the program that may not be clear.

Students need to know these realities, know them not for the sake of knowing, but for the confidence they give in an idea, and as tools they too can use in furthering comparable developments over the world. Norris never knew of the scores of T.V.A.'s that would be developed along the same plan. Some of these dwarf the T.V.A., as the Volga-Don complex, as the Aswan High Dam with a single reservoir half the length of the Tennessee River.

A part of the learning will be the discovery that here is a concept that is universally valid, a connecting link of identity between all national and ideological groups which the student will experience as he advances around the world. He looks to areas in other lands, as in Africa where the Congo River flows into the lower Congo with potential power enough to energize eleven industrial empires the size of Detroit, but not a kilowatt is being developed. That is learning, too, to feel the potential power in a plan, an idea, a concept that hopefully invites investigation and further preparation.

Going farther South, the students see the reality of the statement they heard during the first six weeks of resident study "the South is one region made up of four sub-regions (not counting the T.V.A.") : the mountain region which they have seen; the piedmont region which they observed in passing through; the plantation area, and the coastal plain. They gradually come to see that each of these regions has its own history, its own problems, its own resources, and its own solutions.

But the sickness of slavery has left its deepest marks on the plantation area. These are the Somervilles, the Selmas, the Hattiesburgs, the Jacksons, the Bogalusas, the Orange-burgs. Here is strife that freedom marches may help, and school integration ultimately help deeply. But the causes go back to Eli Whitney, his cotton gin, and the demand for millions of laborers who could be controlled. Remedies will come with the moving out of Negroes for wider op-portunity, with the coming of industry that demands an educated and a skilled people, with labor unions, and practice in economic and political democracy. At places like Koinonia, near Americus, Georgia, students sense the bitterness of antagonisms in the many dynamitings, the burnings, the shootings, all because a small group with the Clarence Jordans and Martin Englands decided they would set up a community to practice what the local reli-gion had long taught.

When the first group of students went to the Koinonia Community in Americus, Georgia, they met a high school graduate named Greg Wittkamper. He wished to attend Friends World Institute. To make this feasible financially, Koinonia sent out the following letter.

141

For four years Greg Wittkamper, who grew up in Koinonia Community, attended Americus High School. Because he shared the Community's belief in racial brotherhood, he was completely ostracized by his white classmates. He was beaten up, pelted with stones, called filthy names, smeared with barbecue sauce, and endured countless other indignities. But Greg faced it with unflinching good will and humor, and in the process became a mature person.

Having now graduated, he has been offered an opportunity to attend a unique school—the Friends World Institute, which is described on the enclosed sheet. Because this school combines education with building peaceful relations with nations and races throughout the world, it has a special appeal for Greg and he is elated over the prospects of attending.

Greg cannot afford the $2,625 yearly tuition, and since the Institute is just being launched, it has no scholarships to offer. However, the school desperately needs books with which to begin its library. So the President, our good friend Morris Mitchell, has proposed to credit Greg's account with $1.00 for each usable book which friends of Koinonia donate to the library. If 2,625 books come in, then Greg's expenses for the year will be paid. If more than that, they will be credited to the following year's tuition.

Enclosed is a book-mark, which describes the four classes of books needed, and also a label for shipping. If you send more than one package, be sure to mark on each label "for G.W." so that Greg's account may be properly credited. Also write on it "Books—Library Rate" in order to get the rate of 4¢ first pound and 1¢ each additional pound.

By donating books to the Friends World Institute you can do several worthwhile things at once: you can make more room on your own bookshelves, you'll give a boost to the library of a very fine young institution, you'll add your bit toward creating a more peaceful world, and you'll send a courageous lad to school to develop even further his understanding of the things which belong to peace.

With warm greetings, from all us at Koinonia.

In consequence, 18,000 volumes arrived, and the Trustees gladly assured Greg that his way for the four-year program would be provided.

At this writing, having been in Scandinavia he is now in Eastern Europe. The post office complained a little that books for Wittkamper were daily overloading the springs of their delivery truck, and several times the school sent a truck to take the small mountain of packages out of their way.

And so to the piedmont area, most advanced in the South, where industry balances agriculture, and scarcely a family is farther than 12 miles from a factory; where labor unions give wider experience in voting, and where Negroes first won the right to vote. The group goes through a typical factory, at least half comprehending the process, with its gainful boredom of highly repetitious work, organized or unorganized, paying little but paying more than the workers had known, the women nicely dressed and all with hairdos, a far cry from a generation earlier.

Then on to the plantation area, the toughest to solve of them all; the area that has spawned most of the racial conflict. Visit a plantation, see the old slave market in Macon, Georgia, visit Koinonia, talk with sheriffs, live at Freedom House in Selma, Alabama, wonder how much longer before this black-belt area heals the wounds of despicable slavery.

Most of the study of the coastal plains, centers in the Beaufort, South Carolina, area, through Penn School on St. Helena's Island. Friends have been working for a century, most recently under the leadership of Elizabeth and Courtney Siceloff, Director of Penn Community Services. Opportunities are afforded to study that program in an area where, following the Civil War, land was granted Negroes, land they still hold. Surplus population has, through the decades, poured out; but those remaining have retained the charm of early days, and the singing remains of high order.

The Spring group, '66, spent a week in Selma, Alabama. They were under the direction of heroic Septima Clark, who in Charleston, South Carolina, defied the authorities and lost entitlement to a pension just prior to retirement by refusing to withdraw from N.A.A.C.P. membership. She was, and is, with the Southern Christian Leadership Conference.

Following is Septima Clark's report, which I include because it shows the realities of the process of involving young people (who have known mostly comfort) in the struggle for equal rights and opportunities.

The Southern Christian Leadership Conference through its Citizenship Education Department made available to students of Friends World Institute a training program of one week duration in Selma, Alabama, with all expenses paid.

1. Local problems and Citizenship Education.
   The program centered around the following topics:

2. How to teach reading and writing to illiterates.
3. The Constitution as it relates to the movement.
4. Organizing a Community for Voter Registration and other efforts.
5. Canvassing a Community for Voter Registration.
6. New Civil Rights Legislation.
7. Consumer Education.
8. Simple Banking (making out deposit slips and checks).
9. Negro History.
10. New Trends in Politics.
11. Films and discussions of them.
12. Role Playing for canvassing.
13. Tours and visitation.
14. Power of Non-Violence.

The group was extremely tense; they lived in the homes of Negroes who are low-income citizens of the community. It was hard for them to adjust to the living conditions, being mainly upper middle-class and having had many luxuries.

As we tried role playing, only two members volunteered to role play with the community people who came in to each of the sessions. To be consistent with the implementation of the planned program was hard. They wanted to stroll around or swim or sit on the steps of the church and talk.

On the guided tour to Tuskegee, some strayed away from the group and showed little interest in learning about a great scientist—George Washington Carver.

The showing of the films (*Right Now*, a story of Savannah, Georgia, and the *Nashville Sit-in Story*) provoked little discussion. In fact, even the leader of your group was anxious to leave immediately after the Nashville showing for a social event being given by one of the community workers.

On the visits to Citizenship Schools in the area, we

145

looked around and found many missing without any knowledge of why they were not there.

Three, to my knowledge, left the group before canvassing started. They seemed afraid to go into various communities, although each team had a local person along.

The first night, after canvassing during the day, brought glowing reports from many brave teams, and I felt doubly rewarded for having patience to consistently work with them and telling them the true facts about Negroes and Whites in that tense community.

Such statements as—"I never believed that Negroes could be so friendly." "Many asked me to come in and sit down, many told me of the kinds of harassment they've lived with." "I know now what alienation means."

One young man called his father the first day and told him about the living conditions he found. He decided that he had to help people because he loved them, and that he wanted children to have a better life. One young woman and man volunteered to help the teacher teach writing.

There was some hostility from Negroes, and these were well-handled. They listened and did not try to educate. They kept wondering if the SNCC worker was right by not wanting them there. They felt that first they have to change values and morals.

There was hostility from Whites also. They were refused service in the Pancake House, because they were seen associating with Negroes at the Negro Church. They were followed and watched continuously by the police force. They have not learned to live with fear inside as we have. This was a good experience.

The canvassing went well, and they, those who worked ardently, made excellent reports. We are now using these survey sheets to flush out the unregistered in Dallas County.

One woman who very graciously kept four in her

146

home told me how one girl cried before leaving. She regretted leaving. She felt that she had a great concern for these people and could make a greater contribution. The Rev. Harris speaks in glowing terms of the boys. They lived with him and were most hospitable.

The money S.C.L.C. spent, $600.00 for one week, was highly significant to me of our philosophy and principles when I think of human beings like Adams, Jane, Ellen, Mara, Barb, and Loomis growing to such marvelous proportions in such a short time. No money to me is wasted if one human being sees the light of "A Great Society."

P.S. They were glad that Friends World Institute gave them the opportunity to gain such experiences.

I was happy for Myles Horton who helped them to understand why some Negroes are hostile.

There are those who protest the rebellion of today's youth by saying, what leadership do they offer in rejecting ours; would they have us smoke pot, let our hair and beards grow, and generally defy convention? The question is unfair. Youth is rebelling, understandably, against a generation they hold responsible for today's war, poverty in the midst of affluence, race hatred, increasing crime, avoidable disease. It is those of us oldsters who also rebel against this chaos who should offer alternative leadership.

While the group was in Selma, James Meredith was shot. Ruby Magee, a faculty member and close friend of Meredith, hurried to him. The students resolved to follow and join the March.

Parents phoned, some wrote, asking if the students would be accompanied by "senior, experienced leadership." I have fought this fight for a score of years and so

147

joined the March. It was on my seventy-first birthday; I walked with the group 18 miles to Canton. The atmosphere was tense with defiance on both sides. A mile of marchers converged on the grounds where quietly determined men stood along the iron fence with rifles ready. There were strong speeches from the Negro leaders. An advance group had tried to put up a tent on the Negro school grounds had been arrested and the tent impounded. Now the large tents would be erected, come what would.

The story has been too often told to warrant detail.[19] The leaders were on trucks equipped with loud speakers. Hundreds of us were gathered round as cars filled with about seventy patrolmen swung into military formation on the windward side of the grounds and prepared their rifles with gas canisters. King practiced the group in getting down.

I was holding one of the poles of the tent when the gas canisters ripped through the group. No one can resist tear gas. Most ran in the opposite direction from the officers, which kept them in the slowly moving gas. Confusion, sneezing, vomiting, falling, running. I quickly circled out of the gas and headed for the officers, there to see two husky, helmeted troopers carry an unconscious man to the edge of the grounds and, with the butts of their rifles, each deal two horrible blows to the head and the sides of the victim of the law's protection, the man presumed to be Charles Meyer, a white pre-med student, who suffered two fractured ribs and partial collapse of one lung. "Stand back," I was told, "or I'll put the butt of this gun into you."

---

19. See *New South*, Southern Regional Council, 5 Forsyth Street, N.W. Atlanta, Georgia, Vol. 21. No. 3, Paul Good, "The Meredith March," pp. 2-16.

What was the responsibility of a "senior leader" at this juncture when the Negro leaders disclosed they would put up the tent the next day? I pondered that question as the protestors reorganized and marched round the school grounds before the menacing, burly officers, all in the same alert, defiant position, feet apart, guns ready.

The students and faculty had been really hurt by the gas, and a few had been carried from the field. But when I announced that this was a school for experience, not war, and while I thought they had all been magnificent in the march and under gas, I felt we should now return to Selma to complete our assignment there and carry further our study of the causes of tension and the possible remedies. But not a student nor faculty member agreed. They were in it and were opposed to leaving. I was deeply moved by this courage and knew they were all now "involved," beyond a doubt. Concluding that none were children and were not to be told what they could or could not do, I resolutely closed the school and impounded the buses and the funds (neither needed on the march, where food was provided by volunteers). And so all, except for a few under strong parental pressure, continued on to Jackson. Such is the story of student involvement in one social problem.

Finally we turn toward home base, pausing to see the Magnolia Gardens or Middleton Gardens; old Charleston; a Negro College; Williamsburg, Virginia. In the library of William and Mary College, we see the bust and portrait of George Wythe, teacher of Edmund Randolph, James Monroe, John Marshall, and Thomas Jefferson.

During this six weeks of travel, no one will have accepted segregation for meals, or lodging, shopping, or recreation. Teaching under such circumstances involves elements quite different from classroom lecturing.

No attempt will be made here to list the kinds of growth that result from such travel study. They have to do with the intellect and the emotions. They tend to motivate, to direct, and to inform. And they are an introduction to the study of many of the same problems and processes that, under different guises, will be encountered in each of the remaining six regions.

Reflection tells me that the preparation at the campus at Mitchel Gardens, then Selma, and then Mississippi graphically illustrates some of the aspects that will, over the face of the earth, characterize World Education. Rebellious youth, conventional or not, wants a positive direction.

The Trustees of the Research Vessel, "Thunderbolt," through Professor Morris Newman, the Director, have offered this facility to Friends World Institute.

The "Thunderbolt" is a converted mine layer, 186 feet long. Its main function has been to study lightning phenomena, and it is equipped with a ten million volt static electric accumulator.

The school has used the vessel, docked now at Miami, Florida, for the study of marine biology, oceanography, and to conduct various scientific projects.

The ship has been reconditioned to accommodate 40 students and faculty. There is equipment for the biological sciences on one side, physical sciences on the other. In the center is a common room with T.V., electric organ, and fireplace.

Specialized faculty members are brought in to lead these studies, an important aspect of the school's cultural approach to science.

Faculty

Nearly 500 applications have been received to teach at Friends World Institute. But the problem is to find faculty less interested in teaching than in learning; faculty who have attained a new kind of scholarship, that of knowing thoroughly some problem areas, some workable solutions. Scholars in the old sense by the hundreds of thousands have turned out millions of "educated" graduates who have been impotent to cure the glaring social ills or wisely direct social growth. With all New York City's schools of higher education, the slums of Harlem have, through the decades, grown larger, worse.

Thoroughness of learning is essential, and high degrees are a practical necessity. But it seems clear that if we are to help build an effective, orderly world community, made up of ever-planning regional (rather than national) communities, and those of intentionally self-directed local communities, we must have faculty members experienced and "scholarly" at each of these levels. There is even thought that the wisest strategy might well include, at the local level, perhaps 50 chosen community workers who remained in as many communities within each demonstration region. They would earn much of their living through their specialty, be it in industry, weaving, ceramics, bookkeeping, plant breeding, farming, forestry. Students would come on occasion to live and work in these communities, to try to help, but essentially to learn. Fortunately, there are many such suitable community worker-leaders all over the world, and frequently they are glad to have students work with them.

A beginning has been made on this plan. In the first of

151

man's great, deliberate, planned regional developments, Friends World Institute has acquired, through the gift of Barnicle and Tillman Cadle, 66 acres, 40 miles South of Knoxville, Tennessee. The Reverend Conrad Browne is the Director of the development of this Sub-Center. Conrad Browne is now the Director of the highly controversial Highlander Research Center, 1625 Riverside Drive, in Knoxville. A camp on the Cadle property was raided by officers of the law, and the campers were arrested in protest to the group being interracial. Shortly thereafter, the buildings were burned. The plan is not to rebuild of asbestos, but to exercise a conciliatory attitude without yielding on principles of moral values, and thereby make of being there, an educational experience. This site will provide a laboratory for study of ecology, silviculture, conservation, community recreation. And it will provide one center from which to go out in study of the T.V.A.

Finally, the faculty needs also to be balanced in other respects as in age, the sexes, and background in the chief areas of knowledge, the arts, sciences, social studies, and the humanities.

Latin America

Just before the Spring group arrives at the North American Center, the Fall group leaves for Mexico.

The program will change from term to term in order to avoid imposing on the hospitality of the many communities and the many leaders who are willing to help.

Robert Duckles, Director of Development for the Latin American Center, arranged for the first group to spend considerable time in Patzcuaro in the State of Michoacan, Mexico. There UNESCO has its training center for the

152

development of community leaders for Central and South American countries. It is called CREFAL, and the Directors have proved most cooperative in permitting Friends World Institute students to use their facilities, including a library, and have helped them understand the nearby community projects in a score of villages.

But the students, after an introduction to the Spanish language, soon move out into individual and group undertakings. One worked with a sculptor; some helped in a brick factory; others taught in schools or helped villages make carp pools. Not all acquired the use of Spanish as rapidly as might have been. But some of them gained remarkable facility, and when the group met with "El Presidente" of a municipality, all of the questions and answers were in Spanish. A few students even read profound volumes in Spanish; others wrote both prose and poetry.

In Patzcuaro, they met Hugo and Helen Van Arx who are identifying with the local community and offering leadership for the development of a remarkable library and in many other ways. The following letter from Hugo Van Arx indicates his estimate of our program.

Mrs. Van Arx and I have been living in Patzcuaro for the past eight years, and we have seen many groups of youngsters coming down from the North, in one capacity or another—to rebuild stone walls, help farmers with some of their chores, or just trying to create good will.

Some of these groups reminded us of babes lost in the woods, lacking complete knowledge of the Spanish tongue, not knowing just where to start to accomplish the basic purpose of their visit.

I can state in all sincerity that the members of your group, under the able leadership of Mr. Duckles and Mr. Meyer, have proven to be the great exception. We think that no other group in recent years has created so much good will among the people of Patzcuaro and has shown such initiative, ingenuity, and courage. In no time did these youngsters become part of the town. This statement of mine has been confirmed by many of our friends here, Mexicans, Americans, and town officials.

We thought you might want to hear about this, and that you may be pleased to know that your group reflected most favorably on your splendid institution.

From Patzcuaro, the group moved to Camomihla near Cuernavaca, not far from Mexico City. Here they had access to those who could help them understand the history and resources and problems of Mexico. And they went out from Camomihla to study the constructive ideas that have resulted so largely from the Revolution of 1910 to 1917, as: the industrial city of Ciudad Sahagun, Tlax.; the cooperative sugar center, farms and factories as at Ciudad El Mante and the Instituto Nacional Indigenista, also Cultural Missions. Mexico has many experimental projects to study, including the extensive Social Security system and remarkable slum clearance program. The Revolution itself broke restraining influences, and the effort to halt it were comparable in effectiveness to the peon who, when the Paracutin volcano erupted in the field he was plowing, tried to stop it by covering the spot with his sombrero.

Antiquities are studied also: the Mitla ruins and the Teotihuacan Pyramids; the Museum of Anthropolgy in Mexico City which as an institution comprises a museum within a museum; works of art in all fields.

The students see and study much more and, in the thousands of miles of travel, come to feel the ruggedness of the terrain and the immensity of that land. They come to know many of its people and begin to assay the deep-seated conflict between the retarding influence of four centuries of ruthless exploitation and the revolutionary urges toward a better society.

Former President Aleman, learning of the T.V.A., arranged with anthropologist Dr. Villa Rojas to visit the T.V.A. and to see it from a plane. Returning to Mexico, they flew together in search of a site for a comparable regional development and decided on the drainage area of the Papaloapan. Former President Cardenas similarly has fostered the development of the Tepalcatepec River basin development, now enlarged to embrace the entire Balsas. At present, plans are being laid to develop also the Chiapas River which flows southwest through San Cristobal de la Casas, Chis. This regional development, unlike the others, will embrace a tropical area.

In most parts of Mexico, local community development has been attempted through the *ejido* system. And besides, a number of local workers have provided exceptional community leadership.

It is the hope that Friends World Institute may decide on one of these three great regional developments and then, as a matter of strategy in the art of education for building a better world, engage as part-time faculty members perhaps a half hundred of these community leaders. Students from the school would have the opportunity to visit and work with these persons. And these leaders would visit one another to share ideas and to seek ways, at the local level, of furthering local and regional purposes, thus to further the dream of local community developments, within regional community developments, within a world community development.

We plan that some students may drive to Santiago to

155

see, and hopefully work with, a group of seventeen Jesuit priests, all well-educated specialists, trying to demonstrate a better way of life, better than any political or economic extreme. The drive to Santiago involves following the Pan-American Highway, with stops at interesting places, to Panama, where the car and group go by boat to pick up the highway again in Colombia.

Another group may go to Puerto Rico, that superb demonstration of what can be done democratically to advance a culture in a quarter century—almost unbelievably. All phases of Operation Bootstrap deserve close study; the work of the Community Education Division under Fred and Carmen Wale and the Health Program that, since 1942, has lengthened life expectancy in that commonwealth from a tragic low to a point now a little longer than that of the States.

Then there is Cuba, which should be studied sympathetically but objectively. No government has a moral right to say that students may not go where they will as students, to study. But wherever the group, under the direction of Robert Duckles, decides to go, the six months will comprise study, travel, work, play, and contemplation in singling out problems and finding hopeful solutions, especially those that point toward universal concepts.

Robert Duckles is laying careful plans at the Mexican Center for the study of all Latin America. He is coping with such questions as the legal aspects of incorporation, the development of a board of Trustees, the acquisition of ground and buildings, and the wise choice of a place between already existing language institutes and programs of social orientation.

There is a real problem of cultural adjustment for some students in moving into other areas of the world. This adjustment can also be difficult for the school, for irresponsibility of a few students can reflect discredit on the administration and the program. In order to lessen this cultural shock, we sought recommendations for the Latin American Center from Ed and Jean Duckles, Representatives of the American Friends Service Committee in Mexico and Quaker Advisers for the Friends World Institute program in Mexico.

1. We will expect the students and faculty of Friends World Institute to be sensitive to and willing to adapt to what the people of Mexico consider appropriate in the way of dress, behavior, and appearance. Most of the people of Mexico dislike intensely such things as the use of beards, evidences of lack of cleanliness, and loud talking, especially in a language foreign to them. They are embarrassed and repelled, especially in rural Mexico, by physical expressions of affection between boys and girls in public, because this is contrary to their ideas of what is correct. They also expect girls to dress much more modestly than is the current practice in the United States.

   Since one of the marks of a mature and educated person is that he or she has learned to have consideration for the feelings of others and respect for the mores and customs of other cultures, we will expect the students of Friends World Institute to show evidence of these qualities, especially while they are the guests of Mexico.

2. We will expect that the students and faculty of Friends World Institute have grasped adequately the principle of freedom in human relationships, and that they have not confused it with license. Every person of conscience should feel free to decide upon a course of action or

behavior consistent with the dictates of his conscience. At the same time, this should include a willingness to accept the consequences of one's actions which in some instances may result in a loss of freedom to act in the name of the society or institution of which he forms a part. This may happen when the welfare of the group is seriously injured by the actions of any of the individuals in it.

We are aware that mistakes may be made by the students of Friends World Institute as they learn to adapt to a new culture. We expect, however, a degree of maturity which results in not having mistakes intentionally repeated unless the person making them is willing by his own decision to separate himself from that point onward from membership in the group.

The following was the schedule for the Latin American Program, February 1 - June 30, 1967.

February 1-28	8:30 - 9:00	Meditation
	9:00 - 10:00	Seminar on Mexican History, with particular attention to the background of contemporary Mexico.
	10:00 - 1:00	Spanish—two beginning and one slightly advanced classes.
	Optional:	Classes in painting, folk dancing, papier mache, and guitar lessons.
		Field trips to Xochicalco, Oaxtepec, and Zacatepec.
March 1-April 12		*Community projects in two villages:* Santa Maria, Acuexcomac, in the state of

Peubla lies at the foot of the snow capped volcano, Popocatepetl. Students will cooperate in building a public laundry area, using water from a spring in town and improving the streets.

Toluca de Guadalupe in the state of Tlaxcala. Students will cooperate in cindering the recently community-built road with tezontle, a locally hand-quarried red, volcanic cinder, to make the road passable in any weather. Also landscaping around the new health center.

April 13-May 7	Mexico City evaluation leading into small group research projects in Mexico City.
May 8-24	Camohmila. Group reports on projects. Seminars to tie together the Mexican experience. Final work on and evaluation of journals.
May 25-June 23	Southern Studytrip.
June 24-30	Semester evaluation at Mitchel Gardens.
July 1-September 8	Vacation.
September 9	Leave for East-West European Center by student ship "S.S. Aurelia."

West Europe

In Scandinavia the pattern is different again, as it will be in each region. There we work through Scandinavian

Seminar.[20] Flying to Copenhagen, the first week is spent at the headquarters, Scandinavian Seminar College, in Holta, a comfortable suburb of the capital city. After a week's briefing, the students elect one of the four countries: Norway, Sweden, Finland, or Denmark. Then each of these groups undergoes an intensive three week language program. This is followed by a three weeks' home stay to try out and improve language skill and experience home life in a new culture.

The students go, usually individually, to a Folk School that has been selected as suitable for the particular student. There the student is immersed in the culture of his choice. During the nine months' period there are three conferences of orientation and evaluation, two near large cities, one in a remote rural area. At Christmas time, it often happens that the students are invited to return to the family of their home stay. This part of the program is extended by three months, because it has been found that nine months are required for students to become fluent in the language and really accustomed to the culture. In this way, many Americans overcome the fear that they cannot learn a foreign language.

East Europe

With present tensions over the war in Vietnam, several years may be required to mature plans for a Center in the U.S.S.R. Dr. Samuel Corson is at work on this purpose.

For the present, and at least through 1966-67, we shall think of an East-West Center in Vienna, with Dr. Ernst

---

20. Scandinavian Seminar, 140 West 57th Street, New York, New York, 10019; Dr. Adolph Anderson of New College, Hofstra University, Director.

Winter as Director. Students who wish to move, after Latin American study, to Scandinavia will be able to enroll in the Scandinavian Seminar program; others will go directly to Vienna. From Vienna they will study both West and East Europe and travel in each direction.

Dr. Ernst Winter is Director of the Diplomatic Academy, Favoritenstrasse 15, Vienna, and lives at Castle Eichbüchl, 2801 Katzeldorf/Leitha, Niederösterreich, Austria. These facilities, including libraries and language laboratory, are being made available to the students of Friends World Institute.

Students are now with Dr. Winter and his assistants, and, equipped with five microbuses, are following this schedule:

April 25-Sept. 17, 1967

April 25-30	Final evaluation period for Scandinavian Seminar Program to be held at Lerdalshöjden, Rättvik, Dalarna. Students arrive the evening of April 25 and leave after breakfast April 30.
April 30-May 14	West European Studytrip from Scandinavia down through West Germany, Holland, Belgium, France, Switzerland, to Vienna, Austria.
May 15-June 25	*LANGUAGE TRAINING AND DEVELOPMENT SKILLS* This period will be divided into two parts. Half of the students will live and study at the Diplomatic Academy for three weeks while the other half lives and studies at

Castle Eichbuchl. At mid-point they will trade places. At the Academy the schedule will be:

8:00 a.m.-1:00 p.m. Intensive language study.

Afternoons: Reading and discussions on the Soviet Union and Africa.

Evenings: Take advantage of Austria's cultural season of ballet, opera, concerts, etc.

AGRICULTURAL DEVELOPMENT SKILLS

The period at the Castle Eichbuchl will be spent:

8:00 a.m. to 1:00 p.m. Learning agricultural development skills.

Afternoons and evenings: Language study and reading about Africa and the Soviet Union.

June 26-
July 23

Students will go out on small group research projects offered in Spain, Greece, Italy.

July 24-
August 13

Vacation. Parents may wish to join the students in Austria for this three week period if they wish.

August 14-
September 17

Eastern European Studytrip through Czechoslovakia, Poland, the Soviet Union.

September 18

Leave for African Center.

162

"F. W. I." Students In Mexican Village —

When there is a Center in Moscow, it is planned that students and buses will be transported from Stockholm to Helsinki by ferry, then driven to Moscow.

If the Center is at Patrice Lumumba Friendship University, it is anticipated that three months will be spent in language study and in the study of the history, resources, and problems of the Soviet Union. Wherever we travel we shall do so basically to learn, not to transform the socio-economic systems we encounter.

After these three months in Moscow, with study of Moscow itself included, we shall begin a three months studytour. We shall drive to Leningrad, living in a camp outside that city, and going in daily to study. Such camps have tents for rent, cots, blankets, toilets, showers, commissary, and a building for use of individuals or groups in cooking and eating. The balance of the time will be spent in study of various developments over the country in keeping with the problem-centered approach. Special attention will be given to the utilization of the Volga and the Don as a drainage area development in comparison with the Tennessee River.

We shall observe again how man has moulded nature to his needs, conserving moisture, generating power, preventing floods, creating industry, planning cities, providing navigation, irrigation, recreation, improved health facilities. In this case, the Volga, flowing into the Caspian, has been joined with the Don at a point before the Don flows into the Sea of Azov, a point at which the rivers are only twelve miles apart. By this means, water has been drained from the Don, but with care not to deplete the waters of the Sea of Azov enough to injure the shell fisheries. We shall follow the rivers to see what has been made of a land once poor, part of it most terribly battered by Germany during the war. So with patterns of rural and urban development in the three months of travel.

Africa

The African Center is being developed by George Delf and will be in readiness for the first group to arrive September 20, 1967. George Delf is furthering preliminary exploration made earlier by Morris Mitchell and more recently by Mary-Cushing Niles, Vice-Chairman of the Board of Trustees.

George Delf wrote one of the first sympathetic biographies of Mzee Jomo Kenyatta and is author of *De-Canting Britain*. He has lived in Africa and helped establish a Social Studies Institute near Niarobi. It is presumed the Center will be near that city.

One purpose of the program will be to help the students see how illogically that great continent is now divided. Once there were indigenous tribal subdivisions. But colonialism carved Africa into political units that have little or no logical basis.

Who has really thought, for instance, of the Nile River basin as a whole from the Mountains of the Moon and huge Lake Victoria, down through the Sud to the joining of the White Nile and the Blue Nile, down through a narrow, parched valley to the Mediterranean? Man has dabbled here and there in the water of the Nile: 2,000,000 or so acres of irrigation at Wadi Halfa, ancient local irrigation schemes along the northern stretches, the Aswan and the Aswan High Dams, a channel through the Sud, some power at Jinja. But no one has bothered to help the people see how interrelated they all are from source to mouth of

165

the Nile; how with comprehensive planning that basin could flourish throughout its reaches. Now 800 billion cubic feet of water evaporate annually from the Sud, and that vast swamp clogs the channel with huge, floating islands of organic matter and vegetation. Drained, the Sud, about 400 by 800 miles, could produce food to feed all Africa. Now tribal, religious, and national hostilities divide the people with tragic consequences. And bilhartzia debilitates the people now, and needlessly, as for thousands of years.

And so we would see Africa whole, with natural subdivisions by regions, and these subdivided into communities, each seeking deliberate fulfillment.

So rich is Africa in resources and problems, that, that continent will surely provide a rewarding laboratory for our problem-centered curriculum.

South and West Asia

Mary-Cushing Niles, a Friend from Baltimore and the Vice Chairman of the Board of Trustees of Friends World Institute, spent five months in India in 1967 on the most recent of a number of trips. During that period, the groundwork was laid for the establishment of the South and West Asian Center, with its own Board headed by Nanu B. Amin and the Executive Committee with Ramesh Pai, Chairman. The Principal of that Center is L. A. Vyas, who will prepare the staff and program in anticipation of the arrival of the first group of students by ship from Africa in March 1968. The Registrar of Bangalore University had resolved on the 28th of January 1967 "that such assistance and facilities as might be desired by the Institute be extended to them by the Bangalore University to the extent possible."

While it is contemplated that the "home base" for the Center and the registered office of the Center shall be situated in Bangalore in the State of Mysore, there will be extensive study trips through India for which detailed itineraries are being prepared and arrangements being worked out with a number of other educational organizations. It is hoped that the initial group of students, who will have already studied and traveled in the U.S., Mexico, Europe, and Africa, will be joined by some students in India and other countries of South and West Asia to continue eastward around the world.

IDEAS FOR STUDENTS' STUDY IN INDIA, MARCH-SEPTEMBER, 1968

by Mary-Cushing Niles

The problems which seem to me of greatest importance for exploration in India are:

Population growth and control and effect on family; women's role in society, etc.

Agricultural development.

Community development, both rural and urban.

Industrialization—changes in family, caste, area and national consciousness.

Urbanization—the problems of the persons displaced into cities by the agrarian and industrial revolution.

Problems of democracy, political and otherwise, with so large a heritage of hierarchy and domination from the top.

The education system—problem and promise.

Group and individual relationships—*panchyats* (village councils), *sarvodaya* (Gandhian ideals of social reconstruction), etc.

Planning—national and regional.

Central-State relationships.

Problems of managing large groups of people—how to keep things small enough to be manageable at all.

Problems of language and communication—unity and diversity.

The Cultural side: The deep effects of a pluralistic society—tolerance, interchange; co-existence.

Religion as a part of life; meditation; pilgrimage; yoga; japa; tolerance and mutual interplay.

The rich cultural life of dancing, art, architecture, music, ancient and modern.

ROUGH CALENDAR AND ITENERARY FOR FIRST GROUP OF STUDENTS

Based on probable arrival in India on or about March 26, 1968. If as early as March 19, transpose dates for earlier arrival in Banaglore and cut out extra trip July 5-12. Convene in Benares September 6 and leave India September 19.

March 27, Wed. BOMBAY
Probably use Bharatya Vidya Bhawan as headquarters.

March 31, Sun.	Perhaps use Rotary hospitality.
	Meet Board Members Mahindra, Shah, and Vicaji and Sponsors Mafatlal, Mehta, Munshi, and other friends. Meet members of the Religious Society of Friends.
	Tour of city. Trip to industrial estate with explanations (R.R. Vicaji would be good). Problems of the great city and industrialization. Place of handicrafts and small industry (Prabha Shah).
	Tata Institute of Social Science.
	Bombay University.
	Juhu beach outside of Bombay, perhaps as guests of Ramakrishna Bajaj or the Tatas.
	Elephanta Caves. Fishing village. The port.
	Atomic Energy Commission (Dr. Vikram Sarabhai, Chairman).
	See one or two Parsee institutions.
	Attend a cultural event—get idea of interchange amog cultures.
March 31, Sun.	Night train to BARODA.
April 1, Mon.	Baroda, care Nanu B. Amin, Board member, and the Lowell Wrights of the American Friends Service Committee's Community Service Project. Hospitality at Uni-

versity or in homes. See the urban community development and a pharmaceutical factory (Sarabhai).

April 2, Tues. Bus to Amul cooperative (cheese) and on to AHMEDABAD, care of Board member Uma Shankar Joshi, Vice Chancellor, University of Gujerat, and Sponsors Gurdial Malik and Smt. Mrinalini Sarabhai. Probably stay at University.

April 3, Wed. See Sabramarti Ashram (of Gandhi) and visit with Gurdial Mallik, Hindu Sufi Quaker saint. See a textile mill (preferably one where the Tavistock Human Relations studies were made) and the Ahmedabad Textile Industry's Research Association (Dr. Kamala Chaudhry) and the Institute of Management. If possible, see dancing at the Sarabhais' private theater through Smt. Sarabhai.

April 4, Thurs. Proceed to UDAIPUR by train or bus.

April 5, Fri. Udaipur, care of Dr. Mohan Sinha Mehta, Board member, and see the rural institute and efforts to build up the countryside. Also see the beautiful city.

April 7, Sun. Arrive NEW DELHI to stay until Saturday night, April 20. Use prayer hall at Sannidhi, Rajghat (near Gandhi memorial museum), for briefings and probably stay at Birla Temple Hall.

Meet Board members Dr. V. S. Jha, Dr.

170

K. G. Sayidain, R. L. Tuli, M. S. Thackor and Sponsors Dr. Bharat Ram, Dr. C. D. Deshmukh, the Venerable Vira Dharmawara, Kakasaheb Kalelkar, Ravish Siddiqi, S. K. De, and Douglas Ensminger, and many other interested persons.

Worship at Quaker House, 224 Jorbagh, and meet Friends and friends of Friends. Hear Harold Snyder on relations between India and Pakistan.

Visit Rajghat and the memorials to Nehru and Shastriji, the Gandhi Memorial Museum, Gandhi Peace Foundation, etc.

Lectures on Vedanta by Kakasaheb Kalelkar; also on nonviolence and reminiscences of Gandhiji. Social teaching of the Gita by Dr. Smt. Ratnamaya Dixit.

Several talks on Islam by Ravish Siddiqi, leading Urdu poet; and Islam in India and also Sufism by Kumari Raihana Tyabji.

Visit to Jama Masjid and Red Fort. Trip to Agra to see Taj Mahal and to Fatchpur Sekri. Visit Jama Milia University.

Visit the Venerable Vira Dharmawara at Ashoka Buddhist Center, Mehrauli, and spend most of the day with him on Buddhism and on meditation. Visit the Qtab Minar and the Ashoka Pillar.

Visit Delhi University. See the Council for

171

Economic Growth, the Education Res. Council, the Dehi School of Economics, and the School of Business Administration and of Social Work. See the social work generated from Jeannette Bossert's concern.

Get briefings on economic situation and on sociology, etc., in India.

Political and constitutional briefings. Visit to Parliament and President's house. Hopefully meet the President and the Prime Minister.

Get the relationship of the States to the Center. Planning and the Planning Commission. Urgent problems, such as language, minorities, education, food, prices, etc.

Faridabad or Okla industrial estates. The Federation of Indian Chambers of Commerce (P. Chentsal Rao).

Village development. Visit to Bazitpur with Karan Singh. Cooperatives.

Cottage Industries emporium and other arts and crafts outlets.

The old city.

Ford Foundation.

Attend an event at the India International Center.

A visit to the American Embassy and Roosevelt House to see the notable architecture. Other arts.

Medical facilities and developments. Family planning.

April 20, Sat.   Train to HOSHANGABAD.

April 21, Sun.   Hoshangabad. Worship with Friends at Rasulia. Explanation of the British and Canadian Friends projects there on tube wells latrines and health clinic and family planning clinic. Meet Board member Smt. Paulina Titus and other Friends. Train to AURANGABAD.

April 22, Mon.   See the famous ancient AJUNTA and ELLORA. Train to HYDERABAD.

April 23, Tues.   Hyderabad. See our Board Member Dr. Khan and our Sponsors Dr. C. D. Deshmukh and Mehdi Nawab Nawaz Jung, and Dr. D. S. Reddy. Program at Osmania University and at Central Institute for Community Development and Small Industries Extension Training Institute. See Islamic culture and blending of peoples.

April 28, Sun.   Train to BANGALORE.

April 29, Mon.   Bangalore with residence in hostels of
   to July 5   Bangalore University.
                        Worship with Friends. American Friends Service Committee VISA program (Volunteers for International Service Abroad).

173

Study of Indian culture, history, economic and social problems, arts, etc.

Opportunity to get to know the industries, social life, and social work of this city with its people from many states. Study government enterprise as well as private.

Indian Institute of Science. University of Agricultural Sciences. National Institute of Social Science.

Ramakrishna Mission. Buddhist Society. Opportunity to study Hatha-Yoga (physical exercises) under a competent teacher. Relations with Christians, including Syrian Christians and Roman Catholics.

Agriculture and rural life. Syndicate Bank's developmental work.

Gandhi Center: International Sarvodaya Center.

Contacts with Board and Executive Committee members.

Arts, music, dancing. Artist Svetoslav Roerich and actress Devika Rani Roerich.

Big newspapers.

Visits to Mysore City. (See Maharaja and his palace, University of Mysore, Central Food Technological Institute), old temples, Manipal (Academy of General Education),

174

	Cochin, Trivandrum, Kanyakumari, Madurai, Gandhigram, Chidambaram, Madras. Meet Board member A. Sivasailam and Sponsors Smt. Rukmini Devi, D. C. Kothari, and S. Naryanaswamy.
July 6-12	Complete these travels.
July 13 to August 11	Field work in small research projects.
August 12 to Sept. 11	Vacation. Accent on Himalayas.
Sept. 12, Thurs. to 15	Reconvene at BENARES. Program at Gandhian Institute of Studies, Bharat Sewak Samaj. See Benares Hindu University, temples, ghats, pilgrims, shops; visit the Buddhist shrine at Sarnath.
Sept. 16	Go to BUDHGAYA, the place of the Buddha's enlightenment; thence possibly to see Vinoba Bhave, Shantiniketan (Tajore's University), possibly Jamshedpur (the steel city), the Damodar Valley and its fertilizer plant and electrification and Durgapur (steel plant).
Sept. 19, Thurs. to 26	Arrive at CALCUTTA. Possibly stay at the Ramakrishna Institute of International Culture. Meet Board Member Pabitra K. Sen and others. Friends Center. Ramakrishna Belur Math and Dakshineswar Temple. Jain Temple. Kali Temple. Botanical Garden. Ford Foundation and the Metropolitan

175

Planning Organization. Slums. Traffic. Refugees. Industrialization. Institute of Management. Water supply. Health problems. Financial center. "The managing agency"— as a holding company device.

University of Calcutta and Jadavpur University. Unions. Communist Party and its importance in Calcutta. Relationships with East Pakistan, China, Sikkim, Bhutan.

Evaluation and Journals. Might shorten vacation and have several days on Evaluation and Journals.

Sept. 26, Thurs.   Leave Calcutta for next area, South and Southeast Asia.

East Asia

The first group will reach East Asia in September 1968. Dr. Earle Reynolds spent more than a year in laying plans, particularly in Japan. Morris Mitchell left New York in May and will be in Hong Kong, Japan, and Korea furthering these plans. It seems likely the first group will be highly mobile, spending some of the six months period in each of the areas.

The Final Six Months

Under this plan of studytravel, each student is automatically returned for the last six months to the Center in the region of his origin. The problem is well-known of students from less privileged areas not wishing to return after study in a more privileged one. The plane carries him on the last lap of his global journey, home. But he should return, eager to be of help, armed with a cultivated spirit of seeking: the habit of recognizing problems for what they are, obstacles to be defined and thought through, not fought through, and eager to enter a planned service or go further in more specialized education.

For at this point he has had a liberal education in the sense of a liberating education and should be ready to enter graduate school. To such a school he would carry his standing on the Princeton Graduate Record Examination and his own transcript of credit from the Friends World Institute.

It will readily be seen how well these plans for world study correspond to the following remarks of Dr. Anthony Pearce, a member of the faculty of Friends World Institute.

When Queen Victoria was ruling over the vast British Empire, one of her distinguished subjects, Edward Augustus Freeman, Regius Professor of History at Oxford, insisted that "the only history which counts is that of the Mediterranean and European races." Since then, most of the characteristic opinions of the Victorian age have been overthrown, and the British Empire has given place to a Commonwealth of free and equal nations. But the narrow opinion expressed by Freeman seems to have remained; indeed, it appears to be the principal unspoken premise of what passes for a liberal education in our time and place.

The "history of races" has a particularly unpleasant ring to our liberal ear. Yet, even in this crude and arrogant sense, we cannot deny that the history of America has, until recently, been restricted to the history of its European immigrants and their descendants. In our histories, as in a great part of our society, the American Negro has been "an invisible man." And as Africans forcibly constrained to participate in the blessings of Western civilization have been overlooked, so African civilizations have been, until very recently, overlooked and even denied existence in Western eyes. Westerners, who have encountered first-hand the civilizations of India, China, and the lands which lie between and around them have been less disposed to overlook or deny Asian civilization. Yet openness to the ancient and rich civilizations of the East has remained the privilege of a tiny minority of Westerners. The Victorian prejudice persists; a man is labeled educated, liberally educated, even if he has never once been asked or even encouraged to open his mind and his imagination to the world outside the West.

At last our universities and colleges have begun timid ventures in "non-Western studies." Still our undergraduate students are unusual if more than one scholarly course, that is, some three per cent of their formal college education, directs their attention steadily beyond the West. The prevalent practice remains unshaken: American colleges still teach history as if Freeman's opinion were almost a law of nature, teach music as if the voices and sithars of India had been forever mute, teach economics as if the awesome experiments in mainland China were irrelevant to the most urgent needs of mankind, and teach philosophy as if Socrates were a creature of a different planet than Confucius.

Slowly our colleges will become more liberal; slowly our universities will become more universal. But there is little or nothing in the development of "non-Western studies" that promises justice to the condition of mankind in our age. Throughout our childhood we are filled with largely unconscious opinions of Western superiority. Even when we are asked to look beyond our direct heritage, it is usually under the negative heading of "non-Western," that is, not the West, not the best, but not to be entirely overlooked. How can our new generations begin to undo the yet uncounted harm wrought upon mankind by generations of Western arrogance?

There have always been some Westerners who have gone out to the peoples of the world in the spirit of John Woolman going among the Delaware Indians: "I went to them to find out how the spirit of God moved within them and to learn from them. And if by chance my coming should be the occasion of some openings of the spirit among them, I shall be content."

So in our time, the members of our new Quaker school go out among the peoples of the earth to learn from them and perhaps repay their learning by service. Experience is the surest judge in human matters, heart-felt experience, and so our communities will move to experience the ways and the wisdom of the principal civilizations of earth. We will go in belief that every human person contains the seeds of goodness, and every human society treasures the works of love.

In four years thus spent in traveling around the world and scouring over seven of its vast regions, students meet everywhere the reality of local problems, always seeking their solutions, visiting various hopeful frontier projects. Not only will they become aware of the repetition of the same problems, even their ubiquitousness, they will perceive, each for himself, as reward for his seeking, a repetitious pattern of seeming solutions. These will doubtless emerge as vast concepts.

These concepts will form the core of his social concerns, will direct him in his life as a useful WORLD CITIZEN.

179

FRIENDS WORLD INSTITUTE AS SEEN BY A
STUDENT—JOHN PHILLIPS

"Former Grinnellian finds challenge in truly liberal education
of Friends' college"

by John F. Phillips

Ed. Note: John Phillips was dismissed from Grinnel at the end of last year for "academic reasons." During this three years here he was involved with the yearbook and the newspaper, and last year he was co-editor/photographer of the 1966 yearbook. After leaving Grinnell, he chose to attend the Friends World Institute because of its "realistic look at life and education."

Phillips commented, "It is the application of one's education that is really important in life. Knowing a great deal and then not being able to apply it to one's life and community is an educational failure."

Phillips is now with the school in Mexico where they are living in small groups in remote villages, learning the language and mores of the people.

Some of Phillips' photographs are currently being considered for use in a story about the school in *Mademoiselle* magazine.

"She looked like a pile of rags, lying there on the sidewalk. We almost kept on walking, even after we realized

180

she was a human being. That's a strange impulse to have felt, wanting to leave her there. Perhaps we rationalized that she was drunk or else dead, or that someone else would come along soon. Maybe we just didn't want to get involved. It took a lot of courage to walk over and bend down and see if she was breathing. The smell of alcohol was very strong. Good thing we stopped. Judging from the dried blood no one else had stopped for quite a while and might not have for quite a while to come. It was 3:00 in the morning. A chilly morning. She had apparently stumbled on the decaying sidewalk, striking her head as she fell. We got her address out of the purse she held in her half delirious grip. It was hard to guess her age. She looked very old and very tired. With our help she was able to walk, after a fashion. Her apartment was about two blocks away. As we walked along, she began to talk, not to us, but to God—'Why did you take him away from me, we had so many good years together, he said life in America would be better . . . and we got along . . . it was hard but we were happy . . . and then you took him after I prayed to you to take me first . . . please let me die. . . .' Not without difficulty we got her into her apartment and into bed. We washed her face. The head cut didn't appear to be very serious. She was able to thank us, after assuring herself that we had appreciated the wedding portrait on her dresser of what had once been a truly handsome couple. We then found ourselves back in the middle of Harlem. But we weren't quite as chilled as before, nor nearly as tired."

The above is an excerpt from the journal I keep as a student at Friends World Institute. FWI urges its students to keep some sort of record of their "intellectual growth." This journal can take just about any form that the student wishes and constitutes the only formal written requirement the school imposes on its students. Just what I and the two girls that accompanied me learned that night is hard to say. Perhaps I learned how dangerously tempting it is—how easy it is—to avoid involvement, to ignore the humanity that lies beneath that pile of rags across the street. Surely I learned how fulfilling it is to recognize that humanity, even in so small a way.

5 dollars for 3 days

The kind of painful but fulfilling confrontation with conscience that I have described happens to everyone from time to time, regardless of who they are or where they go to school. The difference with FWI as a school is that it wants this kind of thing to happen to its students and, as much as possible, provides for it. As part of our study of "problems on the city level," each student in my class (about eighteen girls and twenty-two boys) spent two to three days living in Manhattan with a total of $5 to spend per person for food and lodging. Well-armed with emergency addresses and telephone numbers, we set off to discover, however briefly, the less pleasant and most often ignored aspects of this ultimate example of a metropolis. My little group of three decided to walk the streets for 24 hours or so to get at least a taste of the eternal struggle for life that the over 7,000 homeless of Manhattan know as their entire existence. It's the kind of thing that's hard to get through vicarious description alone. It may even sound corny. But try it, and you may discover as you finally sit down for a nap in Grand Central station (go to sleep in about 30 seconds, and the policeman tells you to produce a train ticket or get the hell out of there) why a lot of people don't like cops. I mean, like, he was a real bastard; he didn't even understand at all when I said that it was all a sort of game and we really had nice clothes at home and parents with lots of money and we'd been walking for hours and hadn't been eating very well and Laura is *really* exhausted and its just a game and can't we stay here for just a half an hour and then. . . .

The faculty at FWI call this sort of thing a "learning experience." The school believes that the most basic and universally understood knowledge has to be individually discovered to have any realistic meaning. Before visiting New York City we spent several weeks in our seminars discussing "the city" as an abstract concept. We heard a number of speakers, were exposed to an appropriate reading list, and saw a number of films dealing with the city. We learned funny, silly, little things, for instance, the whole population of the United States could live in the metropolitan area of New York City in the buildings already existing there if they were distributed at the same density in which people *are* living in certain blocks of Harlem. Then we went to Harlem. . . .

---

7 campuses around the world

FWI went into actual operation not quite two years ago under the auspices of the New York Yearly Meeting, Religious Society of Friends. It was the brainchild almost seven years before of the Westbury (Long Island) Friends

Meeting. The guidelines set up by the New York Yearly Meeting stipulated that FWI be: 1) A four year liberal arts college Quaker in spirit; 2) A world college, international in character and outreach. In 1965, the State of New York granted to FWI a provisional charter which lasts for five years, during which time the school is being developed into Friends World College. Degrees granted during the time FWI is not officially a college will be retroactively validated when FWI receives a college charter. Rather than having a single campus, FWI will ultimately have seven campuses in different parts of the world. Each student will attend each of these campuses for six months and then return for the last semester to his original campus to complete a final thesis or project concerning a specific subject he has become interested in during his travels and previous study. Ultimately it is hoped that classes will originate from each of these seven different campuses. However, for the present all classes are beginning from the North American Center located near Westbury, New York, in an old deserted air base known as Mitchel Gardens. Headquarters of FWI are at Harrow Hill, Long Island, at the home of the director, Morris Mitchell, former director of Putney Graduate School. I'm writing this in Cuernavaca, Mexico. At present there is no Mexican campus as such. Our time in Mexico is being spent between studying Spanish and Mexican history at the Institute and direct living experience in Indian villages, in addition to study trips to surrounding points of historical and intellectual interest. During the next three years the schedule of my class at FWI includes study and travel in Eastern and Western Europe, Russia, Austria, Kenya, India, and Japan.

A new class begins at the North American campus every

six months under the present schedule. I'm in the third class. The first two classes are in Europe, presently, while the fourth is still at the North American center on Long Island. The classes have varied in size averaging around 35. As planned, they will gradually get larger until reaching a maximum of around 100 students per class, half boys and half girls. FWI was started as an experimental college and certainly hasn't left the experimental stage. At times this is hard on students and faculty alike, but it makes FWI an exciting place. Anything can happen. While the second class was traveling through the southern United States in Volkswagen buses studying racial problems and the South in general, they temporarily dropped their work of voter registration in Selma, Alabama, to observe (and participate in, as it turned out for the majority) the Meredith March through Mississippi. The journals of the several FWI students who were tear-gassed in Canton, Mississippi, make very interesting reading. The fourth class of FWI, which is still based on the North American campus on Long Island, has just recently altered its schedule to provide for three weeks of working intensively on the planning and organization of a major national peace demonstration set for the middle of April. The school is negotiating for a castle in Austria for the permanent European center. There have even been rumors that future classes may sail a small schooner from Florida to Acapulco in order to get to Mexico. I wouldn't be surprised, anything can happen at FWI. . . . When traveling we camp out wherever possible and do our own cooking. For longer stays, such as our present month in Cuernavaca, we stay in groups of one and two with local families. This makes for a good experience; it's also financially efficient, making possible an all-inclusive tuition of

$2,600 per year. The American Friends Service Committee provides invaluable information and assistance for FWI in foreign countries as well as in the United States.

Marine biology study
while living on boat

For three weeks before coming to Mexico my class lived on a 185-foot boat in Miami, Florida, studying Marine biology, taking advantage of the many Marine Museums and laboratories in that area, and getting a taste of the necessity of cooperation and cleanliness when living in close quarters. The ship was a lightning research vessel and was offered for temporary use to our school during the "non-stormy" season. In addition to several hours of classes and seminars every day, numerous short study trips, and the inevitable reading lists and available books (always encouraged but never required), we were given the opportunity for skin and Scuba diving and observed several demonstrations of artificial lightning phenomena. To get from Miami to Mexico City, each student in my class was given a plane ticket to Houston, $40, the usual supply of emergency addresses and telephone numbers, and one week. The class split into small groups to travel beyond Houston, some taking a week to get to Mexico City and some going directly. Several students hitch-hiked, and the rest took buses. Students such as myself who rode in buses became well impressed with the necessity of learning Spanish for efficient survival in Mexico. Crossing the border on foot with backpacks and then getting proper bus connections to Mexico City required

186

"Thunderbolt"—lightning research vessel also equipped for the study of oceanography and marine biology. Miami, Florida

Spontaneous "community meeting" Miami, Florida, Jan. 1967

"Conversation" with Normar Thomas—Mitchel Gardens

some fancy dictionary-page flipping for "non-Spanish speakers" such as myself.

Everyone is equal

The concept of each FWI class as a community is strongly stressed. This is not only an efficient necessity since each class is independent of other classes, truly living as an independent unit for four years, but it is a monumental learning experience in itself. How can one expect to work toward a world community until one has learned to truly act out of love towards one's neighbor? As much as possible in a given cultural context, our class attempts to regulate itself as a social entity. We've spent more time in "community meetings" than in any other collective activity. For many this has been the most significant experience thus far. Following someone else's rules without considering their foundations is the easy way out. A FWI community meeting is carried out "after the manner of Friends." Every one is equal; everyone has a voice. The issue is discussed, *really* discussed, until the "sense" of the meeting is achieved. True communication is almost like magic. It eliminates the need for ever voting on an issue. After honest discussion, the decision, if one is required, is obvious to everyone. Someone may well disagree with a decision arrived at in a meeting, but they'll recognize through the discussion why their opinion cannot, and should not, be accepted by the rest of the meeting. Needless to say, these meetings are often long and difficult, but they're rewarding.

After leaving Cuernavaca in the next few days my class

will divide into two separate groups, going to two different and relatively obscure Mexican villages. We will assist with work projects already begun in these villages under local leadership. In the case of my village, this will mean building a road—which means carrying crushed rock from a nearby quarry and spreading it on the road-bed. My village will have no electricity, a minimum of water, and a population of about 1,500, the majority of whom have never been exposed to North Americans in any form. We'll be living in adobe huts and cooking our own meals. For six weeks we'll have direct and inescapable exposure to the subsistence level of living shared by two-thirds of the population of the world. We will be teaching classes of art and English in the local school and, in general, having an experience not unlike the Peace Corps. Because my special interest is photography, I look forward to this village experience as a unique chance to intimately portray in photographs, as much as possible, the essence of peasant culture in Mexico.

Camping in New Hampshire

During the first semester at FWI my class spent a week camping out in New Hampshire, just when the leaves were turning. This was a quiet and beautiful trip as well as an educational one; it culminated a series of seminars back at Mitchel Gardens on Man and Nature and intelligent use of natural resources. On this "New England Study Trip," we camped near an experimental forestry station and attended seminars concerned specifically with forestry conservation. This was a restful time with lots of

copies of Walden available, singing around the fire at night, and lots of free time for individual meditation. It was an experience on many levels; I watched beavers working on a dam and learned how to prune a tree; I learned how valuable beavers are and the necessity of pruning for proper forest conservation and, most important of all, I learned that forest production over most of the world could be doubled and consistent production in the future guaranteed by the mere application of already understood techniques of forestry conservation. We run into that kind of thing quite often at FWI, an awareness that in any number of contexts the sacrifice of an extra bit of effort combined with a proper bit of knowledge can provide for the future welfare of mankind rather than *ignoring* it. Perhaps after four years at FWI all that I'll really be aware of for sure is that two-thirds of the population of the world is barely surviving from one day to the next simply because of hunger and disease, while the other third of the world has the means of both helping to correct this situation and of literally destroying the whole world. But of course . . . everyone knows that. . . .
In its applied philosophy of education, however, FWI makes an interesting distinction between knowledge and awareness; *knowledge* is what you have when you've mastered facts and theories while *awareness* is what has happened when an individual is somehow motivated to act on his knowledge in a rational and human way. Awareness has an extra and almost mysterious element; you might call it emotion, or even love. . . . FWI is dedicated, as an educational institution, to the increased awareness of its students to the very real problems which presently face mankind. At the same time, FWI hopes that its students will become motivated to achieve, in whatever way

192

they are able, the hard facts required for the execution of the specific discipline through which they want to express their "Awareness." This is openly recognized as one of FWI's major problems at present. While the "freedom" from requirements is considered a necessity for a student's growth to be correctly motivated and for him to learn to *truly* think for himself, this freedom demands of the student the maturity to develop self-discipline with regard to his field of special interest. In light of this, it's anticipated that a more formal education may often follow the FWI experience. The beauty of this, however, is that such graduate study will be geared to specific ends and motivated by individualistic and humanistic ideals, rather than being executed out of habit as an aimless extention of a formalized undergraduate pattern which has often been motivated by little more than a desire to achieve an arbitrary social and/or financial status defined by parents and contemporaries. FWI believes that one takes a real chance to promise himself that he will act on his knowledge in a truly constructive and unselfish way after receiving a formalized education. Uninvolvement is a difficult habit to shake. In the words of director Morris Mitchell, FWI is a school designed to produce "agents of social change" and in the process teach the "joy of purpose." The *joy* of purpose. If you can give someone these sorts of orientation, then formal, traditional education will become a means to specific ends and not a "necessary evil" or, even worse, an end in itself. The problems that our generation faces, if it does face them, are war, race prejudice, waste of natural resources, hunger, housing, education, population explosion, pollution of air and water, poverty amidst affluence, and, in general, a disastrous intolerance of and insensitivity to both local and foreign cultural patterns which in any way deviate from the familiar. These problems are the subject matter of FWI. The fact that students in general in the United States have one of the least influential voices of any student group in the world is frightening testimony to the apathetic and often selfish attitude that American education is giving to its products. Increasing affluence in the U.S. is used as a perverted excuse for escalating greed, rather than as a responsibility and opportunity for the furthering of the humanity of men everywhere. Whatever disadvantages its approach may involve, FWI hopes to avoid this trend and give its students an awareness of the constructive potential of wealth and knowledge.

LA MOND—INSTITUTO EL AMIKOJ

Planado por la Mond-Instituto el Amikoj komencis antau sep jaroj per komitato de la Novjorka Ciujara Kunveno de la Religia Societo de Amikoj (Kvakeroj).

La Mond-Instituto el Amikoj (kiu farigos kolegio kiam gia aktivo rajtigos cârton) diferencas kompare al aliaj institutoj de alta edukado en tri rilatoj.

1. La studentoj veturas tra la mondo kaj ne estis alportitaj al unu centro. La kampuso (usona vorto kiu num signifas la tuta funkciejo de la kolegio) estas vere la tuta mondo. Estos sep regionaj centroj: Norda Ameriko, Suda Ameriko, Okcidenta Europo kaj Orienta Europo, Afriko, Hindio kaj Japanlando. Fincele estos 750 studentoj po ciu centro-entute 5,000. Ciu studento komencos en sia hejma centro, restos tie dum ses monatoj kaj same en la aliaj centroj kaj dum la lastaj ses monatoj, li ankau studados en la hejma

194

centro. Krom veturante cirkau la mondo, ciu studento veturos 5,000 mejlojn kap studados en ciu el la sep regionoj.

2. La programo estas bazata sur problemoj anstatau temoj. Studante tiajn problemojn kiaj dangeroj de nukleara milito, kostego de armiloj por la homaro, malriceco meze de riceco, explodo de popolkreskado, malsparo de naturaj provizoj, sano, nescio, rasa antaujugo k.t.p., la enhavo de la studplano estos vivplena kaj tre signifa. Sed la scipovo ne estos la celomemsed ilo al celoj. Tiuj oi daurantaj problemoj estos studataj kiel trovitaj tra la tuta mondo.

3. La baza motivo emocia kaj intelekta estas serci la fundamentajn universalajn verojn kiuj nun eligas novforme en nia epoko—la ne tiom evidenta akompananta forto kontrau la detruemaj fortoj de la Industria Revolucio, nun intensigataj de automacio kaj sibernetiko. Meditado, studado, veturado, diskutado kaj laboro estos la vojoj al la elkovro de la ekvenantaj konceptoj universalaj, kiuj povus helpi en detruo do la homa bedaulinda rasaparugo, timo kaj malamo, kaj tiel konduki nin en amantan kooperantan komunumon.

Kveekarien Maailmaninstituutin perustamista ruvettiin suunnittelemaan seitsemän vuotta sitten, jolloin Kveekarien uskonnollisen ryhmän New Yorkin vuosikokouksessa valittiin tarkoitusta varten komitea.

Kveekarien Maailmaninstituutti (josta tulee yliopisto heti kun on saatu tarpeeksi varoja peruskirjan hankkimiseksi) eroaa muista korkeammista oppilaitoksista kolmessa suhteessa:

1. Opiskelijat tulevat sijoittumaan keskuksiin eri puolille

maailmaa; yliopistosta tehdään kirjaimellisesti maailmanlaajuinen. Keskuksia tulee olemann seitsemällä alueella: Pohjois-Amerikka, Latinalainen Amerikka, Länsi-Eurooppa, Itä-Eurooppa, Afrikka, Intia ja Japani. Kussakin tulee aikaa myöten olemaan 750 opiskelijaa; kaikissa yhtennsä n. 5000. Kukin opiskelija alkaa opintonsa lähimmässä aluekeskuksessa. Siellä samoin kuin jokaisessa toisessa keskuksessa hän viettää kuusi kuukautta; sen jälkeen hän palaa vielä kuudeksi kuukaudeksi omaan aluekeskukseensa. Jokainen opiskelija tulee siten matkustaneeksi maailman ympäri, mutta sen lisäksi hän joutuu kullakin seitsemällä alueella tekemään viitisen tuhatta mailia opintomatkoja.

2. Opinto-ohjelma perustuu ongelmiin pikemmin kuin oppiaineisiin. Tällaisia ovat mm. ydinsodan uhka, aseistautumisen kustannukset ihmiskunnalle, korkean elintason keskellä vallitseva köyhyys, räjähdyksenomainen väestön kasvu, luonnonvarojen tuhlaus, terveydelliset olot, tietämättömyys, rotuennakkoluulot. Niiden tutkiminen johtaa luontevasti elävään ja monipuoliseen tietojen omaksumiseen. Tieto sinänsä ei kuitenkaan ole päämäärä vaan ainoastaan keino tavoitteen saavuttamiseksi. Ongelmia tullaan tutkimaan sellaisina kuin ne esiintyvät eri puolilla maailmaa.

3. Liikkeellepanevana voimana kaikessa tulee olemaan pyrkimys löytää ne yleispätevät perustotuudet, jotka ilmenevät uusissa, ajallemme ominaisissa muodoissa, ehkä vähemmän silmiinpistävinä kuin niitä vastustavat, teollista vallankumousta seuranneet hävittävät voimat. Mietiskeley, opinnot, matkat, keskustelut ja työ ovat keinoja tuollaisten totuuksien löytämiseksi, jotka voisivat auttaa ihmisiä luopumaan valitettavasta hajaannuksen, pelon ja vihan tilasta ja tehdä meistä kaikista sellaisen yhteisön jäseniä, jossa vallitsisi rakkaus ja yhteistoiminta.

INSTITUT MONDIAL DES AMIS (des Quakers)

Les projets en vue de la fondation de l'Institut Mondial des Quakers ont commencé il y a sept ans. Un Comité a été établi lors des Réunions Annuelles de la Société Religieuse des Quakers à New York.

L'Institut Mondial des Quakers (qui deviendra une Université quand les fonds le permettront diffère des autres institutions d'enseignement supérieur sous trois aspects:

1. Les étudiants vont à travers le monde et ne sont pas cantonnés dans un seul centre. Leur campus est littéralement le monde entier. Il y aura sept centres régionaux: l'Amérique du Nord, l'Amérique du Sud, l'Europe de l'Ouest, l'Europe de l'Est, l'Afrique, les Indes et le Japon. Il doit y avoir 750 étudiants par centre et 5.000 étudiants en tout. Chaque étudiant débutera dans le centre de son propre pays; il y passera six mois et six mois dans chaque autre Centre. Il passera les derniers six mois au Centre de sa région. En plus du voyage à travers le monde, chaque étudiant devra faire environ 5.000 miles (...... kilomètres?) de voyage d'étude dans chacune des 7 régions.

2. Le programme est basé sur des problèmes plutôt que sur des sujets. En étudiant des problèmes tels que: dangers des guerres thermo-nucléaires, effets détrimentaires des armes sur l'humanité, pauvreté au milieu de l'opulence, explosion de la population, gaspillage des ressources naturelles, santé, analphabétisme, préjugés raciaux, etc. . . . La matière à étudier sera vivante et importante. Mais l'objet de l'étude sera l'étude des moyens à employer pour les buts à atteindre plutôt que le but lui-même. Ces problèmes persistants seront étudies tels qu'ils se rencontrent dans le monde entier.

3. La raison fondamentale de cette entreprise émouvante et intelligente sera la recherche pour les vérités de base universelles qui aurgissent à notre époque, tant soit peu sous de nouvelles formes et sont la contre-partie des forces destructives qui ont accompagné la révolution industrielle, intensifiée maintenant par les aspects de l'automation et de la cybernétique. La méditation, l'étude, les voyages, les discussions consisteront un travail d'approche pour la découvette de nouveaux concepts universels pouvant aider l'humanité à rayer la déplorable ségrégation, la peur et la haine, et nous amener tous à coopérer à l'éstablissement d'une communauté basée sur l'amour du prochain.

DAS WELTINSTITUT DER FREUNDE—Verzeichnis

Die Pläne zum Weltinstitut der Freunde wurden vor sieben Jahren von einem Komittee in der New Yorker Jährlichen Versammlung der Religiösen Gesellschaft der Freunde unternommen.

Das Weltinstitut der Freunde (das ein College werden wird, wenn ihm einst ein genügendes Vermögen zur Verfügung steht, um eine Verfassungsurkunde zu garantieren) unterscheidet sich von anderen höheren Bildungsanstalten auf drei Gebieten:

1. Die Studierenden gehen hinaus in die ganze Welt und werden nicht in einem Zentrum zusammengefasst. Die Schule ist buchstäblich die ganze Welt. Es wird sieben regionale Zentren geben: Nordamerika, Süd- und Mittelamerika, Westeuropa, Osteuropa, Afrika, Indien und Japan. Es sollen schlieblich 750 Studierende in jedem der regionalen Zentren sein, insgesamt also 5000 Studenten und Studentinnen. Jeder Studierende wird an seinem eigenen Zentrum anfangen, er wird 6 Monate daselbst vel oringen

und 6 Monate an jedem der anderen Zentren; die letzten 6 Monate wird er wieder an seinem eigenen Zentrum sein. Ausser seinen Reisen um die Welt bekommt jeder Studierende 5000 Meilen Fahrt und ein Studium an jedem der sieben Weltzentren.

2. Das Programm beruht auf Problemen und nicht auf Fächern. Indem man Probleme wie die Gefahren eines thermo-nuklearen Krieges, die Bevölkerungs-Bombe, Vergeudung der Naturschätze, Hygiene, Unwissenheit, Rassenvorurteile, usw. studiert, wird das Lernen des Lehrstoffes lebendig und anschaulich gemacht. Das Wissen wird dann ein Mittel zum Zweck und nicht der Endzweck selber sein. Diese dauernden Probleme werden untersucht wann immer und wo immer sie sich in der Welt begegnen lassen.

3. Der seelische und geistige Grundantrieb ist dann das Suchen nach jenen fundamentalen, allgemeinen Wahrheiten, die in etwas neuen Formen in unserem Zeitalter auftreten und die die weniger deutlich erkennbaren Gegenstücke jener zerstörenden Mächte sind, welche die industrielle Revolution begleiteten, heutzutage aber noch verschärft durch die Automatisierung und Kybernetik. Meditation, Lernen, Reisen, Diskussion, Arbeit werden zur Entdeckung der aufkommenden universellen Begriffe führen, welche dem Menschen helfen könnten, die bedauerlichen Zustände der Rassentrennung, der Angst und des Hasses zu überwinden und uns alle in eine liebende, zusammenwirkende Gemeinschaft zu führen.

Si cominciò sette anni fa a progettare il "Friends World Institute" con una commissione dell'incontro annuale a New York della Societa Religiosa di Amici (Religious Society of Friends).

Friends World Institute (che diverrà un collegio quando gli assetti autorizzano la carta) differisce da ogni altro istituto di educazione elevata sotto tre aspetti:

1. Gli studenti vanno dapertutto il mondo. Non sono riuniti in un centro. Il mondo è il loro centro di riunione. Ci saranno sette centri regionali: il Nord America, l'Europa Occidentale, l'Europa Orientale, l'Africa, l'India e il Giappone. Ci saranno 750 studenti ad ogni centro, 5,000 studenti in tutto. Ogni studente incomincerà nel centro situato nel suo paese, passerà sei mesi là e sei mesi in ogni centro; e poi ritornerà al centro del paese nativo per gli ultimi sei mesi. Non soltanto viaggeranno attraverso il mondo, ma anche viaggeranno circa 5,000 miglie in ognuna delle sette regioni.

2. Il programma si base su problemi piuttosto che su soggetti. Nello studio dei problemi, ad esempio il pericolo della guerra thermo-nucleare, il costo delle armi, la miseria, l'esplosione della popolazione, lo spreco dei risorsi naturali; la salute, l'ignoranza, pregiudizi razziali, etc., le materie da studiarsi saranno vive e grandiosi. Però, il sapere sarà un mezzo da arrivare alla meta, non la meta in se stessa. Questi problemi persistenti saranno studiati man mano che vengono incontrati attraverso il mondo.

3. L'ispirazione emozionale ed intellettuale sarà la ricerca per quelle verità fondamentali, universali che emergono in qualche nuova forma nella nostra epoca che sono le controparti meno ovvie delle forze distruttive che hanno accompagnato la rivoluzione industriale, ora intensificate dalle fasi di automazione e "cybernetics." La meditazione, lo studio il viaggiare, la discussione, il lavoro, saranno tutti modi da usarsi per scoprire i concetti universali ora emer-

genti che potranno aiutare a mettere fine allo stato dispregevole dell'uomo: la segregazione, l'odio e la paura, e potranno riunirci tutti in una communità amabile e cooperativa.

EL INSTITUTO MUNDIAL DE LOS AMIGOS

Los planes para el Instituto Mundial de los Amigos empezaron hace siete años con un comité de la Junta Anual de la Sociedad Religiosa de los Amigos de Nueva York.

El Instituto Mundial de los Amigos (que es de estudios universitarios) es diferente a otras instituciones universitarias en tres respectos:

1. Los estudiantes viajan jor todo el mundo. No son traidos a un centro. Su lugar de estudio es realmente el mundo. Habrán siete centros regionales: Norteamérica, Latinoamérica, Europa Occidental, Europa Oriental, Africa, India, y Japón. Finalmente, habrán 750 estudiantes en cada centro, 5000 estudiantes en total. Cada estudiante empezará en su centro nativo, permaneciendo allí y en cada uno de los otros centros seis meses, y finalmente, los últimos seis meses en su región nativa, una vez más. Además de viajar alrededor del mundo, cada estudiante tendrá 5000 millas de viaje y estudio dentro de cada una de las siete regiones.

2. El programa está basado en problemas, en vez de materias. En el estudio de problemas, como són: el peligro de la guerra termo-nuclear, el costo de los armamentos a la humanidad, la pobreza en medio de la abundancia, la explosión de la población, el desperdicio de los recursos naturales, la salud, la ignorancia, los perjuicios raciales, etc.,

los recursos en materias serán grandes, pero los conoci-
mientos serán métodos para un fín y no un fín en si. Estos
problemas persistentes serán estudiados como se encuen-
tran por todo el mundo.

3. La motivación básica emocional e intelectual será la bus-
queda de esas verdades universales y básicas, que están
saliendo en formas algo nuevas en nuestra edad, y que són
contrapartes, sin ser facilmente reconocidos, de las fuerzas
destructivas que han acompañado la revolución industrial,
hoy intensificados por faces de la automación y del uso de
computadoras electronicas, sofisticadas. La meditacion, el
estudio, el viaje, la discusión, y el trabajo serán los métodos para descubrir los conceptos universales que están
saliendo y que podrian ayudar a acabar con la deplorable
segregación, el miedo y el odio del hombre, para traernos
todos a una comunidad amorosa y cooperativa.

VANNERNAS VARLDSINSTITUT

Planerandet av Vännernas Världsinstitut började för sju är
sedan i samband med Vännernas Samfunds arliga möte i New
York.

Vännernas Världsinstitut (vilket skall bli college sa snart de
ekonomiska tillgangarna medger registrering dartill) skiljer
sig fran andra högre utbildningsformer pa följande tre om-
raden:

1. Studenterna beger sig ut i världen och är alltsa inte sam-
lade till endast en speciell plats. Bildligh talat blir "studie-
orten" hela var jord med sju regionala centra i Nordamerika, Latinamerika, Västeuropa, Osteuropa, Afrika, In-

dien och Japan. Fullt utbyggt skall antalet studenter vid varje sadant centrum uppga till 750, totalt 5000. Varje student skall borja vid istt hem-centrum, tillbringa 6 manader dar liksom vid varje annat centrum. Forutom resorna mellan de olika centra kommer varje student att inom var och en av de sju regionerna företa studieresor pa c:a 800 mil.

2. Studiemalsättningen är baserad pa problem istället för ämnen. Vid studierna av problemen, sasom faran för kärnvapenkrig, mänsklighetens kostnader för militära rustningar, fattigdom mitt ibland överflöd, befolkningsexplosion, förslösande av naturtillgangar, hälsovard, allmän okunnighet, rasfördomar etc. skall kunskapsinhämtandet kring ämnena bli levande och vittomfattande. Men kunskaperna skall bli medal för nya malsättningar snarare än nagon form av självändamal. Dessa problem kommer att studeras som man möter dem runt om i världen.

3. Den bakomliggande emotionella och intellektuella drivkraften kommer att bli sökandet efter de grundläggande, universella trossatser, som har uppstatt i delvis nya former under var tid. Med dessa har följt destruktiva krafter som fögo uppmärksammade följdverkningar, vilka intensifierats genom den industriella revolutionens nya faser av automation och elektronhjärnor. Genom meditation, studier, sesor, diskussioner och arbete skall man närma sig upptäckandet av de universella regler, som skulle kunna hjälpa mänskligheten att upphöra med förödmjukande segregation, fruktan och hat och leda oss in i ett samhälle med vänskap och konstruktivt samarbete.

203

教友會世界學院

教友會紐約區年會於七年前專設委員會負責籌建教友會世界學院、現一俟資金籌竣，即可正式立案。教友會世界學院不同於其他高等教育學府之方面有三：

一、本院學生均將於在學期內遍遊世界，而不滙集於任一中心，即以全世界為其校園。本院將設北美、拉丁美洲、西歐、東歐、非洲、印度與日本等七個區域中心。每區域中心之學生數額最高可望達七百五十人，而全校學生總額將達五千人左右。每一學生將先就學於其本區域中心；六個月後，分往其他區域中心各就讀六個月；但結業前之六個月仍返回其本區域中心攻讀。每一學生環繞全球，將在每一區域內遊歷五千英里，從事研習活動。

二、本院學生研習對象為各種專題，而非傳統學科。研討諸如熱核戰爭之危險、軍備對全人類之損耗、富庶中之貧匱、人口之爆炸性增加、天然資源之浪費、衛生無知及種族歧視等等問題，可使各種知識之研習生動而具有意義。然而知識僅被視為達成目的之手段，而非目的本身。本院學生將就上述各久懸未決問題分別在世界各地加以研討。

三、此一努力內蘊之感情與理知之動力在於追求現時代中正以新形態出現之基本普遍真理，略與工業革命導發而為機械自動化與電子計算應用所加强之破壞性力量形成對比。本校將以沉思、研習、遊歷、討論及工作等方式試圖發掘行將出現之普遍性理念，從而有助於結束人類之不幸景況諸如種族隔離：恐懼及仇恨，並促成一互愛而合作之社會。

204

МИРОВОИ ИНСТИТУТ ДРУЗЕЙ /КВАКЕРОВ/

Семь лет тому назад, в Нью-йоркском Ежегодном Митинге Религиозного Общества Друзей, был учреждён комитет с целью основать Мировой Институт Друзей.

Мировой Институт Друзей /который со временем станет колледжом/ отличается от других высших учебных заведений в трёх отношениях.

1. Студенты разъезжают по всему свету; не занимаются только на одном месте. Место занятий – буквально весь мир. Основаны будут семь районных отделов Института: в Северной Америке, в Латинской Америке, в Западной Европе, в Восточной Европе, в Африке, в Индии и в Японии. В конечном счёте 750 студентов будет заниматься в каждом отделе, а всего будет 5.000 студентов. Каждый студент начнёт занятия в том отделе Института, который находится в его районе; позанимается там 6 месяцев, потом 6 месяцев в каждом из других отделов, а последние 6 месяцев проведёт опять уже в отделе своего района. Кроме путешествия кругом света, каждый студент проедет около 5.000 миль в каждом районе, где будет заниматься.

2. Вместо того, чтоб проходить строго установленный учебный план, студенты изучают проблемы. Предметное обучение станет ярким и обширным в изучении проблем, как например, опасности термо-ядерной войны, стоимости вооружения, бедноты среди богатства, увеличении населения, растраты природных богатств, здравоохранения, безграмотности, расовых предрассудков, и т.д. Знание будет скорее средством, которым можно достигнуть цель, чем целью самой по себе. Эти постоянные проблемы будут изучаться во всех их видах кругом света.

3. Основное духовное и интеллектуальное стремление будет состоять из поисков тех основных, всемирных истин, которые проявляются в новых видах в наше время и, которые являются менее заметной соответственной частью разрушительных сил, которые сопровождают индустриальную революцию и усиляются автоматикой и кибернетикой. Работа, размышления, занятии, путешествия, разговоры и обсуждения будут подходами к открытию проявляющихся универсальных понятий, которые могли бы положить конец ужасным отчуждению, боязни и ненависти, и привести нас всех к братственное и согласованно-действующее. общество.

CHAPTER IV

A Rash of World Education Plans[1]

Hundreds of plans have been developed attempting to realize the revolutionary concept of World Education. Efforts to meet the problems of our world in crisis have taken the form of exchange programs, work camp experiences, educational seminars, research teams, art exhibitions, and scholarship funds. Some programs are privately sponsored, some are sponsored by religious groups, some underwritten by large corporations, and others are the work of national governments themselves. Diverse in form and method, all have emerged as part of the concept of World Education.

Proposals for world colleges date back at least 55 years. After the closing of the League of Nations, a number of persons proposed that the League buildings at Geneva be made into a World University. But the world concept was hardly known until recently. In 1958, Carol Stanley McHenry located about 65 such proposals. Now it is believed that there are over a thousand individuals and groups working to establish various forms of world colleges. A study made in connection with Eisenhower College when it was conceived of as having world scope indicated that, in terms of popular approval for fund rais-

---

1. Carol Stanley McHenry in 1958 wrote a thesis on World Education at the Putney Graduate School, Putney, Vermont. It was probably the first thesis on this concept. Much of the research in this chapter is to be accredited to her.

ing, the world college idea carried the strongest of all motivations.

In 1922, at the first session of the League of Nations, the term "International University" was first used by M. Destree. Each year, for fear of universal standardization of teaching, plans were lost in committee.

In 1925, Professor Barany of Sweden suggested a special university in a neutral country which would study courses of international import, especially the cause of peace.

At the invitation of the Radio-difusion Française, broadcasters met at Nice in February, 1949, to discuss the possibility of a World University of the Air. As before, no results materialized.

According to UNESCO, four noteworthy plans have been drawn up by Dr. George Huthsteiner, Dr. Karl Ewerts, Dr. Max Bedrosian, and E. H. Avery, TH. D. Dr. Ewerts is the head of the International University Foundation which hopes to have a university housing four centers: an international research center, an international training center for leaders, a center of theoretical and practical learning to develop "world-men," and a research and training center of world service.

The International School, at 62 Route de Chene, grew up in Geneva largely for the children of those connected with the program of the League of Nations. It continues and serves also as headquarters for the International Schools Association, which in a 1961-62 report stated: "A true international school is one in which neither a nation or national grouping controls the Board of Management, in which more than one national system of education is utilized, and one in which no religious or political approach is dominant."

Also during League of Nations days there was a vigorous and excellent Graduate Institute of International Studies under the able direction of Dr. William E. Rappard. The approach of the faculty and staff was worldwide. Lectures, seminars, and library work were provided on an interest basis with a minimum of courses for credit.

Among the problems of each of these endeavors are questions of sponsorship, location, administration, finance. Language also poses a problem at the present stage of our cultural development, when two and one-half billion people speak at least a thousand tongues. This is a temporary problem born of the isolation produced by such barriers to communication as bodies of water, deserts, mountains, distance, and resulting prejudices. But these age-old tendencies are being reversed. Already a few languages are familiar the world around. Others, for better or worse, are doomed. First dialects will go, then small-group languages. Nations with only five or ten million inhabitants can ill afford preparation and publishing, in their vernacular, of the vast literature now proliferating and essential to cultural understanding and scientific progress. Wisdom would suggest permanent recording of such literature as the best, untimate hope of preservation.[2]

Many nations teach their own and several major languages. Telephones are being automated for world-wide dialing. Radio and television know no political boundaries, especially since the emergence of communication satellites. Travel grows faster, cheaper, more convenient. International trade and world government are linguistically unifying factors. If we survive, it would appear that

2. It was in this spirit the author recorded ten stories in a passing dialect. "Joel Chandler Harris' Uncle Remus Stories as told by Morris Mitchell," Vol. 1, Pathways of Sound #1028.

a Slavic amalgam, a derivative of Chinese and Japanese, and a modified English will dominate in world communication. Finally, within a few centuries, a fusion of these three will emerge. Some believe Esperanto to be the answer, but few if any World Education plans are based on Esperanto, and there is no effective sponsor to create the rich diversity of materials that would be necessary. Most schools of the World Education pattern will make their choice of three or four languages, for learning a language is time-consuming, and, when learned, is mainly a tool for intercultural understanding.

Above all, one great realization has taken place regarding World Education: the need for a new concept of the material to be taught. It is obvious that the narrow brand of national or vocational curricula now employed is not sufficient. The current move is away from the "three R's" towards concepts such as peace research, world law, foreign culture, and the like. This trend occurs in many degrees: from a position of relative conservativeness by schools which start with a standard program and stretch it to include subjects such as philosophy and languages never encountered in standard schools, to the position taken by Upland Institute, in which subjects for seminars are "The Function of the Individual in a Changing Community," and "Concepts and Practices of Non-violence."

It must be made clear that the plans which follow merely show a representative group, a sampling of what is now in operation. Calling this a "Catalogue of World Educational Programs" would be like trying to call a list of important phone numbers a "telephone directory." It is simply an outline, a sketch, of things to come.

Let us look ahead in the spirit of Lewis Mumford, who in 1951 wrote:

In time, these planetary student migrations will, let us hope, take place on an immense scale, comparable to the comings and goings of unskilled labor from Europe to America at the beginning of the twentieth century; but now worldwide in scope, and with teachers, not labor bosses, to lead them. The result of such transmigrations would be to enrich every homeland with mature young men and women who knew the ways and farings of other men, who would bring back treasures with them, songs and dances, technical processes and civic customs, not least, ethical precepts and religious insights, knowledge not taken at third hand from books, but through direct contact into every village and city, a touch of the universal society of which they form an active part.

Such people would be ready for further study, further travel, further research, for further tasks and adventures, as the harried young people of today, threatened with the horrid compulsions of war, caught in the bureaucratic routine of school, office, and factory, are not. They would no longer live in their present parochial world: that world whose narrow limits are not in fact extended by the vague dribble of information and suggestion that reaches them by way of books or radio, filtered through many political and ideological sieves.

The present trickle of students already passing back and forth between certain parts of Europe and America under the Fulbright Act are still caught by the routines of conventional education. But in time, their studies, their civic responsibilities, and their vocational interest will be united in a new kind of education; and mighty streams of such students, flowing back and forth along the seaways and skyways, will eventually irrigate the parched cultural soil of many lands.[3]

3. Lewis Mumford, *The Conduct of Life*, Harcourt, Brace & World, New York, 1951, Harvest Book Edition, pp. 278-279.

Currently, UNESCO, the United Nations Educational, Scientific, and Cultural Organization, takes the position that there is a need for a World University, but many considerations must be taken into account, and consequently there now exists no United Nations University, nor are there plans for one as such. One of the main stumbling blocks is the sheer vastness of the financial requirements of such a project. But there are also many other, deeper considerations:

> While, theoretically, the idea of an international university is not incompatible with the concept of the United Nations and UNESCO, it is one which would be exceedingly difficult to put into practice. Even if the major . . . political problems involved could be solved, others would still remain. Would it be possible, for example, to obtain agreement between the scholars of different countries on the concept of such a university? Though they may have much in common, there are unquestionably fundamental differences in educational theory and practice between the universities in various countries.

> The formulation of internationally acceptable admissions requirements would be, in itself, most difficult, and these could only be applied successfully if secondary schools throughout the world were prepared to modify their curricula and conform to comparable standards of scholastic achievement.

> It would also still remain to be seen whether, in a given country, a degree or diploma awarded would be equiva-

lent in value to those awarded by the universities of the respective countries which are naturally better able to adapt their courses to meet local professional requirements.[4]

So, as it stands now, the United Nations serves through UNESCO to try to get the existing universities throughout the world to work within their structure to promote World Education. However, many suggestions for United Nations Schools have been presented:

1. In 1946, at the first of the UNESCO general conferences, there was discussion of the future establishment of a UNESCO educational center dedicated to international cooperation and the development of a world outlook in education. The center would train graduate students for international service.

2. In 1958, the Federation of American Scientists suggested the establishment of a United Nations University. The purpose of the University, which would be on the graduate level, would be to eliminate war by making a major effort to reduce tension, to find ways to resolve conflicting ideologies, to build up international institutions, and to join together in research on world problems such as nuclear testing, food shortage, overpopulation, etc. The school would probably be located in Switzerland, since it is neutral, and the money for financing the project would come from the U.N. member-states. The faculty and students would be drawn from as many countries of the world as possible. Graduates would be qualified for foreign service.

3. An International Federation for the United Nations

4. Communication from Anita Frykholm of UNESCO, March, 1966.

has been organized by Dr. George Huthsteiner of California.

4. Mr. H. Larry Winecoff of New York University has proposed that secondary schools in the United Nations member-states be encouraged and aided in conducting mock United Nations meetings in order to learn more about world affairs and to stimulate interest in the United Nations and its workings. Such a program could be organized like the High School Council for the United Nations, which was established in New York in 1953. Each year a series of workshops are held dealing with world problems, and these culminate in a model U.N. meeting with discussion on topics ranging from disarmament to Vietnam and politico-economic self-determination.

Man's Greatest Effort at World Education

The Unesco House
2, Place de Fontenoy
Paris 7, France

The foremost effort at World Education man has ever undertaken is the United Nations Educational, Scientific, and Cultural Organization. Everyone knows something of Unesco, but to most the workings of this vast, complex organization are vague. And so we present this brief, comprehensive account by Tor Gjesdal, assistant director-general in charge of communication, Unesco Headquarters, Paris:

A 20th ANNIVERSARY must necessarily be a milestone in the life of any organization—a vantage point from which to look back on the past, assess the present, and attempt to extrapolate the future.

The United Nations Educational, Scientific, and Cultural Organization, born in 1946, has now reached such a milestone. Twenty years ago, it came into being when the 20th acceptance of its Constitution—appropriately, by Greece—was deposited in the British Foreign Office in London. It had 30 founding members; a budget, for 1947, of $7,000,000, adopted by its first General Conference; and a home in a converted Paris hotel.

Today, Unesco has 120 member-states, total financial resources amounting to some $50,000,000 a year—comprising budgetary contributions from its own members and funds from the United Nations Development Programme (UNDP)—and a headquarters that has become a Paris landmark.

But this headquarters is only the upper part of the iceberg. Of Unesco's professional staff, 1,067 are now working in the field and only 635 in Paris. At the start, Unesco had a staff of nine professionals, eight of them in headquarters. Two-thirds of all the funds at the disposal of the organization are now allocated to field work with direct impact on development.

I bring in these comparative figures to make a first point: The momentum of change over the past 20 years has been so great, that one can only assume that equally profound transformations are in store for Unesco in the future. But the thread of the principles on which the organization was founded has never snapped, and it must remain unbroken if the organization is to maintain its identity and serve its purpose.

These basic principles consisted of a heritage from the prewar Institute for Intellectual Cooperation associated with the League of Nations, and a Constitution designed to adapt this heritage to the requirements of a post-war world. The preamble to this Constitution stated, "It is in the minds of men that the defenses of peace must be constructed . . ." and the story of the past 20 years of Unesco is an unrelenting effort to erect these defenses through international action in education, science, and culture. One need not be reminded that the task is far from finished.

Historically speaking, Unesco first began to work in the domain of intellectual cooperation, although, even in its earliest years, it soon found itself meeting practical emergency situations. Devastated by war, the schools of continental Europe and Asia were crying for aid. In the form of textbooks, libraries, and teaching materials, help was given by and through Unesco. Such emergency action has continued—once might call it Unesco's "fire department" function in education—in other stricken areas of the globe. Under an agreement with the United Nations Relief and Works Agency, since 1950, Unesco has provided the technical advice and executive personnel needed to carry out the agency's educational program, which now maintains 180,000 Palestine Arab refugee children in primary schools, 74,000 in secondary schools, and 1,800 in universities.

In fact, one could very well say that the world has been in a state of educational emergency ever since Unesco was founded. All the problems that had been swept under the rug and comfortably ignored in the past soon came into glaring daylight. Education was no longer a privilege but a right, and most of the world's population was deprived of it. In its early years and with extremely modest resources, Unesco sent teams to individual countries requesting help in organizing and expanding their school systems. But then, in 1960, two significant events

215

took place that were to prove closely related: (1) the United Nations Special Fund, (now the United Nations Development Program) came into being; (2) a large number of newly independent countries, mainly African, joined the ranks of Unesco's member-states. Education was recognized as an essential cog—if not a motor—in national development. A piecemeal approach, no matter how well intentioned, was not enough.

Since 1960, regional educational conferences at a ministerial level have been organized regularly by Unesco in Asia, the Arab States, Africa, and Latin America. They have brought about a policy of long-term planning education and an awareness of its direct economic returns: Today, developing countries devote from 15 to 25 percent of their budgets to schools, and the number of school-age children actually in classrooms is rising. This is true even in Latin America, which has the world's record rate of population increase, where a 10-year Unesco "major project" in educational expansion will be completed this year. In Latin-American primary schools alone, the number of pupils has increased by 12,000,000 since 1956.

Regional conferences have been followed up by field operations. In Khartoum, Bandung, and Mexico City, regional centers are conducting research on specific problems of school construction where imported solutions cannot be used. Yet the human factor still prevails in education, and, as everyone knows, it is easier in the end to build schools than to provide the teachers to man them. Consequently, Unesco's field program in education has a heavy accent on teacher training. As part of the major project in Latin America, associated normal schools were established in Colombia, Ecuador, Honduras, and Nicaragua to influence methods throughout the area. In Asia, there is a regional center for training teacher educators in the Philippines, and in the Arab world, training colleges have been set up under UNDP in four more countries. The most crying need was in Africa, and there the impact of this aid has been the greatest: Twenty colleges in 17 countries to train secondary school teachers, with an output of 1,500 last year and a present enrollment of 7,400.

This brief summary of Unesco's field operations in education would not be complete without a mention of its new functional literacy effort, which has begun with five pilot projects in Algeria, Ecuador, Iran, Mali, and Tanzania, aided by UNDP. Briefly stated, the old shotgun approach of the mass literacy campaign (which often broke down through lack of incentive) has been replaced here by an attempt to bring literacy to people who can apply it immediately to direct economic purpose in their lives.

But this educational emergency I mentioned has required qualitative as well as quantitative action. To construct the defenses of peace in children's minds, nearly 500 schools in 54 countries have joined Unesco's Associated Schools system, created in 1953, to give pupils a clearer idea of other nations in general and the United Nations in particular. Such action has been taken at the governmental level as well, notably through Unesco's sponsorship of the International Convention and Recommendation Against Discrimination in Education. And, fittingly enough, only a few weeks before the celebration of its 20th anniversary, Unesco saw the adoption by an intergovernmental conference in Paris of a "Magna Carta" for teachers, setting forth recommendations to protect the status of the profession and to define teachers' rights and responsibilities.

217

It is certain that Unesco's operational activities in the field will expand as increased funds become available, for there is a constant and increasing demand from member-states for international assistance. However, Unesco will be playing the role for which it was originally created only if it continues to act as a conscience on human rights for the world community.

Other Proposals

In 1942, *Bertrand Russell* proposed the establishment of an International University, the purpose of which would further the development of world government and do away with the nationalism that leads to war. He proposed that there be a central university in a neutral country open to all races, religions, and political groups except those who reject the idea of a world government. The University would be administered by international authority and would function on the graduate level so as not to compete with existing colleges and universities. All students would be required to know English and one other language.

* * *

Albert Marble, while President of the Michigan Credit Union League, proposed the founding of the People's University of the New World. This plan would not require the development of a new campus, since it would combine the already existing educational facilities of institutions such as the Cooperative Schools in Scandinavia, the International Cooperative Alliance (London), the Putney Graduate School, and the Rochdale Institute. There would be no separate faculty or student divisions—it would simply be a meeting place and a coordination center with a Secretary-General whose function it would be to communicate the ideas of the university to the public. Violence would be renounced and no religious or political system would be favored.

The hopes of *Frank Sutliff Hackett*, Headmaster of Riverdale Country Schools in New York, were expressed in his *Guide for Riverdale, an American World School*. He called upon education to take the lead in bringing about world cooperation. His dreams for international education at Riverdale did not materialize, but the school did maintain a student body of international background and studied the work of the United Nations.

* * *

A plan calling for the creation of a World University was proposed by *Joe Weingarten*, late of Houston, Texas. The school would be devoted to problems of world peace, with Chairs for World Peace or Visiting Professorships for Peace in this and all universities.

* * *

Robert Beggs has called for the incorporation of a Center for the Study of World Community at Cornell University as the first chapter in an Association of Universities, Sciences, and Religions, of Ithaca, New York.

Communication with Mainland China

A. Burns Chalmers, Secretary of Education, the American Friends Committee, has proposed that American colleges and universities in the United States invite scholars and professors from mainland China to come to this country both to study and to lecture. "Human encounter and communication are of the highest importance in relation to mainland China."

International Medical School

Claude E. Forkner, M.D., of New York, has proposed the establishment of an International Medical School as part of an International University, in the belief that science is one area in which it is possible to develop international cooperation.

International Education Center

Sargent Shriver, former Director of the Peace Corps, proposed that an international education center be set up for the purpose of integrating foreign students into the American academic community. International Houses already exist, but they have been criticized because they tend to keep foreign students together rather than help them to actually enter into the American way of life. The center suggested by Mr. Shriver would bring together, for a limited amount of time—a year, a semester or a seminar of a few weeks duration—an equal number of American and foreign students. They would live and learn together, both at the center and in participation in the cultural, social, and political life of New York City. Returning volunteers from the Peace Corps could also attend. The purpose of the program would be "to teach these students to become broader and more effective citizens of the world."

International Communications Network

Now that television can be transmitted by satellite, thought must be given to the idea of global networks. Robert Sarnoff of NBC has expressed the following:

"Through satellite TV, different societies will be brought into direct and daily contact. This may mark the beginning of a vast re-education process for all of us on earth; a re-defining of old relationships and a searching for new ones. Out of this interplay, a global culture may begin to emerge, and perhaps, in time, a global language."

The Federation of the United Nations Universities
c/o The Institute for Psychological and Social Research
914 South Robertson Blvd.
Beverly Hills, California 90211

This development, guided by Dr. George Huthsteiner, is in the planning stage. There is thought of having a land center on Baja Peninsula. But the unique part of the plan is to have the headquarters on shipboard, as the only available neutral location. The equipment will be kept as light and mobile as possible, and the administrative headquarters will remain aboard ship until such time as the nations of the world can declare a number of areas neutral and free from national pressure.

On September 2, 1967, in Los Angeles, this group will hold a meeting, "A Conference for a World University."

Ogontz Plan for Mutual International Education
International House of Philadelphia
140 North 15th Street
Philadelphia, Pennsylvania 19102

As part of International Cooperation Year, Carl Stenzler, Chairman of International House of Philadelphia, has proposed that there be greater emphasis on the International Humanities as part of our existing school curricula in order to prepare our students to understand and cope with world cultures and values different from their own. Foreign students, who identify with world people, about whom we know too little, should be brought into elementary and secondary schools, not just colleges and universities, as visiting teachers. This Plan, projected with warmth and understanding as suggested by Mr. Stenzler, would broaden the perspective of both American and foreign students, greatly enrich our American educational system, and make the achievement of international understanding a reality.

World College

A World College on the former World's Fair Grounds is being planned by the Metropolitan Area Council for International Culture and Lifelong Education, Incorporated, 51 East 90th Street, New York, New York 10028. Under the leadership of Robert M. MacIver, President, and Harry H. Lerner, Executive Vice President, efforts began in 1965 to save some buildings in the Belgian Center for a World Educational Center. Lack of unity with some persons of influence led to the destruction of the Belgian Village, as of many other buildings that might have served this purpose. But there is an able group of Officers, Board of Directors, and Board of Advisors, and progress is being made toward the founding of a World College on the former World's Fair Grounds.

A United Nations University
2534 Student Activities Building
University of Michigan
Ann Arbor, Michigan 48104

In February, 1962, the Association for Commitment to

World Responsibility, ACWR, published the third draft of a proposal for a United Nations University. In the foreword, Kenneth Ewart Boulding, Professor of Economics, University of Michigan, credits this serious study to a dedicated group of students at the University of Michigan: "The world is in desperate need of a symbol of unity of knowledge which transcends all diversity of interest and belief. The truth, whatever it is, is One."

The study deals with the need, objectives, and functions of a United Nations University, the effect it would have on existing universities, and prospects and strategies. There are valuable appendices and a bibliography.

An International College
Abid Al-Marayati, Ph.D.
Department of Political Science
Arizona State University
Tempe, Arizona 85281

Dr. Abid Al-Marayati, formerly of the Center for Middle Eastern Studies at Harvard University, has proposed the establishment of an International College, the purpose of which would be "to prepare students in professional competence and, at the same time, create a greater awareness of international affairs. . . . It can also serve as a means for the training of persons in various fields urgently needed by the developing countries." Dr. Al-Marayati points out that there has been, in the past, some problem in that students studying abroad often do not wish to return to serve their own countries where help is most needed. Therefore, it would be wise to establish such a college within a developing country with a curriculum based on local as well as international problems. The college should have an internationally-oriented faculty and administration, and students should be drawn from as many areas of the world as possible.

World University Committee
Prof. C. M. Bedford, Past Chairman
1030 Idylwyld Drive
Saskatoon, Saskatchewan
Canada

Since 1964, the World University Committee of the Canadian Home and School and Parent-Teacher Federation has been promoting the concept of a World University. In a brief to the External Affairs Minister of the Canadian Government on April 29, 1965, it proposed a feasibility study as to the Canadian Government, in the name of the Canadian people, initiating and sponsoring a World University "devoted to the Arts of Peace:" the curriculum to include the humanities, the behavioral sciences, international law, and the study of peacekeeping operations. The Minister approved in principle and suggested that the Federation should continue its efforts.

The Canadian Home and School and Parent-Teacher Federation World University Committee is still active. It was instrumental in establishing a Canadian World University Committee, organized at Montreal on June 12, 1966. The idea has also been taken up by a group of young people in Saskatchewan who in 1966 established a Committee for the Establishment of the World University. These three committees are collaborating on the furtherance of the concept.

Université Internationale du Développement

An International University of Development was proposed, in 1965, by Josue' De Castro, world-renown nutritionist, presently associated with the University of Brazil. Dr. De Castro suggests that the University be established in some neutral country, perhaps Switzerland, and that it serve as a liaison between universities and other educational institutions the world over.

The plan is that the university grant two-year scholarships to graduate students interested in helping the developing countries. Each student would spend one year studying at the most highly qualified university in his particular field of interest. Then, four months would be spent at the International University studying world problems. Finally, the student would live and work for six months in a special area, so that he might better understand a country's specific problems. Here he would apply his highly specialized knowledge to help start what Jose' De Castro calls "the education of a village," thereby raising their standard of living, especially in the area of nutrition. The establishment of a village school would also help to provide a socio-cultural milieu where a child could grow, learn, and work without being separated from his native environment. In addition, these schools would be a place to educate local leaders who would then be prepared to guide their own people wisely and well.

World University
James B. Hilton, Ph.D., D.Sc.
State University of New York
College of Medicine
Brooklyn, New York 11203

A World University, with the expressive name of Abraham Lincoln University of the World, to be founded by the United States of America, was proposed in 1961 by James B. Hamilton. A booklet of thirty-nine pages was published by the Harris McLaughlin Foundation and examines the following areas of concern.

1. The value of, and need for, a World University.
2. Some prerequisites of a World University if it is to fulfill its potential.
3. Aims, composition, role, and relationship to other international organizations.
4. Problems that may be encountered and,
5. Support and implementation.

International Peace University

"An International Peace University as a Means Leading to the Elimination of War" has been proposed by Lieutenant Colonel Edward M. Strieber, USAF. His 122 page volume begins with an "Abstainer" of responsibility by the War College, Air University, and the Department of the Air Force for the views expressed. The treatment is broad in historic perspective, imaginative in approach, and realistic in design.

In essence, Lieutenant Colonel Strieber holds that war cannot unite man, only destroy him; that institutions have arisen in the past because they were needed; that the need is now imperative for an International Peace University, to do for peace what universities have been doing for the furtherance of knowledge in other areas. He believes that the most able scholars must learn to work together in a university that should be established now by the United Nations under UNESCO; that such an institution should embrace the focusing of all disciplines on peace, and that it should expand to possess offices in all schools of higher learning throughout the world. Progressively, this would develop into a multi-trillion dollar organization operated by the people, for the people of the earth, and for the progress of mankind within a peaceful world community.

Peace Institute

Sweden plans to establish an international research center in Stockholm for the study of the causes of political conflict and means of settling them. It will be directed by Mrs. Alva Myrdal, Sweden's top disarmament negotiator. She hopes to bring together well-known scientists, scholars, and diplomats so that the Institute will play a large role in furthering efforts toward disarmament, and hopes also that it may be allowed to act as a control station because of its location in a neutral country. Other members of the planning committee include: Professor Hannes Alfven of the Royal Institute of Technology; Karl Birnbaum, Director of the Swedish Institute of International Affairs; Martin Fehrm, Director-General of the Research Institute of National Defense; Professor Bror Rexed of the Government Science Advisory Council; and Professor Anders Wedberg of the University of Stockholm.

World Center

Robert Yeaton of the American Friends Service Committee has proposed the founding of a World Center dedicated to securing world peace through developing points of view which are fair to all nations, and the acceptance of these views by people all over the world. The Center will be developed in Baja California Sur, where there is an ideal climate for outdoor living. At first it will be used as a recreational center and as a means of support for the World Centers. Developed in cooperation with the Mexican government, it will contribute considerably to the Mexican economy.

The Center will attempt to bring together future world leaders from all nations to work with outstanding world thinkers. There will be four different organizations: The World Center Governance to plan necessary constitutional changes which govern the center; the World Study Center to spread world points of view through mass media; the World Market to support the Center through commercial activities; and the General Services Contingent to provide supporting services for the Market and the Center.

World Coordinating Center

In his address, *An International Approach to Higher Education: The Emergence of a World Perspective*, at Cornell University, in 1965, Morris Mitchell proposed that means of communication should be established to make a community of many centers for a World Community. He suggested open-wire phone connections; electronic service for inter-library exchange of microfilm; closed circuit TV; plane service between centers; hospitality facilities for exchange students, faculty, administration; publication of a Journal of World Community to hasten the growth of the movement, prevent duplication, and avoid repetition of error; preparation of texts, development of audiovisual material and other matter designed to replace the present provincial treatment; operation of a peace research center of world proportions with inter-center connecting service for computerized aspects of research; coordination of the now scattered and piecemeal research in all the fields of human knowledge; and perhaps publication of a daily paper at each center written from the world point of view, carrying UN and UNESCO news, but also local news placed in world perspective.

Religious Ventures with World Outreach

There are far too many such projects inspired by the many faiths to attempt a listing. World Education is, by definition, moral education. But it cannot be doctrinaire for the obvious reason that the world will never agree on doctrine. If Quakerism rested on dogma, then the name *Friends World Institute* would be a contradiction in terms. While Quakerism was Christian in origin, increasing numbers of Friends are humanist and hold a cosmic theology. Quakers do believe in the dignity, worth, and beauty, call it "divinity," of all people, and that conflicts should be resolved peaceably.

Religious advocates are often unaware of their sectarianism. When Kagawa arrived in America from Japan, and was asked why he had come, he replied, "I have come to Christianize Cooperatives and cooperatize Christianity." A nice sounding phrase, but false. For while all people are consumers, all people will never be Christians. One beauty of Consumer Cooperatives lies in the fact that persons of all faiths, and none, have worked together since 1944 without so much as a recorded fisticuff, while the history of many religions, including that of Kagawa, has been writ in blood.

An example of a sincere school of religious motivation and would-be world outreach, is The Unity School of Christianity at Lee's Summit, Missouri. In summary, "The Unity School of Christianity is a religious educational institution devoted to demonstrating that the teaching of Jesus Christ is a practical, seven-days-a-week way of life. Because of its nonsectarian emphasis on Christian teaching and healing, it is, as its name indicates, a school rather than a church, prepared through its activities to help anyone, regardless of church affiliation, to find health, peace, joy, and plenty through his day-by-day practice of Christian principles."

In contrast, being far broader, is the Unitarian Universalist Association: "One of the aspirations of the Unitarian Universalist Association is to encourage the formation of an international community of religious liberalism. This does not imply a missionary endeavor to bring converts into the "one true faith" as developed by American and Canadian liberals. What is envisioned is the creation of a voluntary world-wide fellowship of all those who have discovered and prized free religion in its various modes and expressions. There is an inter-continental dimension of our faith that needs to be reckoned with."

World Citizens
c/o Marjorie Barter
9 Jackson Place
Moonachie, New Jersey 07074
or
c/o Guy Marchand
208, Rue LeCourbe
Paris V, France

World Citizens issues an international passport, a double card, cream-yellow, folded, with the words "World Citizen" in several languages: French, English, Russian, Chinese, and Arabic. There is a spot for a passport picture, a statement of allegiance to the people of the world, a line for signature. The non-recurring cost is $1.00 and entitles the owner to representation in a world parliament of peoples (if and when held). For now, this is a psychological device. Border officials are puzzled when it is presented. But if thousands regularly carried and presented these unofficial passports, they might help nudge along the cause of world realignment from irrationally drawn national boundaries to a world community comprised of natural regional communities comprised, in turn, of countless local communities.

Friends World Institute
5722 Northern Boulevard
East Norwich, New York 11732

On behalf of the Committee on a Friends World College, Morris Mitchell proposed that, at the White House Conference on the Year of International Cooperation, a carefully prepared paper be presented on the concept of World Education. To this end, it was proposed that nominations be solicited and funds procured to bring to a conference twenty-five pioneers in World Education, who would spend several days together on this paper. It was further proposed that the White House Conference consider means of setting up, through UNESCO, an association of World Education Institutions which would contribute sufficient dues to cover the costs of office staff and the publishing of a Journal of World Education. The Journal would solicit and promote resources such as a world-minded faculty; world communication facilities (such as Telstar); documentary films; ideas on significant areas of study; shared housing and transportation; and further promote local, regional, national, and world conferences on this newly emerging concept and movement.

I

Mobile Campuses

(1) Introduction

More and more emphasis is being put on travel as a means of world education. The problems of the world have been studied in the clinical atmosphere of a stationary campus. Sometimes foreign students and exchange professors have been used and courses taught with a world outlook and a world interpretation. In conjunction with this, the idea of exchange programs developed. One student changed places with another in a foreign country, concentrated on the culture and language of that country, lived in the homes of its citizens, and attended its schools. This excellent system has two drawbacks: first, the participant gets only a contrast between his country and that of his host; second, such programs have been, numerically, limited. The program becomes, in part, a goodwill mission between the two countries, with the participants acting as personal ambassadors. Exchange programs have relevancy in the world today; they promote international understanding, though not a world outlook.

Extensive study-travel, on the other hand, tends to develop this world outlook. Students are immersed in the cultures of many countries, study their traditions, mores, folkways, social problems. Increasingly, the emphasis is on the global view, breaking from the kind of provincialism which characterizes limited exchange programs.

Within the traveling campus, course work is continued and is coordinated with actual experience. Instead of studying from a distance, the same type of study is undertaken within the physical context of the material which is being presented. The traveling campus brings new perspectives and a sense of immediacy to the material.

There are several types of mobile campuses. In some, the students move from one center to the next; in others, the students take their campus with them. Friends World Institute is an example of the first type and the University of the Seven Seas is characteristic of the second. Some study-travel programs are supplements to regular college work and others are colleges.

Whether these different schools offer conventional courses or take a radical turn from contemporary education, all emphasize world-mindedness.

II

Mobile Campuses

(2) Examples

The International School of America
50 West Gay Street
Columbus, Ohio 43215

The ISA's program is designed with the specific purpose of making our students aware of the complexity of some of the world's problems and, hopefully, of motivating them to want to prepare themselves to better deal with these problems. We are not trying to make experts of them in an eight month period, nor do we look at our program as

233

a terminal one in any sense. Most of our students return to colleges and a great many of them have become involved in special curriculums, graduate work, and other special activities, whereby they have managed to continue to develop their competence and background.[5]

Within an eight month world tour, the International School attempts to create an experience which is both intense and, at the same time, clearly meaningful to the student. First, the students live with families and become as immersed in the life of the country as is possible within the two to four weeks spent in the area. Second, the small size of the group (24 students and four faculty members) contributes to the type of program which can be developed. The school is able to deal with the students as a homogeneous entity, and this tends to improve the quality of the experiences which the school can provide.

The faculty offers basic courses in the humanities, natural and social sciences, and French. With the exception of French, each course emphasizes the country which is being visited. Outside of the normal course work, students concentrate on the major current issues relevant to the areas. The East-West struggle, under-developed countries, the impact of technology on agrarian cultures, foreign aid, religion and social customs, Indian democracy, Egyptian nationalism, the legacy of ancient civilizations, the Common Market, and international economic competition are just a few of the issues examined by the students and faculty.

Coupled with on-the-spot field trips, tours, orientation periods (including lectures and addresses by leading citizens in the different countries), and course work, the

---

5. Communication with Karl Jaeger, Executive Director, March, 1965.

students live with native, English-speaking families for the two to four week period spent in each study area. The school feels that living with families is one of the most valuable experiences of their students. Through this part of the program, the students experience a certain immediacy of involvement in each new area.

The school provides a teacher/student ratio which is rarely found on any university or even small college campus. Moreover, since the faculty members travel constantly with the students, a certain rapport between the students and faculty is developed. The teachers are responsible for teaching only one course during the full eight month period. This enables a teacher to work individually with students who may be having difficulty with the material and with those whose interest in the subject extends far beyond the classroom.

Much time is spent in specific cities in as stable a situation as can be developed. Some of the cities visited are: Tokyo, Kyoto, Taipei, Bangkok, New Delhi, Teheran, Cairo, Jordan, Istanbul, Athens, Rome, Berlin, Warsaw, Moscow, Paris, and London.

The International School of America was founded in 1958 by Karl Jaeger, now Executive Director. Originally, many of the students were those who wished to take an extra year between high school and college, but now the program is intended primarily for those who have completed a year or two of university undergraduate study.

The tuition for the eight month program is $4,450. This covers all transportation, room, board, and textbooks. It is suggested that each student have $400 for other incidental expenses. The school offers some scholarships to outstanding students where need is evident.

> The College Cruise Around the World is a new method
> of education—the coordination of travel and study. . . .
> Travel is made more valuable because it is intelligently
> directed; study more interesting because the student sees
> with his own eyes what textbooks and lectures can only
> partially help him to visualize. The benefits of acquiring
> this breadth of view at an age when he is planning his
> life are incalculable.[6]

In 1926 a pioneer experiment in World Education was
begun under the direction of Dr. Charles F. Thwing of
Western Reserve University and Dr. John Carleton Jones
of the University of Missouri, along with other educators
from well-known colleges and universities, i.e. Williams,
Yale, Dartmouth, Oberlin, and the University of Michigan.

In that year, the *S.S. Ryndam* made its first voyage as a
University Afloat. The cruise lasted one year and the ship
stopped in thirty-seven ports in twenty-eight countries
around the world. Side trips included visits to seventy different cities. The students and faculty were royally welcomed at the various ports and were accorded banquets
and addresses by the local officials.

The schedule of the cruise provided for one hundred
and eight working days at sea and one hundred and four
days on land for observation and field work. During the
time at sea, courses were conducted in accordance with
the academic standards and methods of a conventional
college, but with a special emphasis on the countries

---

6. *The College Cruise Around the World,* University Travel Association, 1928-1929, 285 Madison Avenue, New York, New York.

visited. Teaching was done by means of general lectures by the faculty of the Cruise and by faculty members and officials of foreign countries wherever visits were made to other institutions of learning. Field trips supplemented regular course work and provided actual contact with, and observation of, peoples in other cultures. Quizzes, midyear and final examinations were held exactly as in land-based colleges.

The *University Afloat* survived two years and then ran into difficulties, the nature of which has not been easy to determine.

Chapman College
Seven Seas Division
333 N. Glassell Street
Orange, California 92666

> It is the belief of the founders and developers of the University that our rapidly expanding private and governmental agencies exist for the preservation and development of the individual's dignity, responsibility, and earned freedoms.

> The University of the Seven Seas is a challenging experience in international living and study using the world as its laboratory. It offers on the spot study for intercultural concern and understanding of the problems of man in his search for truth and meaning in human experience.[7]

The Floating Campus on the "M.S. Seven Seas," a division of Chapman College, was formerly the University of the Seven Seas and, most likely, an outgrowth of that

---

7. *University of the Seven Seas*, Walker-Smith Co., March, 1964, p. 13.

earlier experiment aboard the S.S. *Ryndam*. The Floating Campus was organized in 1963 and has enjoyed far greater success. Although the earlier experiment on the *Ryndam* failed, the idea did not become obsolete. A similar experiment was undertaken by Donald D. Davis, G. Walter Dow, E. Woody Roberts, George D. Smith, and several others with the same philosophy of education. They shared the common idea that education means more to the student when it is coupled with actual experience, ". . . that behavior is the only true index of intelligence, and that the academic program must be related to all aspects of individual development . . . that man's intelligence increases as he develops new tools . . . that the student in such a program has an added stimulus to learn and relate his learning to his behavior."

This philosophy became a reality in the form of the University of the Seven Seas, now the Seven Seas Division of Chapman College. Using a former passenger ship, the "M.S. Seven Seas," which was specially remodeled to serve as a mobile classroom, the founders began to realize their dream of an international experience-related education. The academic year was divided into two semesters and two voyages, each approximately 108 days in length. In 1964-1965, the itinerary began in New York and ended in San Diego with the emphasis of the voyage on the Mediterranean and Southeast Asia. Among the ports visited were: Lisbon, Barcelona, Naples, Rome, Athens, Beirut, Alexandria, Port Said, Suez, Bombay, Colombo, Singapore, Bangkok, Saigon, Hong Kong, Inchon, Yokohama, Honolulu, and San Diego. The following voyage began in San Diego and moved around the world westward to New York, emphasizing study of Southeast Asia, Africa, and Latin America.

Classes are held on board ship every weekday. Students and faculty go on relevant field trips in ports of call. Each member of the cruise is expected to participate in all school activities. While in port, each student works on an assigned project related to his course of work. He also gathers information within his major area of interest, whether or not a special field trip has been scheduled. Interviews, conferences, and lectures with leading citizens form an important part of the program when the ship is docked. Research papers are required of the student with emphasis on relating specific information with personal experience. This promotes an in-depth attitude toward learning.

The philosophy of curriculum development in the Seven Seas Division is: "that those courses will be offered primarily which can be taught better aboard ship or can be otherwise enhanced by the itinerary. In addition to courses which fall in this category, a modicum of general education courses is offered in order to make it possible for the student to continue his progress toward a Baccalaureate or Master's degree." Typical courses are: Anthropology, Area Studies (required of all students), Art, Economics, Education, English, Foreign Languages, Geography, History, Political Science, Sociology, Speech, and Drama. Costs: Tuition, field trip expenses, and visa fees, $805. Room fees range from $1690 to $2490. Total costs per semester range from $2500 to $3300.

Student Travel

With increased mobility, students are on the move as never before and the world over. There is a surge of such motion. The motives vary from sheer restlessness to serious study. Not all of it will help build a world community; some will hurt. Some such travelers are poor ambassadors, disregarding the impressions they make, carrying with them blinding prejudices. Even with the high-minded of these groups, too much of the motivation rests on the assumption that familiarity leading to friendships will ease tensions. That assumption over-personalizes the forces that now so dangerously divide mankind. The most helpful travel will have as its object recognizing the problems that cause conflict, defining them, and seeking everywhere appropriate remedies.

Too frequently, political prejudices impede such travel, and many nations, including the U.S., impose severe legal restrictions, such as withdrawing passports as a penalty for visiting "enemy" nations. The assertion of the inalienable right to travel, at one's own risk, must be pressed. For we desperately need such communication if we are to become, while there is time, a world community.

The *Saturday Review* for February 28, 1967, carried an excellent article *Where and How of Student Travel*. This article describes many organizations such as the *Institute of International Education, Council on Student Travel, U.S. National Student Association, American Youth Hostels, The Experiment in International Living*, and others.

Stationary Campus Schools

Introduction

Most schools that are moving toward World Education operate from an established center, a campus. Students are gathered from many lands and, after completing the program, are expected to return to their homes. The travel costs are often high for the limited, round-trip fare. And after the students become enamored of newly experienced conveniences and luxuries they do not want to return to more primitive conditions. There are variations in stationary campus plans, as with Scandinavian Seminars, where students from America go individually to different folkschools.

III

Stationary Campus Schools

(2) Examples

Callison College
University of the Pacific
Stockton, California 95204

"The Callison Concept . . . Creative ferment is characteristic of higher education in America today. The knowledge explosion, our rapidly changing world, and the recent student unrest have all influenced American educators to re-examine current practices. Those responsible for planning the Callison College Program believe the current ferment will eventually lead to positive and healthy innovations in the curricula of American colleges. Though they do not claim final answers, Callison's administrators are bold enough to try to answer the questions raised by the ferment in three ways: 1. Reverse the current trend to anonymous education by creating a personalized living-learning community serving a maximum of 320 students. Since 80 students will be abroad during any given year, the student body residing in Stockton will number about 240, with a faculty of 18 or 20 persons. 2. Depart from outmoded but prevalent tradition by giving the student as thorough an understanding of the non-Western world and the problems of emerging nations as of his own Western heritage. 3. Give more than lip service to the obvious truth that the development of man's capacity to make enlightened value judgments, after a critical examination of evidence, is far more important than the mere accumulation of facts.

"A Living-Learning Community . . . Each Callison class will be comprised of about 80 students. Students will live in newly constructed buildings on the University of the Pacific campus. They will share meals with the Callison faculty in a spacious new dining room and will attend lectures, seminars, and tutorial sessions in the new Academic Facilities Building which Callison will share with Pacific's two other cluster colleges. The entire community will gather from time to time in the Callison Lounge for cultural events and for a monthly lecture series. These lectures will present world leaders in politics, art, literature, and social change.

"The Year Abroad . . . Because those planning the Callison program consider it impossible for an American student to acquire the capacity to empathize with, and understand, peoples of the non-Western cultures through course work, no matter how creatively taught, the college will require each sophomore class to spend the year in residence in a non-Western country as a group. The Charter Class will spend its year in an emerging nation. Though this experience will be under the supervision of the Callison faculty, there will be several scholars from indigenous universities on the teaching staff of the overseas campus. The cost of the year abroad, including transportation, probably will be near the normal costs for a year's residence at the University of the Pacific. The trip abroad, which will be by air, will be arranged with visits to several Asian nations. The return trip will be by way of Europe. This will constitute an around-the-world experience.

"The Callison Student . . . To be accepted in Callison College, a student must present evidence of maturity and academic achievement, a capacity for creativity, and a motivation for service. Because of the responsibility which the college will assume in taking a student into another culture for a year's residence—where he will represent not only his college but his country—Callison will limit enrollment to students willing to discipline themselves for the purposes of a creative college community. The opening date for Callison College is September 16, 1967. About 80 students will be accepted for Callison's Charter Class."[8]

Blake College
342 East 10th Street
Eugene, Oregon 97401

This is a new venture which advocates a world point of view. It's philosophy is based on William Blake's attitude toward education, but draws from other sources, including Whitehead, Bergson, Rodgers, and the Gestaltists. The school seems to have also been influenced by Summerhill ideas. It was founded in 1962 in Mexico but has recently moved to Oregon.

---

8. 1966 Bulletin-Callison College, University of the Pacific, Stockton, California.

Institute for Research on International Behavior
San Francisco State College
San Francisco, California 94132

The Institute for Research on International Behavior was established in 1958 by Professor Charles A. McClelland in connection with a research project under a grant from the Carnegie Corporation. The Institute conducts research and training on topics related to the psycho-political aspects of international relations. Institute projects are primarily concerned with decision-making, communication, and perception studies. These areas are analyzed, particularly as they apply to the management of international conflict and the development of conditions conducive to the achievement of international arms control.

Plans are now being made to broaden the activities of the Institute into a Center for Advancement of Studies in World Integration and Development. A number of unique training projects will be aimed at collaborative studies to be undertaken by teachers and graduate students from around the Pacific Basin in conjunction with specially selected American undergraduates.

Foreign Policy Association
345 East 46th Street
New York, New York 10017

The Foreign Policy Association stimulates interest in international relations and assists in the development of a greater understanding of the prerequisites of effective government by encouraging "informed, responsible, and articulate discussion of foreign policy issues." The Asso-

244

ciation serves to accomplish these goals through its "Great Decisions" Programs, School Services Department, and World Affairs Book Center.

*World Confederation of Organizations of the
    Teaching Profession*
1330 Massachusetts Avenue N.W.
Washington, D.C. 20005

The World Confederation of Organizations of the Teaching Profession promotes international understanding and goodwill through education. The Confederation has national, associate, and international members representing four million teachers in 91 countries. WCOTP plans conferences and seminars for educators in various parts of the world to study the special problems of education in an age of rapid change. Its special consultative and associate relationship with UNESCO serves to make the Confederation informed participants in matters related to international education.

The International Association of Universities
6, rue Franklin
Paris 16, France

The International Association of Universities was founded in 1950 and now has about 500 members-universities in every part of the world. This Association is a Twentieth Century recognition that universities are becoming "key institutions of civilization." Supported principally by annual dues which are determined by the size of the school, $150 to $450, the Association also receives grants for special purposes such as research. From the beginning, there has been close cooperation with UNESCO. The third edition of the International Handbook of Universities was published in September, 1965.

International Society for the Establishment of a
World University
The Hague
The Netherlands

Beginning in Zurich, in 1953, with a meeting of persons from eleven nations, the International Society for the Establishment of a World University spent seven years in planning. In 1960, an experimental summer session was held in Strasbourg which was based on the consideration of human problems rather than on subjects. The following summer, the school was moved to The Hague and became a year-long program.

The Experiment in International Living's School
for International Training
P.O. Box 676
Brattleboro, Vermont 05301

Since 1932, The Experiment in International Living has been conducting a variety of highly successful programs for international educational exchange. Particularly within the past few years, as its programs have diversified, the Experiment has felt an increasing need for more adequate orientation and training facilities. As a consequence, in 1962, it acquired an estate of fifty acres overlooking the Connecticut River Valley near Brattleboro, Vermont, which, with one hundred additional acres, has since been developed to comprise classrooms and residence halls;

laboratory, library, dining and recreational facilities.

Essentially, the School prepares people to live and work effectively in a foreign culture. Because of its nature and the variety of training programs it offers, the size of the student body is constantly in flux. There are, however, facilities at the School for two hundred and fifty persons on long-term programs. The School is directed by Otis Wickenhaeuser.

The Upland Institute of the Crozer Foundation
Upland Avenue
Chester, Pennsylvania 19013

The program of the Institute helps students to develop:

1. A recognition of social change as a necessary process in building social institutions and values to cope with the problems of a complex, urban, and technological society.
2. A conviction that man has the capacity and resources to devise constructive patterns that can aid in resolving the pressing problems of contemporary society.
3. A conviction that the greatest possibility for creative social change lies in the development of democratic and nonviolent institutions and values.
4. An increased commitment to become involved in working for social change in some constructive, creative manner.[9]

In attempting to meet the challenge of world conflict and crisis, Upland Institute is accepting about fifteen students for a one-year program with the hope of training these men and women in a non-violent approach to lead-

9. *Upland Institute:* A Program for Leadership in Social Change Bulletin, 1967.

ership in the areas of social welfare, government, peace, and civil rights work. The Institute is looking for people preferably, but not necessarily, with experience in social conflict areas who hold B.A. degrees.

The curriculum evolved through experimental seminars held by the New York Friends Group over a two-year period in four major cities. A permanent program began in September, 1965, with the assistance of the Crozer Foundation, using the campus and facilities of the Crozer Theological Seminary in Chester, Pennsylvania. The Institute is now under the direction of a Council of Fellows, experienced in the ways of social change and academic achievement, who consult with the faculty to determine policies and standards. They call upon visiting lecturers to broaden their scope.

The program is conducted through seminars, individual projects, and reading programs. A student spends approximately three days a week off campus in field work with various social agencies and action groups. The hope is that, through actual involvement and participation, the student will acquire skills and abilities as well as develop a deeper feeling for the problems with which the Institute hopes to work.

The Institute has taken preliminary steps toward accreditation. At present, a student is granted a Certificate of Accomplishment upon completion of the full program of study and field work. Fees per academic year are: Room, board, and tuition $1200. Additional incidental expenses: books, laundry, etc., approximately $500. The Institute states that: "No qualified student should hesitate to apply because of financial problems. The Institute will make every attempt to provide necessary financial assistance to qualified students."

> The aim of the teaching is to free the students from narrowly national or vocational outlooks, widen their horizons, and help them both to think for themselves and to devote themselves actively to the solution of current problems.[10]

Since 1921, this college has tried to follow the goal set by its founder Dr. Peter Manniche—to reduce international tension. Based on the Scandinavian Folk High School, International People's College creates a friendly atmosphere, conducive to learning, and strives to supply an international student body with material on which to form a world approach to the solution of social problems. Instruction is given by means of lectures, tutorials, and discussion groups. The ratio of faculty to students is high, and personal, intimate teaching is therefore possible.

The curriculum is divided into three main groups: social and economic studies, the humanities, and language. Some of the courses offered are: Religion and Churches; Western Philosophy; Danish, German, and English literature; Art, Music, and Drama; Social Psychology; the Co-operative Movement; Danish History; and Languages. Various activities are also offered such as guest lecturers, craft courses, folk dancing, and excursions. No degrees are conferred, but upon completion of extensive study and research in a specific field of study, a diploma may be awarded. The fees are 1500 Danish Kr. per term, approximately $225.

---

10. The International People's College Prospectus, 1965-1966.

In order to extend the international connections of the college, the Danish Ministry of Education is considering a scheme of scholarship exchange. Under this plan, foreign students of the college will be supported by grants if the institution of their native country is willing to offer similar facilities to a Danish member of the college. International People's College will therefore be pleased to hear from similar educational establishments outside Denmark interested in extending their international service by exchanges of this kind. It is preferable that these exchanges should take place on a terminal basis.

International University of Social Studies "Pro Deo"
Rome, Italy

Founded in 1944 by the Most Reverend Father Felix A. Morlion, O.P., now President and Rector, Pro Deo University is an inter-religious, international university. Father Morlion states as their aim: ". . . that men of study and men of action from different nations and those of different social and religious backgrounds, who recognize in God the Supreme Source of authority in public and private life, should join in a common work to establish unity among all those who inhabit the earth."

Pro Deo students represent the faiths of Christianity, Judaism, Islam, Hinduism, and Buddhism. The University's pattern of teaching is designed to train world leaders in subjects important to "freedom's survival throughout the world": democratic governmental practices, modern diplomacy, international trade, industrial management, labor and intergroup relations, and mass communications media.

For some years, Pro Deo has been developing overseas extension programs in North and Latin America. Similar centers in Asian and African countries are now being planned.

An editorial by Norman Cousins, *Saturday Review*, April 8, 1967, reports a special study getting under way at Pro Deo relating to language. We quote a segment of this thought-provoking editorial.

... The role of language in contributing to men's problems and their prospects is the subject of an imaginative and valuable study now getting under way at Pro Deo University in Rome, which is winning recognition in world university circles for putting advanced scholarship to work for the concept of a world community.

... One aspect of the Pro Deo study, as might be expected, has to do with the art of conveying precise meaning from one language to another . . . The Pro Deo study, however, will not be confined to problems of precise translation. The major emphasis has to do with something even more fundamental: the dangerous misconceptions and prejudices that take root in language and that undermine human values.

... The purpose of Pro Deo University in undertaking this study is not just to demonstrate that most cultures tend to be self-serving in their language. The purpose is to give educational substance to the belief that it will take all the adroitness and sensitivity of which the human species is capable if it is to be sustained. Earth-dwellers now have the choice of making their world into a neighborhood or a crematorium. Language is one of the factors in that option.

Scandinavian Seminar
62 West 58th Street
New York, New York 10019

> We believe that an individual deepens and enriches his
> concepts of life in the struggle to become one with a
> new people. The value of your year with the Seminar
> will depend upon your own response to it. You will be
> separated from familiar faces, and you may often feel
> inadequate in making yourself understood and in under-
> standing others. Your beliefs may come into conflict with
> those held by others. You may be forced to search more
> than ever before for strength, tenacity of purpose, and
> tolerance and in doing so, you will gain fresh insights
> into yourself.[11]

The Scandinavian Seminar provides nine months to live
and study in Scandinavia as part of the Folkehojskole
Program. The program involves fifty to one hundred students in a school whose aim is the development of the
whole person, not just the vocational or academic. No
language prerequisite is required. Upon acceptance, however, the student begins an intensive language course and
before entering the folkehojskole, spends three to four
weeks with a Scandinavian family. To many, this is one
of the most unforgettable aspects of the entire school year.
The Seminar's program runs from August to the following
May and operates in Denmark, Sweden, Finland, and
Norway. No more than three foreign students are introduced into any one folkehojskole.

Courses in the traditional American sense do not exist.
The student lives and studies at the folkehojskhole, where
he learns about Scandinavia through lectures, discussions,

---

11. Scandinavian Seminar Brochure.

seminars, tours, and independent study, as well as through daily contact with the Scandinavian world around him. The curriculum emphasizes history, literature, the Scandinavian language, and the social sciences. Opportunities also exist to pursue specialized interests in the "folk arts." During the year, the students involved in the Seminar program are brought together for intensive group work at orientation courses and to trade experiences and review activities.

While credit for the year of the Seminar cannot be guaranteed, there are some eighty colleges and universities that will grant credit for this program. Before completing the term, each student is responsible for a paper in a field of interest to him and related to his Scandinavian experiences. Evaluation of the student is made by the Scandinavian and American staffs on the basis of a report from the academic director, the folkehojskole, the language director, interviews with the student, and from his project paper.

The Seminar has been in existence since 1949, and is financed by student fees and by individual and group contributions. In the hope of enabling people from all economic backgrounds to attend, there is a limited scholarship loan service. The Seminar fee is $1800, plus $150 for travel in Scandinavia and $160 minimum for return transportation. The program is directed by Dr. Adolph Anderson and Dr. Halfdan Gregersen.

New Experimental College
Slotsherrensvej 21
Vanlose, Copenhagen, Denmark

New Experimental College, established in 1962 by Aage R. Nielson, its present Director, is designed to bring together teachers and students from all over the world. Its purpose is to investigate the whole process of learning in the context of a new learning situation. Participants are given the opportunity to study, do research, and work together with the vision of developing a world university.

The curriculum is determined by students and faculty on the basis of interest and has concentrated on the fields of education, language, psychology, philosophy, sociology, and Scandinavian Area Studies.

Since 1962, over 100 persons have participated in the program. The cost for a six-month term is approximately $875, plus transportation.

Royalton College
School of Foreign Affairs
South Royalton, Vermont 05068

Dr. Anthony N. Doria, Director, is energetically establishing this School with a one-world perspective, and property has been acquired for centers in West Africa and Italy. Since its inception in 1964, leading nationals of other countries have been an integral part of the campus in Vermont, exemplifying Dr. Doria's philosophy that only through this direct relationship will the student come to understand his vital role in the world community.

The School of Foreign Affairs provides a center for discussions, instruction, and learning within the context of International Relations: World Politics, International Law, and World Order. Studies are divided into two-year programs. The Junior College offers a broad, basic educational program stressing literature and the liberal arts. The Senior College offers a choice of one of three programs: International Business and Economics; International Politics; and Letters. However, the student is not confined to the formal disciplines but rather encouraged to take part in college and community affairs, as part of his education in the democratic process of American society and of the world.

Tuition for the school year is $2550. Royalton College has taken preliminary steps toward accreditation as a degree-granting institution.

International Studies and World Affairs
State University of New York
Planting Fields
Oyster Bay, New York 11771

The Division of International Studies and World Affairs at Planting Fields is being developed to provide a coordinating function with the United Nations, governments and institutions of other nations, and with other forces in American culture with concerns abroad.

The new Executive Dean, Dr. Glenn Olds, and his staff are responsible for developing international dimensions of the entire University system. These functions include:

1. Encouraging international curricular and co-curricular development.
2. Coordinating study abroad.
3. Coordinating overseas services and contracts.
4. Developing international faculty and student exchange.
5. Developing international library, information, and learning resource services.
6. Establishing the international center, servicing the entire system through conferences, workshops, institutes, research, extension, and experimentation.[12]

---

12. *International Studies and World Affairs*, Bulletin, 1967.

Three regional Centers are proposed in Western Europe, the Middle East, and Latin America. Other Centers are planned in Eastern Europe, Africa, Southeast Asia, and the Far East. The possibility of a campus afloat in collaboration with the Maritime College is being explored. There are also plans for the development of an Institute for Developing Nations and an Institute on the University's Role in the Foundations of Peace.

"With such a foundation in facility, staff, and program the University may confidently claim its rightful mission as *universal innovator*—recreating a distinctly human culture and a global citizen, as well as helping to conserve the hard-won human gains that have brought us to the atomic cloud—veiled symbol in sight and sense—of a more ancient symbol—the flowering tree of knowledge—in man's first tempting garden."[13]

Stanford University
Palo Alto, California 94304

Stanford University has completed the opening of its fifth European campus where about half of Stanford's 5,500 students will have the opportunity to study abroad sometime during their college career. In each six-month period, 400 students are divided among the five Centers: Grantham, Lincolnshire, England; Stuttgart, Germany; Tours, France; Florence, Italy; and Semmering, Austria. Continuing their regular college liberal arts program, with emphasis on the studies related to the countries visited, the students spend four days a week at lectures and have the rest of the week to study on their own and travel.

---

13. *Innovation in International Education*, Glenn Olds, Executive Dean, 1966.

The cost is the same as at Palo Alto, plus $40 for a field trip each quarter and expenses for return transportation. Information from *New York Times,* April, 1966.

Institute of International Relations
Prof. C. H. François Hsieh
Université Nationale du Rwanda
B.P. 200
Butare, Rwanda, Central Africa

Professor C. H. François Hsieh, in 1964, announced the establishment of an Institute of International Relations. Principal activities of the Institute include courses, conferences and research seminars in foreign policy, public international law, and contemporary international economics. Students are prepared to serve in the fields of diplomacy, journalism, international commerce, and teaching.

Institut Européen
Des Hautes Études Internationales
Palais de Marbre
9, Avenue de Fabron
Nice, France

The Institut Européen is a graduate program operating through the University College of Aoste and the European Institute of Nice. Students attend from many nations; knowledge of French is essential. Attention is given to the problems of European unity, but also to the relation of France to various nations including the United States. The program is problem-oriented and relates especially to the less developed areas of the world and to the problems of world organization. Tuition for the session in Aoste—July to September, $750; in Nice—October to June, $2,000.

Coady International Institute
St. Francis Xavier University
Antigonish
Nova Scotia, Canada

The Coady International Institute offers courses in Social Leadership designed to be of particular value to those interested in community development work and allied fields, and to students abroad who desire to apply "the Antigonish Way" to the economic and social conditions of their own countries. The Antigonish Movement is a process of adult education through economic cooperation. Besides studying the history, principles, and philosophy of the Antigonish Movement, case histories are studied which exemplify the Movement's effectiveness in developing the social and economic potential of communities all over the world, especially in the developing areas of Latin America, Africa, India, Pakistan, Korea, and Malaya.

The complete course extends over eight months, a part of which is spent in field work supplemented by discussions with leaders experienced in the practical aspects of cooperative marketing, merchandising, wholesaling, credit union operations, and educational organization and techniques. There also are seminars led by experts in the fields of agriculture, welfare, labor, and community development.

The possibilities for the application of this program to the underdeveloped countries are unlimited. It is a pro-

258

gram of self help and mutual help. It takes the people
where they are, even the illiterate, and leads them to the
highest possible level of performance . . . Inexpensive
and easily applicable to large numbers of people over
wide areas—big enough philosophically and scientifically
to appeal to the most fastidious—suited to democracy in
this scientific and technological age—it is a program of
adult education that begins with the economic and fans
out into every phase of human activity and will give life to
all nations and all peoples, not just the favored few.[14]

Institute for the Study of Nonviolence
P.O. Box 5535
Carmel, California 93921

The Institute for the Study of Nonviolence, which takes
a spiritual approach to the solution of world problems,
came into being "because of the need of our time; and to
understand the nature, principles, and assumptions of
nonviolence: its practical, psychological, personal, social,
political, institutional, and economic applications."[15]
The Institute was organized by folksinger Joan Baez.
Its President and leader of discussion is Ira Sandperl. The
program consists of informal but disciplined seminars and
study for four days a week, with one entire day spent in
silence—reading or writing if desired. Sessions last for six
weeks, with special weekend seminars, and are directed
toward the development of a nonviolent approach to
world peace.

---

14. The late Msgr. M. J. MacKinnon, former Director, after working on
a project in India.

15. *Institute for the Study of Nonviolence*, Bulletin. 1966.

259

World Peace Through Law Center
75, Rue de Lyon
1203 Geneva, Switzerland

The World Peace Through Law Center, through a strong commitment by the legal profession, has organized its worldwide resources in the search for peace through the Rule of Law. Lawyers, jurists, and legal scholars from 125 countries are involved in this movement, which has substantially progressed, within a few years time, toward the development of international law as an essential factor for world peace. More than 3,200 interested persons from all parts of the world attended the Washington World Conference in 1965. The next World Conference on World Peace Through Law will be held in Geneva in July, 1967.

The Temple of Understanding
1826 R Street, N.W.
Washington, D.C.

The Temple of Understanding began in the home of Judith Hollister of Greenwich, Connecticut, and, with the help of the late Eleanor Roosevelt and many others from all parts of the world, grows daily toward reality. This project is dedicated to the construction of a building in the Washington, D.C. area to be a center of scholarship where persons of all religions—Buddhist, Judaic, Christian, Islamic, Hindu, and Confucian—may work and study together in order to achieve a deep understanding of one another's faith. From this center, all forms of communication will be used to convey this message of understanding to mankind the world over.

Council for the Study of Mankind
P.O. Box 895
Santa Monica, California 90406

The United States Committee, Council for the Study of Mankind was founded in 1952. Gerhard Hirschfeld is the Executive Director. Its members are studying the ways in which the major issues of our time may be related to the idea of mankind as a whole and are creating a new philosophy of education based on mankind. The Council is particularly interested in creating better understanding among high school students of the growing trend toward global interdependence among nations and people. Some of the books which have been published by the Council include: *Economics and the Idea of Mankind, Education and the Idea of Mankind, Law and the Idea of Mankind, Mental Health and the Idea of Mankind, Technology and the Idea of Mankind,* and *The Idea of Mankind in World History.* Conferences are being planned to discuss similar works on other subjects, such as art, biology and genetics, the humanities, philosophy, politics, religion, atomic energy, beauty, morality, space, and values.

The Council is also interested in the participation of those persons outside the academic community—professionals and businessmen—who can act as channels of communication between the academic world and the layman.

World Fellowship Center
Conway, New Hampshire

World Fellowship is people working for world friendship and a peaceful existence for all mankind. At this Center, persons of all races, nationalities, religions, and political persuasions meet to discuss their experiences and their social concerns.

In keeping the channels of communication open to everyone, Fellowship participants experience an understanding of the true meaning of brotherhood by working together toward peaceful solutions of the world's problems. World Fellowship is directed by Dr. Willard Uphaus and Ola Uphaus. A stay at this Center in the White Mountains costs between $6 and $9 a day, which includes board and room and attendance at seminars directed by leading authorities on the various subjects concerning mankind and his search for peace.

The Peace Corps Movement

Peace Corps
Washington 25, D.C.

The Peace Corps concept, born at San Francisco's Cow Palace in 1961, is a striking example of burgeoning World Education. At first under Director Sargent Shriver and now Jack Vaughn, in five years the number of American volunteers has grown to more than 10,000 serving in fifty countries. This organization has enjoyed the support of both parties.

The Peace Corps Act, passed by Congress September 22, 1961, gave as the purpose:

"To promote world peace and friendship by making available to interested countries Americans willing to serve overseas who would:

1) Help people of these countries meet their needs for trained manpower;

2) Help promote a better understanding of the American people on the part of peoples served; and

3) Promote a better understanding of other peoples on the part of the American people."

Peace Corps Volunteers go only where they are requested and work for the host government or for a private agency whenever possible. They are not advisors but doers. They receive no diplomatic privileges. They must learn to speak the language of the host country and to refrain from political or religious proselytizing. Volunteers must be over 18, but a college degree is not required. High medical, psychological, and character standards have been established, so selection is careful. Volunteers serve for two years. They are paid $75 a month (plus travel and living allowance) but do not receive this amount until the end of the two-year period.

Among the countries in which we have Peace Corps Volunteers are: Afghanistan, Bolivia, Brazil, Ceylon, Chile, Columbia, Dominican Republic, Ecuador, El Salvador, Ethiopia, Ghana, Honduras, India, Iran, Ivory Coast, Liberia, Malaya, Nepal, Nigeria, North Borneo, Sarawak, Pakistan, Peru, Phillipines, Sierra Leone, Somali Republic, Tanzania, Thailand, Togo, Tunisia, Venezuela, and the West Indies. None of these countries have received as many volunteers as they would like to have.

When the Peace Corps began, it was concerned almost exclusively with education and community development. While these are still of great importance, Peace Corps projects have now become far more diversified and include such projects as public health, geology, home economics, construction and architecture, livestock breeding, mechanics, music, painting, printing, law, engineering, forestry, and educational television.

The Peace Corps idea was conceived in the "cold war" climate, and the motives were doubtless mixed. There was, from the beginning, a lack of willingness to be deeply self-critical of America and of the long-range effects the Peace Corps might have of a negative, as well as positive nature. The "Free World" was confident of its values and its system; this was to be a cultural blood transfusion from the strong to the weak. Of course, it is unlawful to give an actual blood transfusion without first examining the donor's bloodstream for infection. If the donor were erupting with sores over his entire body, then such a test would be the more imperative.

Yet the American scene erupts in the side of every city with a disgraceful slum; not local infections but a bloodstream infection. Then there were other signs of sickness that needed to be guarded against: racism and high crime rate and rural poverty, including 2,000,000 migrant workers; the condition of most of the American Indians and several racial groups, including millions of the 20,000,000 Negroes; perhaps 60,000,000 poor in contrast with about 100,000 millionaires. But such was the unself-critical mood of the times.

Nonetheless, the Peace Corps has done much good. It is a constructive, internationalizing force as beneficial to the donors as to the recipients.

The Peace Corps idea has so caught hold that now, internally, America has its own Domestic Peace Corps, VISTA. And there are a number of privately-sponsored, comparable movements, such as the Quaker VISA. (Actually the work of the American Friends Service Committee, which began during the First World War, was a prelude to the Peace Corps concept, particularly in its domestic and overseas work-camp aspects. Likewise, International Voluntary Services preceded the Peace Corps and served in part as a pattern.)

Still another hopeful sign is emerging. First Wilmington College, Wilmington, Ohio (a Quaker school), has made arrangements for eighty students to enroll for two years in the Peace Corps as an integral part of their college program. Besides the rich experience, service, and financial assistance, students will receive a considerable measure of academic credit. Other colleges are following this pattern. This is a break in the wall of academic formalism.

The world was ready for the Peace Corps idea, which has proved contagious and has spread. About forty other countries have now developed comparable service organizations, such as the Overseas Volunteer Service in Great Britain, the Jongeren Vrijwilligers Programma in the Netherlands, the Zambia Youth service, the French International Volunteer Service, the Cuerpo de Salvadorenos para El Progresso Social of El Salvador, and the German Deutscher Entwicklungsdient. Practically all of them are modeled on the idea of the Peace Corps.

And this proliferation will tend to counterbalance the one-sidedness of a Peace Corps as promoted by any one nation.

Does one not feel in this vast movement, only five years old, the dawning of a day when misnamed compulsory military "service" (to humanity, a disservice) will gradually fade into the background in favor of this new form of voluntary humanitarian service? Indeed, it is thinkable that the pioneer role of conscientious objectors, who suffered the indignity of "alternate service" under near slave conditions in Civilian Public Service camps (sometimes called Chastity, Poverty, and Slavery camps), was another related prelude to the Peace Corps. And now that so many more thousands are objecting to participation in war and are accepting, though not voluntarily, alternate service, the time is clearly ripe for replacing war as a means of settling conflicts with all sorts of World Education ventures. Important among these, clearly, is the Peace Corps concept.

The next great step in the Peace Corps movement should be federation under UNESCO. That will be a great step indeed toward functional World Education.

VISA-American Friends Service Committee
160 North Fifteenth Street
Philadelphia, Pennsylvania 19102

VISA, Voluntary International Service Assignments, is the Quaker Peace Corps. Young people in the 20-30 age group, identifiably motivated by a deep concern for their fellow man, are sent on two-year service assignments in the United States or abroad. Besides being of service, participants share an experience of working and learning in a culture different from their own—an experience which will have an enduring, positive effect on their whole lives. Through these acts of mutual help, sharing a simple and often frustrating way of life, emerge the basic tenets of brotherhood for all men.

Volunteers begin with a month of orientation at Pendle Hill, a Quaker Study Center in Wallingford, Pennsylvania. Living as a neighbor, they may work as community development assistants in rural areas, teaching literacy, demonstrating how to cook more nutritiously, or assisting wherever is the greatest need. The program, with volunteers and a field director, operates in Tanganyika, Guatemala, India, Germany, and the United States and is a branch of the American Friends Service Committee. Volunteers pay for their own clothing and travel documents. The Service Committee provides maintenance, plus $12.50 a month spending money and $75 a year vacation allowance. However, volunteers are asked to contribute whatever they can to their own maintenance.

International Film Seminars, Inc.
1125 Amsterdam Avenue
New York, New York 10025

The purpose of International Film Seminars is to promote the production and study of documentary films. The organization took root in the film making of Robert Flaherty, whose four major achievements: *Nanook of the North, Moana, Men of Aran,* and *Louisiana Story,* represent, through non-preconception, a universal viewpoint. Robert Flaherty's widow, Frances Flaherty, has been the chief inspiration and interpreter of the art of non-preconception, and a Film Study Center at the Flaherty Farm in Dummerston, Vermont, is being planned.

The annual Robert Flaherty Film Seminar brings together film makers from many different lands whose works are shown and discussed. The next seminar will be held in September, 1967.

Center for Cultural and Technical Interchange
    Between East and West
(The East-West Center)
Honolulu, Hawaii 96822

The East-West Center is a project of the United States

government in cooperation with the University of Hawaii. It was established by the United States Congress in 1960 as an educational institution to strengthen understanding among the people of the Pacific, Asia, and the United States. Students come from Australia, Burma, Cambodia, Ceylon, Fiji, Hong Kong, India, Indonesia, Japan, Korea, Laos, Malaya, Nepal, New Zealand, North Borneo, Okinawa, Pakistan, Philippines, Republic of China, Samoa, Sarawak, Singapore, Tahiti, Thailand, the Trust Territory, Vietnam, and the United States.

There are three principal divisions of the Center: the Institute for Student Interchange, which administers student scholarships; the Institute of Advanced Projects, which administers senior scholars' research programs; and the Institute for Technical Interchange, which administers technical training programs. Scholars come to the Center for a year's residence and for attendance at four- to six-week seminars and week-long conferences. A broader approach to world understanding through education is developed and shared through research and study.

Universities and the Quest for Peace
General Secretariat
1400 Hermann Drive
Houston, Texas 77004

Universities and the Quest for Peace was established on a worldwide basis at UNESCO House in Paris in 1963 by Dr. Raga S. Elim of Egypt and a committee of university educators with representatives from Africa, Asia, Europe, and the Americas. Since that time there have been two continental meetings for Africa and the Middle East, and the Americas. A third meeting for Asia and the Far East, a United States-Canadian Conference, and a World Conference in Rome are planned for 1967.

The programs are based on the belief that universities have a role in the removal of obstacles to international education and in the training of future leaders and policy makers. It is felt that Universities must make it part of their planning to educate the public in international conflict and to bring international affairs to the secondary school level, since this represents terminal education for the vast majority of people in the world. Particular attention should be given to those subjects which deal most directly with the international community, such as sociology, political science, and economics.

International Study and Research Institute
41 Central Park West
New York, New York 10023

The International Study and Research Institute, directed by Dr. Arno G. Huth, operates a program that cuts across disciplinary lines and enables adult students and professionals to understand, and to face, the challenge and the problems of our changing world. Offered are non-degree courses on international affairs and orientation for international service, with study of causes and problems of political and economic change. The inter-relation of politics, economics, societies, and cultures is stressed. There are also informal meetings with diplomats, UN officials, and other leaders in business and international affairs. Membership entitles one to free attendance at receptions and lectures and reductions on Institute publications. The cost ranges from $10 annually for Regular members to $500 a year for Patrons.

Education and World Affairs
522 Fifth Avenue
New York, New York 10036

Education and World Affairs is a private, nonprofit educational organization founded in 1962. Its purpose is to assist in strengthening the performance of American higher educational institutions in world affairs—teaching of Americans, conduct of research, exchange of persons, and cooperation with educational institutions and efforts abroad. Its basic support comes from initial grants of the Ford Foundation and the Carnegie Corporation of New York.

EWA's Major Categories of Programs and Activities are:

Consultation and participation in international educational policy-making, including public statements on these issues.

Careful, objective studies of key issues in international education.

Standing committees on major areas of concern, and Regional Councils on educational cooperation with countries of the major world areas.

Problem-oriented conferences, seminars, and working groups as communications bridges between U.S. private institutions and government agencies, and representatives of educational communities in other countries.

Consultations with American colleges, universities, and other organizations for the improvement of international education at home.

270

Dissemination of information—through its own publications, by distribution of other materials, and through library and information center activities—to advance general understanding in its fields of interest.

EWA's Overseas Educational Service

When it became clear in 1963 that the U.S. required a private organization to aid in identifying and placing well-qualified American educators for positions in the universities of the developing nations and in assisting in the eventual reentry of these educators into the United States, the trustees authorized the establishment of the Overseas Educational Service as an affiliate of EWA. In its first full year of operation, OES placed some 50 U.S. academic persons in educational institutions in Africa, received requests to fill more than 200 posts for 1966, and developed a selected national registry of more than 1,400 candidates for one- or two-year educational assignments abroad. OES staff members have visited more than 20 African universities, an equal number in Latin America, and selected universities in Asia and the Middle East, and have visited a substantial number of U.S. universities and colleges to interpret the purpose of OES to the academic community and to search for promising candidates.

OES is presently funded in the main by a grant from the Carnegie Corporation, although it generates a certain amount of self-support in the form of contract arrangements and recruitment fees.

EWA's Universities Service Center:

In the autumn of 1963, under a grant from the Carnegie Corporation, EWA established the Universities Service Center in Hong Kong. The purpose of the Center is to

271

assist scholars to move more quickly into productive research by providing physical facilities and services, contacts and access to research resources, and general advice and guidance. During 1965, as many as thirty scholars at a time, most of them American, but including British, Korean, Japanese, and Chinese scholars as well, made use of the Center.[16]

Hesbjerg College
pr. Holmstrup, Fyn
Denmark

Hesbjerg College was founded seven years ago as an experiment by Jorgen Laursen Vig, who is also the present Headmaster. The direction of the courses is international. Students are accepted from all countries. However, a knowledge of English is required. Examination courses are provided for Danish students, and a wide range of other courses, particularly in the area of International Relations, for English-speaking students.

Typically, the College held a combined Summer School and Work Camp on the topic of *Peace Research*. Resident professors provided an introduction, and then a series of visiting lecturers spoke on such topics as the Economics of Peace, Law and World Order, Mathematics and Peace Research, and Non-Violence. In addition to the regular program, other subjects such as art, religious thought, and Danish life and literature could be studied at the same time.

Last year, Hesbjerg College also held a graduate study course on *British Political Issues*. No formal prerequisites were demanded, but one should have had some previous

16. *Education and World Affairs Information Service*, April, 1966.

political study. The program, directed by Eric Liggett, was designed to help clarify the often confusing face that Britain presents to the continent.

Arts for World Unity
Vally Weigl, Chairman
55 West 95th Street
New York, New York 10025

As the great art of the world is the heritage from many cultures to the world's people, it acts as an effective means of communication and understanding. Art goes beyond the barriers of language, dogma, politics, and prejudice and, therefore, can play a vital role in the cause of peace.

Arts for World Unity is a project of the Peace Institute of the New York Yearly Meeting, Religious Society of Friends, whose main areas of concern are:

> To bring art in the cause of peace to the public and develop mutual understanding and communication; to encourage hope for peace and fear of war; to foster pathos, humor, love of one's fellow man, and respect for people of various cultural background.

> To stimulate creation, production, performance, and exhibition of art work in the fields of drama, film, music, dance, and the graphic arts, highlighting work that is international in scope and presenting such work locally, nationally, and internationally.

> To cooperate with individuals and other organizations in the compilation of a listing, as comprehensive as feasible, of art works, past and present, which express those basic

longings of people for peace and mutual understanding beyond the barriers of prejudice.[17]

Recent activities of the Arts for World Unity include: programs of music, dance, and poetry in churches and institutions of eight different denominations; graphic arts workshops and seminars and exhibits of their results; exchange of works of art by graduate students on the university level. Contacts with like-minded organizations and individuals—also in the U.S.S.R.—have been established, and the exchange of information encouraged.

Among the sponsors and advisers of Arts for World Unity are Adele Addison, Benjamin Britten, Pablo Casals, Aaron Copland, Martha Graham, Yehudi Menuhin, Dmitri Shostakovich, William Warfield, and many others who share AWU's belief in the communicative power of the arts.

Brazil '65 Project

A pilot study and involvement project was sponsored by the Cornell United Religious Work and the Ithaca Westminster Foundation in cooperation with the Cornell Latin American Studies Committee. Its purpose: to interest North American students in the development problems of Latin America by giving them a comprehensive view of the problems of an underdeveloped area of one country while experiencing these problems with student counterparts in that country.

The first project took place in the Spring semester of 1965 on the Cornell Campus and in northeastern Brazil

17. *Arts for World Unity*, Brochure, 1967.

the following summer. The main purpose of the Brazil '65 Project was educational: the correlation of academic knowledge of economic conditions with an understanding of the concrete human problems thereby created; correlation of development theories with value judgments underlying specific development decisions; and comparison and testing of American and Brazilian approaches to modernization and change. The program also assisted Brazil by deepening the understanding of Americans who will enter professions relative to Latin American affairs and by assisting Brazilian counterparts to carry out limited stages of long-range, locally sponsored community-development projects.[18]

The Cordell Hull Foundation for International Education
536 International Trade Mart
New Orleans, Louisiana 70130

The purpose of the Cordell Hull Foundation is to promote understanding among the peoples of the Western Hemisphere and foreign lands by providing scholarships for students from various parts of the world to study in the United States.

The UNESCO Institute for Education
Feldbrunnestrasse 70
Hamburg 13, Germany

The UNESCO Institute for Education is a central university for people of the world to meet and study problems and exchange ideas, particularly those concerning educa-

---

18. *Brazil '65 Project Report*, Ithaca, New York, January, 1966.

tion. The Institute was founded in 1951 to help Germany overcome intellectual isolation, but later became concerned with international understanding. It is an autonomous organization with a governing board of thirteen members and a small staff from all over the world. Its curriculum covers many fields of international understanding: adult education, educational reforms, teacher training, international understanding, and research on scholastic attainments.[19]

Committee on World Education
Glassboro State College
Glassboro, New Jersey 08028

> A new world community is in the making. Will education and those who are principally responsible for it have a role to play in this most significant process? Only teachers and those who are in the educational profession can answer this question. But most of them are still unaware of it. World Education deals with the world as a whole and its problems from the point of view of the whole world or the whole of mankind.[20]

A special committee made up of students and faculty at Glassboro State College was formed in 1965. It defines World Education as an "educational program for the promotion of peace, the development of a world community, and the identification of man with humanity." The Committee has presented a plan which solicits the ideas and help of the whole university in the exploration and im-

---

19. "The UNESCO Institute for Education," *International Review of Education*, Vol. VIII, No. 1. Martinus Nijkoff's, Gravenhage, 1962.

20. *Committee on World Education*, Report, 1965.

plementation of a World Education Program at Glassboro. Some of the proposals evolving from this plan include World Education Leadership Seminars with a group of 25 to 30 volunteer senior students who are interested in becoming pioneers for World Education in public schools after their graduation; World Education Exhibits on art, music, science; Special Activities, such as dancing and concerts, reflecting different cultures; New Courses for Graduate and Undergraduate Studies; Coordination with Elementary and Secondary Schools on World Education projects; Promotion of Programs for Study or Teaching Abroad; and the Establishment of a World Education Library within the College Library. The Committee has collected a bibliography on World Education and published a number of informative newsletters. Dr. George Geng was Chairman of the Committee from 1964-1966. Its present Chairman is Benjamin Hitchner.

Peaceways
Rural Route 1
Box 664
Battle Creek, Michigan

> Peaceways is an Educational Foundation chartered under Michigan law to further international peace and brotherhood: specifically to bring people together for purposes of friendship and intercultural understanding without discrimination of race, creed, color, political belief, or geographical distribution; to promote the dissemination of knowledge for human betterment; to support the United Nations in the struggle to free mankind from ignorance, poverty, disease, and war and build a world community based on the law of human brotherhood[21]

21. *Peaceways*, Brochure, 1965.

Peaceways is directed by Rebecca Shelley and is modeled, as far as possible, after the Ghandian Ashram where volunteer labor is used to maintain the community, and living is simple, frugal, and dedicated. Peaceways occupies a ninety-six acre tract in the country beside Deep Lake.

International Cultural Center for Youth
1 East 57th Street
New York, New York

The purpose of the International Cultural Center for Youth is to promote global understanding and unity through cultural exchange among the youth of the nations; to stimulate them through the related arts—music, drama, dance, films, paintings, sculpture, and literature—to take a more active role in building a peace-loving world.

ICCY proposed, and has been working on, various projects to instill in youth this one-world creed. Some of these are:

1. To erect International Cultural Centers for Youth where the cultures of other nations may be presented.

2. To provide opportunities in music and art for young people who would otherwise be deprived of the privilege of study.

3. To organize and equip mobile cultural caravans, with the cooperation of other agencies, to bring programs and exhibits of culture and the art from nation to nation and from metropolitan centers to outlying communities.

4. To reach the organized young people of church and

synagogue, of mosque and temple, with an awareness of the vast world outside their particular religious experience.[22]

The Asia Society
112 East 64th Street
New York, New York 10021

The purpose of the Asia Society is to bring the people of America and Asia together in their appreciation of each other and their indigenous ways of life. The Society encourages the study of Asia in American schools and stimulates cultural interchange between the United States and Asia.

China Institute in America
125 East 65th Street
New York, New York 10021

The China Institute promotes cultural and educational exchange between the Republic of China (Taiwan) and the United States through lectures on Chinese history and culture, sponsored at their School of General Studies.

The Japan Society
112 East 64th Street
New York, New York 10021

The Japan Society promotes the exchange of information to assist persons interested in furthering cultural, business, and teaching associations with persons in Japan.

22. *International Cultural Center for Youth*, Report, 1966-1967.

American Youth Hostels
14 West 8th Street
New York, New York 10011

American Youth Hostels provides planned itineraries and opportunities for inexpensive living at Youth Hostels and campsites in Europe, Asia, Canada, and the Americas.

National Science Foundation
1951 Constitution Avenue
Washington, D.C. 20550

The National Science Foundation fosters interchange of scientific information among scientists of the United States and foreign countries and serves as a center of information about the training, employment, and demand for scientists and technical personnel.

The Friendly World
GPO Box 1004
Brooklyn, New York 11202

The Friendly World is a privately published, international magazine, "exploring new avenues to international understanding." It has evolved as Alice L. Wood, publisher and editor, has seen gaps in world affairs programs where private citizens have a role to play. The literary content of the magazine is of a three-fold nature:

1. Informative Materials

A lively presentation of information about world affairs programs and, wherever possible, geared to opportunities for specific action. Content is especially developed with regard to the needs and interests of teachers and students, and of world affairs program planners on the community level.

A regular issue of the magazine generally features one or two principal themes, around which the materials of the issue are oriented. Themes have included: the United Nations, Freedom from Hunger, the American Negro and Human Rights, Africa, et cetera.

2. Lighter Features

The informative features are interspersed with lighter features, to entertain and amuse. Folk tales, verse, puzzles, music, "World Affairs Mail" increasingly provides international flavor, since more and more distinctive contributions come from citizens of Asia and Africa, as well as from Americans.

3. Special Issues

Two special issues yearly are the "World Holiday Calendar" and an illustrated catalog of "Holiday Gifts to Promote Peace."[23]

The Friendly World presents a refreshingly intimate view of people the world over, a view which is overlooked by most of our international organizations and news media. "Through *The Friendly World* you may see people as people, with potentialities as well as needs, and the world as a world of challenge and opportunity, not trouble-spots and crises."

A complimentary copy of *The Friendly World* may be

23. *The Friendly World,* Brochure, 1967.

281

had for 50¢ to defray cost. The magazine is financed by a paid subscription of $5 yearly.

Citizen Exchange Corps
550 Fifth Avenue
New York, New York 10036

The Citizen Exchange Corps, organized in 1962, as a non-profit, non-political foundation, has grown rapidly and has immense hopes and objectives. Concentrating now on exchanges in both directions between the United States and the Soviet Union, it is hoped, as soon as possible, to include other countries where relations are sensitive, as in China. Individuals of all ages and from every occupation are included. As to purpose: "Citizen Exchange Corps believes there must be a meaningful build-up in mutual understanding to produce a suitable climate for nuclear disarmament before a holocaust by accident or attack."

Of a bold proposal to use ships from the "mothball fleet" as a floating table for American-Soviet exchanges; surplus food from the Department of Agriculture; training and leadership experts from the Peace Corps, Stephen D. James, Founder and Executive Director wrote:

C.E.C. emphasizes that a prime objective of its program is not merely exchanges, *per se*, but by making a plan of imaginative dimensions in one area of peace activity credible, it hopes to open the way for others. C.E.C. wants to show that it is just as possible to arrange a low-cost trial exchange of 10,000 visitors as to send 15,000 troops to West Germany overnight, as the U.S. did recently in flexing its muscles to reassure its NATO allies; or, that it is as feasible to spend four or five million dollars to re-

282

activate a few mothball ships as to spend one or two billion to develop a new missile which may be obsolete upon
completion.

In short, C.E.C. says it wants to break the imagination
barrier in the social sciences by one successful, large-
scale scheme, so that social scientists will begin to match
the dimensions of experiment in the physical sciences,
which have produced the all but out-of-control pyramid-
ing of weapons systems. Massive exchanges of citizens,
we believe, would fulfill that objective.[24]

In order to help make these exchanges useful in terms
of citizen diplomacy, a series of three-week institutes,
seminars, are organized in Leningrad and Moscow. Cost
and other information regarding the program may be obtained by writing the Citizen Exchange Corps directly.

The American University School of International Service
Massachusetts and Nebraska Avenues, N.W.
Washington, D.C. 20016

The American University proposes to approach World
Education through a School of International Service. In
answer to past and current needs, religious and private
agencies have long been pioneering in the field of international social dynamics. The American University recognizes these broad possibilities and has initiated a course
focusing on:

1. The fact of world human need—both physical and spiritual, or psychological, and conceptions of understanding of widely diverse efforts to meet human need.

---

24. *War/Peace Report*, October, 1964.

2. A survey and analysis of representative case studies to be drawn from important religious and service agencies which are pioneering in, and working with, problems of international service and understanding.[25]

This program began in September, 1966, and is aimed at persons especially interested in the experiment as the basis for further work and possible credit, and at professional, religious, and service agency personnel. The material breaks down roughly into two major areas:

1. The Human Dimension of International Service. This provides a background into the philosophies of the many religions and a study of human needs: food, health, housing, education, as well as political structure and the relationship of war and peace to human need. 2. Human Service and Peace Building Agencies. The study of case histories of many of the religious and social agencies devoted to human need, such as the American Friends Service Committee, the Salvation Army, Young Men's Christian Association, and the Red Cross.

The International School of Geneva
62, Route de Chène
Geneva, Switzerland

. . . the school offers a broader aspect in many courses and several additional subjects which are not normally presented in a national curricula. It should be stressed that the school is neither a language school nor a finishing school, but is a school where an all-round education may be obtained.[26]

---

25. Suggestion for the School on International Service, Darrell Randall, March, 1966.

26. *The International School of Geneva*, General Prospectus, English Language Side, 1920.

The International School of Geneva is an outgrowth of the establishment of the Secretariat of the League of Nations and the International Labor Office in Geneva in 1920. Officials of these organizations did not wish to send their children away to schools of their own country or to the local Swiss schools. The International School was organized in 1924 in a chalet donated by M. Adolphe Ferrière, but was soon moved as it rapidly expanded. In 1929, the Boarding Department was added, and the School is now established on the estate of La Grande Boissière and is flourishing in spite of some difficulties both during the Depression of the Thirties and the Second World War. Since the re-establishment of international organizations and business in Geneva, the need for such a school was clearly shown by its growth and its international character made evident, in that the students which, by 1960, numbered 1,400, represented some twenty-six nations.

Within a decade of its beginning in 1920, the School established certain principles which have proved prophetic as to the needs of World Education: the development and use of French and English as languages of instruction, especially with regard to the needs of students to whom these were virtually a foreign language; the provision of a school program so designed as to stimulate interest in international affairs and at the same time to provide adequate preparations for entrance to national universities; the development of special teaching methods designed to overcome difficulties arising within the group from difference of background and training.

The present program consists of a primary school and a secondary school. Within these divisions, both French and English programs are presented. Through the third grade, emphasis is placed on use of languages and number skills. The children are also given the opportunity for self-expression, being encouraged to express their ideas to the fullest extent in social studies discussions. Instruction in all of these courses is given in the group method, which allows the child to develop at his own speed. From the seventh grade through graduation, the curriculum is basically similar to one that might be found in a good American High School, only in a more advanced form. Classes throughout are kept small: twenty in the elementary grades and about twenty-five in the secondary grades. Knowledge of French or English is essential, and an interview is requested, where possible, upon consideration of an application. Annual fees, including room, board, and tuition, average 10.580 francs ($2200).

Institute of World Affairs, Inc.
527 Madison Avenue, Room 314
New York, New York 10022

The Institute of World Affairs was founded forty-one years ago in Geneva, Switzerland, to promote international understanding and was later incorporated under the laws of New York State. Until April, 1967, the Institute was directed by the late Mrs. Alexander M. Hadden, President and Co-Founder. Facilities at Twin Lakes, Salisbury, Connecticut, include dormitories, library, study hall, a cafeteria, and recreational facilities.

An example of the type of program offered at the Institute was a Summer Seminar in 1966, conducted by Dr. Luther Harris Evans of the Columbia University Law School and former Director-General of UNESCO in Paris. About forty-five students on the college senior or graduate level, from various countries, religions, and cultural backgrounds, participated. The subjects studied were Political Science, Economics, International Relations, and International Law. It is hoped that the Seminar will prepare them for leadership and active participation in public affairs in their respective communities and will be effective in working toward world understanding. Credit may be obtained and full and partial scholarships are available for about thirty-five students. In evaluating applicants, much emphasis is placed on academic standing, creative ability, and adaptability to international living.

Agni Orjansgarden
Ronninge, Sweden

Agni, an International Center for Cultural, Educational, and Relief Activities, was founded as an educational institution in May, 1936, near Stockholm, Sweden. According to the Director, Mikael M. Hoffman, Agni is a combination of an International university, center for international relief, a work camp, settlement, Indian Ashram, and Scandinavian residential folk high school. Young people come from all over the world to participate in international seminars and to work. Agni feels that, with its long, intensive experience in helping to create an international community, it has developed a proved method which can be applied universally.

Patrice Lumumba Friendship University
5 Konskoy Proyesd, 7
Moscow, U.S.S.R.

In February, 1956, the *New York Times* reported the planned opening of a World University in Moscow, the

"University of Friendship of Peoples" which was to provide tuition, medical aid, and free travel to students of Asia, Africa, and Latin America, in an effort to help the developing nations.

This University came into being in 1960 and was named after the Congolese political leader. It is organized to train engineers, doctors, teachers, economists, and specialists in agriculture, industry, and international law in a four-year course, with provisions for a five-year medical degree. The government of the U.S.S.R. pays the entire cost of operating the University, and most of the students have received scholarships from the Soviet government. These scholarships cover tuition, medical care, transportation to and from Moscow, a monthly allowance for spending money of 100 rubles ($112), various excursions throughout Russia, without cost, and an allowance for clothing of 300 rubles ($336). Each student pays for his own board. Five years after its beginning, the University enrolled more than 3,000 students from 80 countries on three continents. Friendship University graduated its first class of 228 students in 1965: fifty-seven students from Southeast Asia and the Far East; thirty-eight from Africa; fifty-eight from Latin America; thirty-one from the Arab countries and the Near East; and forty-four from the U.S.S.R.

World Education Fellowship
Teachers College
Columbia University
New York, New York 10027

The World Education Fellowship, presently with members in some thirty different countries, has been working for nearly fifty years for international cooperation and understanding in the field of education.

According to the Fellowship's plan of action, their aims are:

1. To encourage in children an awareness that peoples and cultures are coming together into one inter-dependent world.

2. To provide a continuing experience of relationships, discovery, and achievement—developing personal confidence, cooperation, and a sense of responsibility—so that young people may emerge into adulthood equipped to deal realistically with the situations and the stresses of a rapidly changing society.

3. To help children and adolescents who are heading for empty, apathetic, lonely, unfilled lives: the child who lacks a warm, dependable home background; the child who fails to make social contacts; the child who is isolated through racial prejudice, et cetera.

4. To help children to discover the principles and moral values they need in order to establish fruitful relationships with others and to make decisions as individuals.

5. To seek to deepen insight about ourselves so that we may be more effective human beings.

In order to realize these aims, the Fellowship plans study-courses and conferences for groups all over the world as aids to teachers, parents, sociologists, psychologists, and students to help them to meet the challenges effected by the urgent need to live with understanding and peace.

World Education Fellowship was formerly the New Education Fellowship and, in the Twenties, took root in the world-wide upsurge of interest in problem-centered, child-centered, interest-centered, purpose-centered schooling. A score of nations developed chapters in the New Education Fellowship. The Progressive Education Association was the vigorous American member and published *Progressive Education*, an able monthly. This important association and journal dissolved during the McCarthy period. The world-wide journal was *The New Era*. Now the quarterly is called *International Bulletin of World Education Fellowship* and is edited by Dr. E. Alice Beard, International Center for Integrative Studies, 14 Fifth Avenue, New York, New York 10011.

Office of International Studies and Programs
Kent State University
Kent, Ohio 44240

Kent State University is currently offering, through its regular curriculum, an opportunity to promote international understanding and world order. This includes an Area Study Program in which the student may elect a second major, either in Latin American Studies or in Soviet Union Studies. There is also a summer Asian Study Program. Six foreign languages are available. During the academic year 1965-1966, there were 190 foreign exchange students in residence. These students were offered special classes in English.

On campus, there are over sixty members of the faculty who have had a year or more of civil service experience abroad. A program of foreign study projects covers Tanzania, Mexico, the Communist countries, Europe, and the

Far East. Some of these foreign programs are offered in cooperation with universities existing in those countries to be studied. A series of seminars are available to Kent State faculty members both here and abroad.

World Federation for Mental Health
1, Rue Gevray
Geneva, Switzerland

The World Federation for Mental Health was founded in 1948; it now has 149 Member Associations in fifty countries, 107 Affiliated Organizations, and several thousand Individual Associates.

Its Aim:

To promote among all peoples and nations the highest possible standard of mental health in its broadest behavioral, medical, educational, and social aspects.

Its Program:

—to work with the Economic and Social Council of the United Nations, UNESCO, the World Health Organization, and UNICEF, with all of whom the Federation has a consultant role;

—to promote mutual understanding and the exchange of knowledge through its Annual Meetings, International Congresses, seminars, and study groups;

—to collect and disseminate information;

—to further the establishment of better human relations in all possible ways.[27]

27. *World Federation for Mental Health,* Broachure, 1967.

The World Federation for Mental Health publishes periodicals which are sent to all members. It also has a program of scientific publications. A list is obtainable from the Geneva Secretariat.

International Student Conference
Post Box 36
Leiden, Netherlands

The International Student Conference is a student organization comprised of national unions of students from every corner of the globe. The Secretariat is centered in the Netherlands. Its Charter states devotion to "the free university, the free society, and world peace and to the struggle against all forms of oppression wherever they may exist." The organization tries to make practical application of its ideals through international meetings, national and regional seminars, technical assistance, scholarship aid, publications, and training projects. The students also organize and operate hostels to promote international student travel.

The Lisle Fellowship
3029 Pittsview Drive
Ann Arbor, Michigan 48104

Lisle Fellowship pioneered in international human relations in 1936 by originating one of the first summer programs in cross-cultural encounter and experience.

The Fellowship initiates International Institutes in Human Relations to provide inter-cultural relationships. Six-week summer programs include community service while living with local families in a foreign country. This is followed by shared living with the larger international group at the Home Center where the experience of each participant is evaluated. As one of the voluntary agencies in international education and as part of the world student exchange program, Lisle Fellowship programs have expanded and developed in four continents of the world, at the request of nationals from the countries represented.

The program is open to college students, graduates, and young adults. Costs vary, depending on location: Colombia, $650; Bolivia, $800; Germany and Denmark, $850.

World Law Fund
11 West 42nd Street
New York, New York 10036

The World Law Fund was established in 1961 as an educational project of the Institute for International Order. The purpose of the World Law Fund:

> To focus the vast educational facilities already in existence in universities, colleges, schools, and in mass media and certain other non-academic structures on the two interrelated problems of eliminating war and establishing a less costly and hazardous system of world order than the international system we now know.[28]

The Fund, accordingly, seeks to introduce the subject of war prevention and world order into the curriculum of all major educational systems throughout the world on all levels of scholarship and to encourage the study of these subjects by students, teachers, and all concerned persons.

---

28. *World Law Fund*, Brochure, 1967.

Besides the dissemination of study materials, the teaching potential of movies and television has been effectively used. A special program with the ministry and a program for writers have been initiated. The former will help provide informed discussion of world order problems, and the latter will stimulate new thinking and new materials. These two groups have been selected because of their capacity to reach others.

The World Law Fund's program endeavors to reach persons both here and abroad who are enlightened about the issues of war and peace, but feel the need of a directive and, through them, to initiate new ideas and new energies to the foremost problem of our time—"the eradication of the institute of organized warfare."

The 1967 *World Law Fund Catalogue of Instructional Materials* is available upon request.

Council on Student Travel
(Changing its name as of November 15, 1967, to the
    Council on International Educational Exchange)
777 United Nations Plaza, New York, New York 10017

The Council on Student Travel is a non-profit federation of academic institutions and educational and religious organizations which sponsor work, study, and travel programs overseas. Dedicated to goals of educational achievement and international understanding, the Council coordinates and assists in the activities of its members in developing standards for, and improving the quality of, educational exchange programs.

As part of its services to educational groups and to the independent student traveler, the Council arranges sea and air transportation throughout the year for students and teachers, including trans-Atlantic charter sailings during the summer. On all charter sailings, the Council coordinates and staffs a shipboard orientation program of educational and recreational activities. The Council also co-sponsors U.S. study and travel programs for foreign students; assists member organizations and institutions in developing and operating overseas educational programs; sponsors conferences in the field of educational exchange; works to expand educational exchange opportunities between the U.S. and Asia, Africa, Latin America, and the U.S.S.R.; and acts as a clearinghouse of information on international study, travel, and work opportunities.

International Union of Students
Vocelova 3
Prague, Czechoslovakia

The International Union of Students is a student organized and operated International Center that is prepared to serve students and visitors from all parts of the world.

United Nations Institute for Training and Research
801 United Nations Plaza
New York, New York

The United Nations Institute for Training and Research (UNITAR) opened in 1965. The purpose of the Institute is to train enrollees from less developed countries for posts with their national government or the United Nations. The Institute hopes, thereby, to build up the staff resources of the UN and so to strengthen its effectiveness. The problems of the UN—maintaining peace

295

and security and the promotion of economic and social development—will be emphasized, so that the trainees will be prepared to operate on an international, as well as a national, level.

In connection with the Institute's research program, several preliminary studies have already been initiated. These involve the evaluation of such projects as the World Food Program, language teaching, and a directory of existing training and research institutes.

Sixty-five countries in Africa, Asia, Europe, and Latin America have already contributed toward the establishment of the Institute. Members of the Board of Trustees include Kenneth Younger of Britain, Director of the Royal Institute of International Affairs; U Thant, Secretary-General of the United Nations; and Abdul Rahman Pazhwak, of Afghanistan, President of the United Nations General Assembly.

Institute for International Order
11 West 42nd Street
New York, New York 10036

> To promote through education support of the United Nations . . . and a wider knowledge of the need and means of securing peace.[29]

The Institute for International Order seeks in various ways to stimulate individual and private action to counterbalance the partiality of nationalistic interests. It encourages through various channels support of the United Nations. Grants are made, usually from $1,000 to $25,000,

---

29. *Institute for International Order*, Brochure, 1967.

to organizations whose programs are in furtherance of the goals of IIO. More than 180 such grants have been made since the founding in 1948. Grants for 1966 included the American Friends Service Committee, League of Women Voters Education Fund, United Nations Association of the U.S.A., and the World Law Fund.

The United States International University
California Western University Campus
3902 Lomaland Drive
San Diego, California 92106

The United States International University has been developed to bring together students from various parts of the world to study and live together in the attainment of degrees in the United States curricula of higher education.

The first division of USIU is California Western University in San Diego, California, a private university which gives graduate and undergraduate degrees in arts and sciences, education, law, business administration, and the performing arts. The second division is the Elliott Campus northeast of San Diego. A graduate campus at San Diego and an arts and science campus in Arizona are planned.

The first Center outside the U.S.A. is in Mexico City. Others are planned for Brazil and Venezuela and five other countries of the world.

Out-of-country Centers will include 100 students from campuses in the U.S.A. and 200 to 300 students from the region around each Center. The curriculum will be two years in length and integrated with all parts of USIU. Students from out-of-country Centers will concentrate on English and U.S. area studies. Those from the U.S.A. will specialize in language and area studies of the Center region. Faculty will move freely within the system. Center students will receive degrees after two years in the U.S.A.

It is believed this approach will enable foreign students to receive the most from their studies in the U.S.A. and then to work in their homelands effectively for international organizations, schools, and business firms.[30]

The bold thinking behind this project is attributed to Dr. William C. Rust, President of California Western University, and the plan involves several interesting innovations. Sponsored by five degree-granting universities in the U.S.A. (California Western University; School of Performing Arts; the Elliott Campus; the Graduate School, all in San Diego, and the Arizona Division), international education with programs in a number of parts of the world is achieved without special problems of accreditation.

Willard Johnson, Director of the program, wrote on January 25, 1967, "Above all, such a university will be one with a world focus, a world perspective, and a globe encircling system."

The World University
P.O. Box 4800-K University Station
Tucson, Arizona 85717

The World University will present its curriculum as a synthesized whole. The disciplines selected for study will reflect the unity of all knowledge, a fully integrated

---

30. *The United States International University*, Brochure, 1967.

298

system of learning which will endow the student with a comprehension of all that is vital to a healthy, peaceful, and orderly world community. Everything will be studied from the viewpoint of what is necessary to the formation and maintenance of a world society that does not require the exercise of force to preserve it. Instead of looking at life from a narrow sectarian or nationalistic view, as so many of the colleges do today, the World University will offer the whole of humanity as the highest consideration, and the greatest good to the largest number as the most sacred obligation. This is democracy in its most ecumenical form.[31]

The idea of the World University was originally proposed by Reverend Albert Sheldon in 1910 as "an institution of higher learning devoted to the study, development, and preservation of peace throughout the world." In 1946, not long after the establishment of the United Nations, Dr. Howard John Zitko again proposed the World University, and plans have been moving ahead since that time. In 1947, the World University Roundtable was established in California by Dr. Zitko for the purpose of developing such a school. It now has members in over sixty countries. In 1954, the Office of International Coordination came into being in California, and in 1960 the search for a campus began. Finally, a six-hundred acre site was chosen near Tucson, Arizona, and the offices and library were moved there preparatory to construction of the campus in the Fall of 1967.

The World University in its beginning will be a liberal arts Junior College. All curricula will conform to the entrance requirements for the University of Arizona. There

---

31. Communication with Dr. Howard Zitko, 1966.

will be no grades or examinations, so that students may progress at their own desired rate of progress toward completion of their academic program. Tuition will be approximately $120 a month, plus room and board. It is hoped that there will eventually be twelve centers around the globe, and that students from all countries of the world will participate.

World Academy of Art and Science
1, Ruppin Street
P.O.B. 534
Rehovot, Israel

The World Academy of Art and Science was established in 1960 as a forum "for distinguished scientists and scholars to discuss the vital problems of mankind, independent of political boundaries or limits, whether spiritual or physical; a forum where these problems will be discussed objectively, scientifically, globally, and free from vested interests or regional attachments. It will function as an informal world university at the highest scientific and ethical level, in which deep human understanding and the fullest sense of responsibility will meet."[32]

In September, 1965, members of the Council for a World University met in Rome to discuss the development of the World Academy of Art and Science. Present members of the Council include Lord J. Boyd Orr of the United Kingdom, Hugo N. Boyko of Israel, Elinar Du Rietz, Carl-Göran Hedén and Hugo Osvald of Sweden, Choh-Ming Li of the Chinese University of Hong Kong, Ivan Malek of the Academy of Sciences of Czechoslovakia, Dato Sir

---

32. World Academy of Art and Science, Newsletter, 1966.

Alexander Oppenheim of Malaysia, Lloyd L. Morain, Stuart Mudd, Hermann Joseph Muller, Robert M. Hutchins, Linus Pauling, and Albert Szent-Györgyi all of the United States.

There is a five-step plan for the development of a World University which is not to be limited to one geographical location, but is rather to be a network of cooperating departments all over the world.

1. A Council is to be appointed. (This has already been completed.)

2. Various colleges and universities will be approached for suggestions of topics which merit world-wide research.

3. Annual or bi-annual reports will be published so that participating institutions will know about what is going on involving the others.

4. Participating institutions will decide upon mutual requirements, degrees, and textbooks which will be of general validity.

5. When sufficiently integrated, participating universities and colleges will declare themselves part of the World University.

Then, efforts undertaken in various parts of the world will be organized and combined into worldwide research on problems affecting humanity. The ethical aims of science could be realized.

Three notable volumes have been published by the

World Academy of Art and Science:

1. *Science and the Future of Mankind*, edited by Hugo Boyko, 1961, Dr. W. Junk Publishers, The Hague, $9.50. The authors comprise 21 of the world's foremost scientists and humanists.

2. *The Population Crisis and the Use of World Resources*, edited by Stuart Mudd, 1964, Dr. W. Junk Publishers, The Hague, $9.50. This comprises chapters by forty leading experts on population growth.

3. *Conflict, Resolution, and World Education*, edited by Stuart Mudd, Dr. W. Junk Publishers, The Hague, 1966, $9.50.[33] This volume, so far as we are aware, is the first substantial presentation of the concept of World Education.[34] And it is the more impressive for its recognition of the problem-solving approach to peace through conflict resolution.

United Nations International School
1311 First Avenue
New York, New York 10021

The United Nations International School was established to meet the needs of members of the United Nations Secretariat and Delegations for the education of their children. From its beginning in 1947 at Lake Success,

---

33. To be published in the United States by Indiana University Press, Bloomington, Indiana, June, 1967.

34. Another book on world education has just been published: *The Idea of a World University*, by Michael Zweig, edited with a Foreword by Harold Taylor, Southern Illinois University Press, Carbondale and Edwardsville, 1967. This the first systematic presentation of the history and development of the idea of world university.

New York, the philosophy of the School has been to retain the cultural values of each nationality while practicing the ideals of international understanding and cooperation of the UN Charter. During the year 1965, there were 568 pupils enrolled from sixty-eight countries. The faculty is also international in experience, with members from Asia, Africa, North and South America, Europe, and Australia. The UNIS serves as a pattern of development for other schools and colleges on other continents with the vision of educating citizens of the world community.

Institute of International Education
809 United Nations Plaza
New York, New York 10017

The Institute of International Education, founded in 1919, is an organization which develops and administers programs of educational exchange for foundations, private organizations, governments, colleges, universities, and corporations in the United States and abroad. Approximately 7,750 students, teachers, technicians, and specialists from about 110 countries study or train through these programs each year. Through its counseling and information services and its publications, the Institute assists thousands of individuals and many organizations with matters of international education here and abroad.[35]

The Institute of International Education is the Western Counterpart, and predecessor of, the Soviet Union's Friendship University, now Patrice Lumumba Friendship University. In a sense, a real sense, they would like to be international on an all-inclusive basis, but each on its own

35. *Institute of International Education,* Bulletin, 1967.

terms. Working closely with American business Foundations and the State Department, IIE has done a thriving business and has recently moved into its present, excellent headquarters building in the United Nations Plaza. Detailed annual reports are made describing the variety and the volume of programs. The Institute has been an important factor in growth toward World Education.

I

Exchange Programs

(1) *Introduction*

Exchange programs have been effective in bringing to a higher pitch international understanding between different cultures and, especially, between individuals of different countries. Often linked with educational efforts, the exchange program comprises possibly the largest part of the international cooperation effort in the world today. Private groups as well as schools, universities, and the different governments of the world have started and carried out such programs.

Although the exchange program is often limited in scope, its value has been extensive. People on an individual basis have been given the opportunity to live, work, study, and travel in situations foreign to their understanding and experience. Through mutual purpose, both the participant and those people with whom he comes in contact are able to gain a better feeling for the cultures from which others come and, hopefully, are able to correlate them with their own realm of experience and understanding—within the context of world peace and brotherhood.

I

Exchange Programs

(2) Examples

People-to-People
2401 Grand Avenue
Kansas City, Missouri 64141

> The activities of People-to-People have a basic denominator; a breaching of the age old barriers of geography, language, race, history, and customs . . . Given a chance, people will make friends across, around, over, and under all the natural and man-made barriers which separate them.
>
> Dwight D. Eisenhower

During his administration, President Eisenhower became convinced that international relations was not only the business of the government, but also that of the people at large. With this in mind, and deviating from the accepted government-to-government approach to international goodwill, President Eisenhower called a conference in 1956 of Americans whom he felt would be most willing to participate in, and support, such a program. His vision of the great good that could come from a program in which ordinary citizens could get to know citizens of foreign countries intimately, initiated a new approach to international understanding.

Since that conference, and all during the following years of "Ike's" administration, the idea grew and became increasingly popular. At the close of his term as President, People-to-People was continued as a non-governmental agency with Mr. Eisenhower as Chairman of the Board. A Board of Trustees was formed consisting of leading American business and cultural leaders.

There are both adult and youth programs. The Adult Programs include community chapters in which groups in the United States arrange hosting for foreign visitors; international festivals; group tours to other countries; a letter exchange between citizens of other countries; and a Sister City Program through which communities in America exchange letters, information, and people with a city in some other part of the world, "building bridges of friendship."

The Youth Programs include campus chapters at universities which sponsor a summer "Student Ambassador" Program, through which college and university students meet their counterparts abroad.

An International Travel Program makes travel in this country and abroad more meaningful for students and adults by sponsoring personal contact and home visits.

American Field Service International Scholarships
313 East 43rd Street
New York, New York 10017

The American Field Service sends teen-age students abroad to spend a summer with private families in foreign lands. Over 900 students between the ages of 16 and 18 participate in this Hospitality Program.

Also sponsored by AFS is a program which involves approximately 300 teen-age students who live with private families and attend the local secondary schools for one year in a foreign country.

In both of these programs, American communities may

submit candidates to be sent abroad when they sponsor the visit of an AFS student to the United States. All students speak English and are chosen for personal as well as academic qualities.

The American Field Service was originally founded in France in 1914 as a Volunteer Ambulance Corps during the war. It was again active during the Second World War. In 1947, it began its work on the teen-age level, and in 1950 the first group of Americans went abroad as part of the Exchange Program. It is through these kind of associations that American Field Service works to further the basic friendship which can exist among all men.

Among the participating countries are: Algeria, Andorra, Argentina, Australia, Austria, Belgium, Bolivia, Brazil, British West Indies, Cambodia, Chile, Colombia, Costa Rica, Czechoslovakia, Denmark, the Dominican Republic, Equador, Estonia, Ethiopia, Finland, France, Germany, Great Britain, Greece, Guatemala, Iceland, Indonesia, Iran, Italy, Japan, Kenya, Laos, Lebanon, Luxembourg, Madagascar, Malagasy Republic, Malaya, Morocco, Netherlands, New Zealand, Norway, Pakistan, Panama, Peru, Philippines, Portugal, Rhodesia, Singapore, South Africa, Spain, Swaziland, Sweden, Switzerland, Syria, Thailand, Turkey, Uganda, United Arab Republic, United States, Uruguay, Venezuela, and Vietnam. A sponsorship cost of $650 per student is donated by the local chapter of AFS. This becomes part of the Scholarship Fund which is used to pay traveling expenses for students whose families cannot afford it. This money does not cover school supplies and personal expenses.

The American Field Service has no religious or political affiliations. In speaking of it, Dwight D. Eisenhower said: "This kind of exchange, as it grows and grows, will have a better effect in advancing the peace of the world and of giving greater promise to each of us, young and old, to live fuller, better lives, free from the burdens of armaments, free from the fears of attack, living together in the confidence that humans can trust and believe in other humans."

The Exchange-of-Persons Program
2101 Constitution Avenue, N.W.
Washington, D.C. 20418

The Exchange Program as planned and administered by the Bureau of Educational and Cultural Affairs of the Department of State, began following World War II. Acting on a proposal of Senator J. W. Fulbright of Arkansas, Congress, in 1946, authorized use of some of the foreign currencies resulting from the sale of surplus war goods to be used to support an international educational exchange of persons.

This program fosters a belief in education, freedom of intellectual inquiry, and the creation of improved relations between the United States and the rest of the world. As a branch of the government, it naturally hopes to disseminate American ideals and to dispel misconceptions and stereotypes of this country and its people.

To accomplish these aims, the program has five specific objectives.

1. To increase mutual understanding.

2. To promote international cooperation for educational and cultural advancement.

3. To work with those nations that seek America's collaboration in economic and social modernization.

4. To increase the competence of the United States in dealing with international affairs.

5. To further and support basic foreign policy objectives of the United States.

From 1949 to 1963, nearly 53,000 foreign visitors came to the United States and over 21,000 Americans went abroad under this Exchange Program of the Department of State. Over 120 countries were involved, among them: Argentina, Britain, Chile, Colombia, France, Ghana, Guatemala, India, Japan, Kenya, Malaya, Nigeria, Philippines, Rhodesia, South Africa, Sudan, Sweden, Tanzania, and Uruguay.

"Important as it is, the exchange program of the Department of State is but a small part of the great flow and counterflow of Americans and people from other countries who, on their own or with private or other government sponsorship, today cross oceans, borders, and cultural barriers in order to see and be seen, teach and be taught, in another land.

"But it is a significant, a selective part. It is not too much to say that it embodies the hopes, the aims, the good will, even the dream of peace, of the American people."

Carl Duisberg–Gesellschaft
5 Köln, Kaiser-Friedrich-Ufer 41-45
Germany

It's one world we live in today; nations are growing more and more together and frontiers are falling. Let's help to build this world of tomorrow with methods of tomorrow.[36]

36. J. W. Funke, Executive Director, Carl Duisberg Society.

The Program of the Carl Duisberg Gesellschaft provides work experience in America for German students and professional people and in Germany for a similar group of Americans.

This non-profit organization was founded in 1949 by German participants in a Work-Study Program who had been in the United States under the auspices of Carl Duisberg. Carl Duisberg (1861-1935) was a German chemist, researcher, scientist, and leader in industry. He was one of the pioneers who first saw the possibilities and pragmatic gains to be reaped by initiating an exchange work-study program with other countries.

The Carl Duisberg program now includes a Study Period to acquaint the student with the way of life unique to the country he is visiting. Participating colleges and universities enroll the student for one special semester for this purpose. During this time, employment opportunities are found within the interest and experience of the participant, and the employer pays the prevailing salary scale according to qualifications. This Work Period initiates the person into the business, agricultural, or university life of a foreign country. The Gesellschaft keeps in constant contact with the students, and an analysis of the experience is made at the conclusion of the program.

Each participant is responsible for his own expenses. However, some of the participating schools and businesses do offer partial scholarships, and the student can often defray a good portion of his expenses through his work experience.

This work-study involvement with the customs, language, and the agricultural, industrial, and educational aspects of a foreign country broadens horizons and hopefully promotes a world perspective on the problems which confront humanity today.

Interested Germans and Americans are eligible. It is required that they be between 22 to 30 years of age and have at least two years of college, some practical job training, and a knowledge of German and English.

The Experiment in International Living
Putney, Vermont 05346

The Experiment in International Living is dedicated to creating mutual respect, understanding, and peace among people the world over. It is based on the idea that "one best learns to understand another people and their culture by living among them as a member of a family." The many, varied programs include travel and study, but homestay is of the utmost importance.

The Experiment in International Living was founded in 1932 by Dr. Donald B. Watt and is at present under the direction of John Wallace. The oldest exchange of persons program of its kind in the country, it is a non-profit, educational organization financed by fees, foundation grants, gifts, and government contracts. Its headquarters are in Putney, Vermont, with regional offices and/or representatives in some 45 countries on six continents.

The inbound and outbound summer exchange of students, young businessmen, et cetera is perhaps the best-known program. Participants spend a month in a home as family members and a month of travel and study with the group or, in some cases, independently. Through another program, the Experiment helps colleges and universities establish and administer their overseas programs. Homestays are also arranged, both for these students and for foreign students. Since 1961, the Experiment has been very active in the training of Peace Corps volunteers.

In 1965, a number of new programs were designed to give participants a chance to "work with their hands and study with their heads as well as to learn with their hearts." These programs include such projects as the teaching of English as a foreign language, work projects, foreign language study, and opportunities to travel and study in the pursuit of special interests in many fields: medicine, political science, social service, et cetera.

Among the countries in which there are Experiment projects are: Algeria, Argentina, Australia, Brazil, Cameroons, Ceylon, Chile, Colombia, Costa Rica, Egypt, Ghana, Guatemala, Iran, India, Israel, Japan, Mexico, Morocco, Nigeria, Pakistan, Peru, Philippines, Poland, Taiwan, Tanzania, Tunisia, Turkey, Uganda, USSR, Yugoslavia, and sixteen Western European countries—Austria, Belgium, Czechoslovakia, Denmark, Finland, France, Germany, Great Britain, Greece, Holland, Iceland, Italy, Norway, Spain, Sweden, and Switzerland. Costs range from $475 (Mexico) to $1350 (Australia). Applicants are encouraged to apply for scholarships.

World Neighbors
5116 North Portland Avenue
Oklahoma City, Oklahoma 73112

World Neighbors is a non-sectarian group which provides assistance for nearly 100 self-help projects in the developing countries of Latin America, Africa, and Asia. The association was founded by its President, Dr. John L. Peters, who, out of his tragic war experiences in the Philippines, pledged himself to the eradication of the causes of war and the search for ways people could live together in peace.

World Neighbors is dedicated to the self-help approach to total community development, offering mutually approved assistance, guidance, and inspiration to villagers who are often poverty-stricken, uneducated, and diseased. Qualified nationals are selected and trained for leadership in projects involving food, family planning, public health, literacy, crafts, and small industry. By choosing nationals, the barriers of language and of local acceptance are avoided.

After benefiting from a World Neighbors' experience, the leader is asked to assume the responsibility of a volunteer. In this role he shares his new knowledge and know-how with others, thus extending the outreach of World Neighbors.

World University Service
1011 Chestnut Street
Philadelphia, Pennsylvania 19107

World University Service, assisted by its several sponsoring agencies, is an international association of students and professors "who wish to share materially, intellectually, and spiritually with their contemporaries around the world." Beginning in World War I, World University Service has carried on mutual self-help programs for fifty years. It is devoted to the cause of improving educational opportunities, so that no person may feel handicapped in the full development of his worth by the crippling effects of poverty, sickness, isolation, and fear.

WUS funds are provided by students and faculty and other interested persons in some 52 countries and channeled to such projects as student housing, student health centers, libraries, and co-operative cafeterias.

The purpose of World University Service is accomplished mainly through its self-help programs, the integral part of which benefits both donor and recipient, and through which the dimension of international education is strengthened.

Work Camp Programs

Co-ordination Committee for International Voluntary Work Camps

6, Rue Franklin
Paris 16, France

The *Handbook on International Study: For U.S. Nationals,* published by the Institute of International Education, states the following about the Co-ordination Committee:

Central information bureau and liaison center for over 80 groups sponsoring work camps or recruiting volunteers for work camps; provides list of organizations abroad where application may be made; enclose international postal reply coupon to cover mailing expenses.

International student work camps are communities where volunteers live, work, and study together in projects which are of service to the local area. The first work camp was founded just after World War I in France, and here students worked on the reconstruction of homes and farms that had been destroyed in the war. Since that time, many more such work camps have provided practical, intercultural experiences under the auspices of various organizations. Among these are the following, with varying costs

314

up to $1,000, including transportation, for a summer program of work, study, and discussion: The Winant and Clayton Volunteers, Inc., 865 Madison Avenue, New York, New York 10021; Ecumenical Voluntary Service, 475 Riverside Drive, New York, New York 10027; American Friends Service Committee, 160 North Fifteenth Street, Philadelphia, Pennsylvania 19102; Brethren Service Commission, New Windsor, Maryland 21776; Operations Crossroads Africa, 150 Fifth Avenue, Room 303, New York, New York 10011.